NEGIMA!

9

Ken Akamatsu

TRANSLATED BY
Toshifumi Yoshida

ADAPTED BY
T. Ledoux

LETTERING AND RETOUCH BY
Steve Palmer

BALLANTINE BOOKS · NEW YORK

A Word from the Author

As of this book, *Negima!* Volume 9, we're heading right into the largest event ever to be held at Mahora Academy, the Mahora Festival story arc!... Or so I complacently thought, before realizing that the entirety of Volume 9 would end up covering only the preparations for the Festival. (^^;) Will Negi and his students make it through all three days in one piece?... All I can say is, I'll draw it for you best I can!

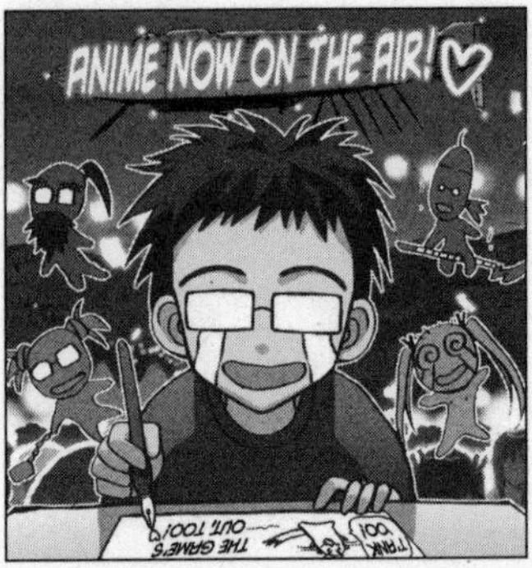
ANIME NOW ON THE AIR!

Oh, and also, before I forget—the animated *Magister Negi Magi* is now on the air (in Japan)! Watching the 31 voice actors play the 31 students is really something, let me tell you. Seriously, it's more like a classroom in an all-girl boarding school than a recording studio. Oh, would that I were Negi...! (Heh.)

Ken Akamatsu
www.ailove.net

Note: The video game and anime are currently available in Japan. At the time of publication, we do not know when they will be released in North America.

Negima! Volume 9 is a work of fiction. Names, characters, places, and incidents are the products of the author's imagination or are used fictitiously. Any resemblance to actual events, locales, or persons, living or dead, is entirely coincidental.

A Del Rey Trade Paperback Original

Published in the United States by Del Rey Books, an imprint of The Random House Publishing Group, a division of Random House, Inc., New York.

First published in serial form by Shonen Magazine Comics and subsequently published in book form in Japan in 2004 by Kodansha Ltd., Tokyo. Publication rights arranged through Kodansha Ltd. All rights reserved.

Library of Congress Control Number: 2004090830

ISBN 0-345-48273-5

Printed in the United States of America

www.delreymanga.com

1 2 3 4 5 6 7 8 9

Translator —Toshifumi Yoshida
Adaptor—T. Ledoux
Lettering and retouch—Steve Palmer
Cover Design—David Stevenson

Honorifics

Throughout the Del Rey Manga books, you will find Japanese honorifics left intact in the translations. For those not familiar with how the Japanese use honorifics and, more important, how they differ from American honorifics, we present this brief overview.

Politeness has always been a critical facet of Japanese culture. Ever since the feudal era, when Japan was a highly stratified society, use of honorifics—which can be defined as polite speech that indicates relationship or status—has played an essential role in the Japanese language. When addressing someone in Japanese, an honorific usually takes the form of a suffix attached to one's name (example: "Asuna-san"), or as a title at the end of one's name or in place of the name itself (example: "Negi-sensei," or simply "Sensei!").

Honorifics can be expressions of respect or endearment. In the context of manga and anime, honorifics give insight into the nature of the relationship between characters. Many translations into English leave out these important honorifics, and therefore distort the "feel" of the original Japanese. Because Japanese honorifics contain nuances that English honorifics lack, it is our policy at Del Rey not to translate them. Here, instead, is a guide to some of the honorifics you may encounter in Del Rey Manga.

-*san:*   This is the most common honorific, and is equivalent to Mr., Miss, Ms., or Mrs. It is the all-purpose honorific and can be used in any situation where politeness is required.

-*sama:* This is one level higher than "-san." It is used to confer great respect.

-*dono:* This comes from the word "tono," which means "lord." It is an even higher level than "-sama," and confers utmost respect.

-*kun:* This suffix is used at the end of boys' names to express familiarity or endearment. It is also sometimes used by men among friends, or when addressing someone younger or of lower station.

-*chan:* This is used to express endearment, mostly toward girls. It is also used for little boys, pets, and even among lovers. It gives a sense of childish cuteness.

Bozu: This is an informal way to refer to a boy, similar to the English term "kid" or "squirt."

Senpai/sempai: This title suggests that the addressee is one's senior in a group or organization. It is most often used in a school setting, where underclassmen refer to their upperclassmen as "senpai." It can also be used in the workplace, such as when a newer employee addresses an employee who has seniority in the company.

Kohai: This is the opposite of "sempai," and is used toward underclassmen in school or newcomers in the workplace. It connotes that the addressee is of lower station.

Sensei: Literally meaning "one who has come before," this title is used for teachers, doctors, or masters of any profession or art.

Anesan: Anesan (or *nesan*) is a generic term for a girl, usually older, that means sister.

Ojôsama: Ojôsama is a way of referring to the daughter or sister of someone with high political or social status.

-[blank]: Usually forgotten in these lists, but perhaps the most significant difference between Japanese and English. The lack of honorific means that the speaker has permission to address the person in a very intimate way. Usually, only family, spouses, or very close friends have this kind of permission. Known as *yobisute,* it can be gratifying when someone who has earned the intimacy starts to call one by one's name without an honorific. But when that intimacy hasn't been earned, it can also be very insulting.

魔法先生ネギま!

MAGISTER NEGI MAGI

9

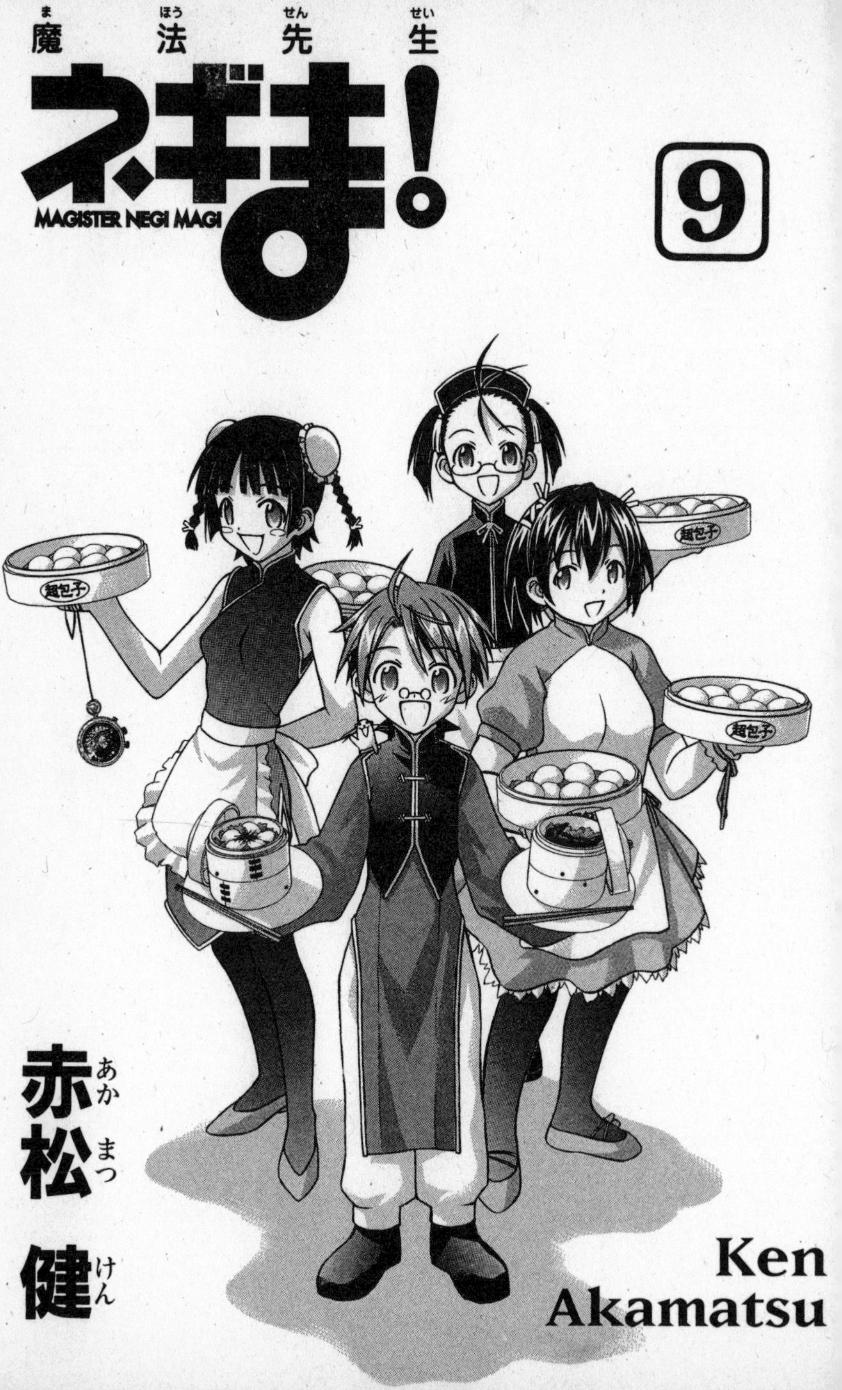
超包子
超包子
超包子

赤松健

Ken Akamatsu

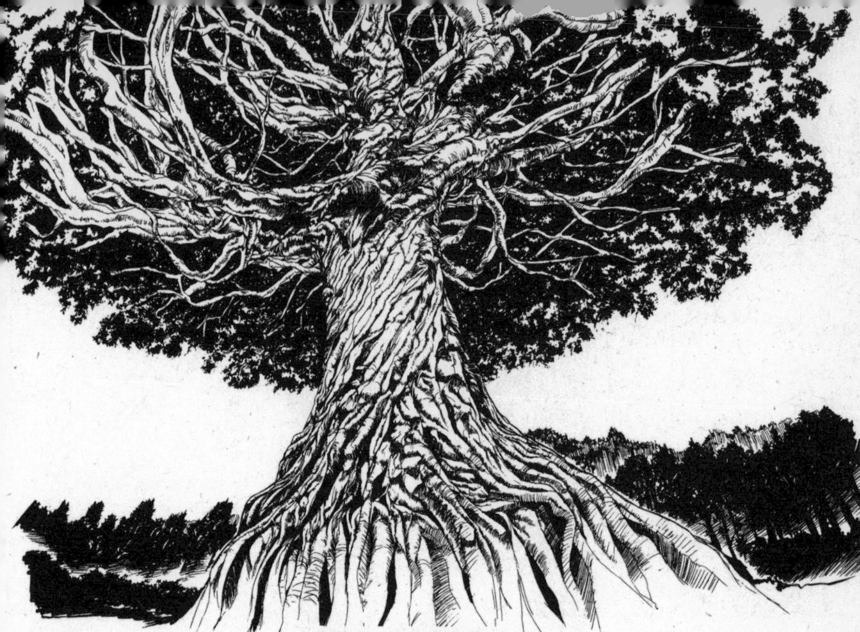

CONTENTS

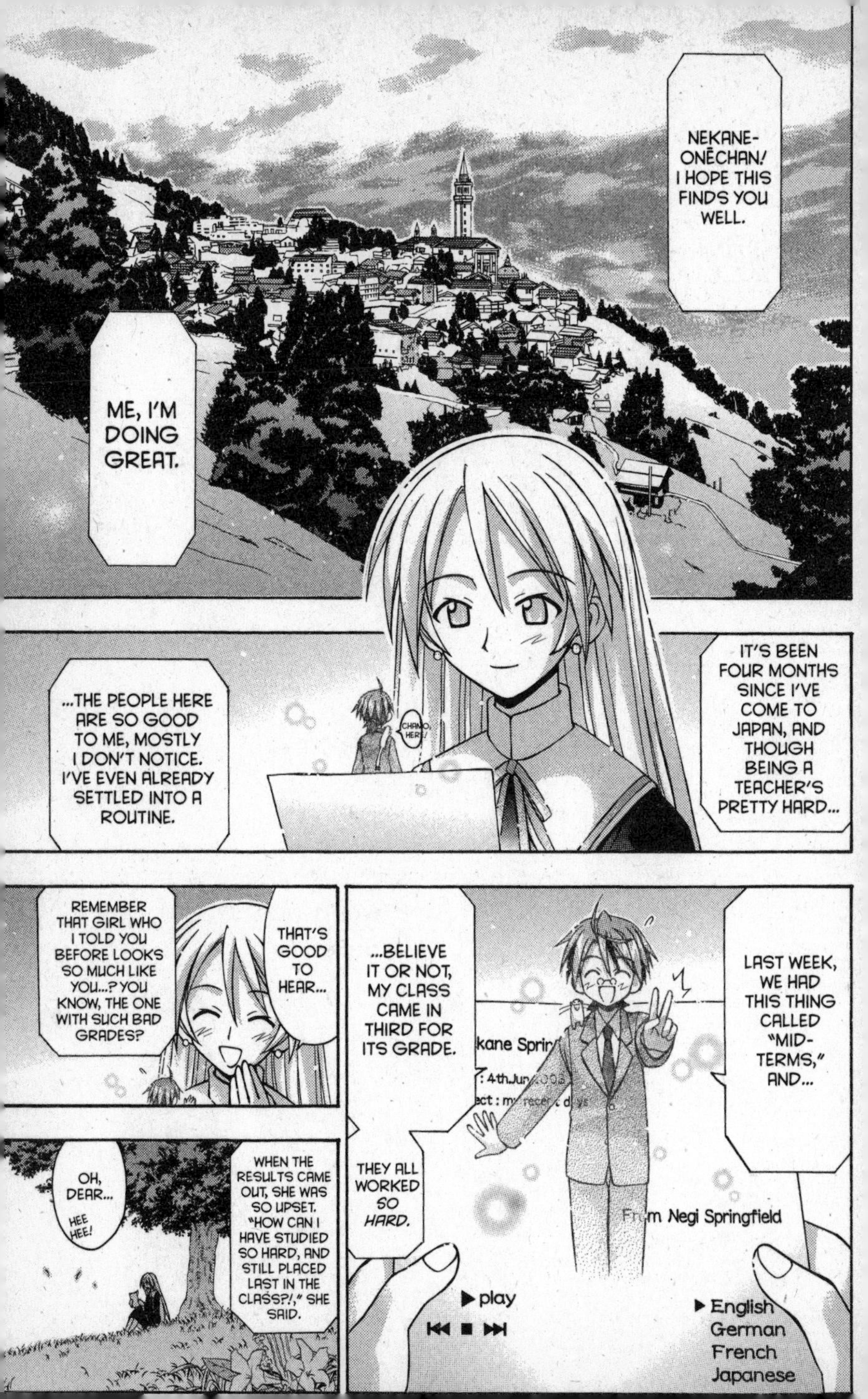
NEKANE-ONĒCHAN! I HOPE THIS FINDS YOU WELL.
ME, I'M DOING GREAT.
IT'S BEEN FOUR MONTHS SINCE I'VE COME TO JAPAN, AND THOUGH BEING A TEACHER'S PRETTY HARD...
CHAMO, HERE!
...THE PEOPLE HERE ARE SO GOOD TO ME, MOSTLY I DON'T NOTICE. I'VE EVEN ALREADY SETTLED INTO A ROUTINE.
LAST WEEK, WE HAD THIS THING CALLED "MID-TERMS," AND...
...BELIEVE IT OR NOT, MY CLASS CAME IN THIRD FOR ITS GRADE.
THEY ALL WORKED SO *HARD.*
From Negi Springfield
▶ play
▶ English
German
French
Japanese
THAT'S GOOD TO HEAR...
REMEMBER THAT GIRL WHO I TOLD YOU BEFORE LOOKS SO MUCH LIKE YOU...? YOU KNOW, THE ONE WITH SUCH BAD GRADES?
WHEN THE RESULTS CAME OUT, SHE WAS SO UPSET. "HOW CAN I HAVE STUDIED SO HARD, AND STILL PLACED LAST IN THE CLASS?!," SHE SAID.
OH, DEAR...
HEE HEE!

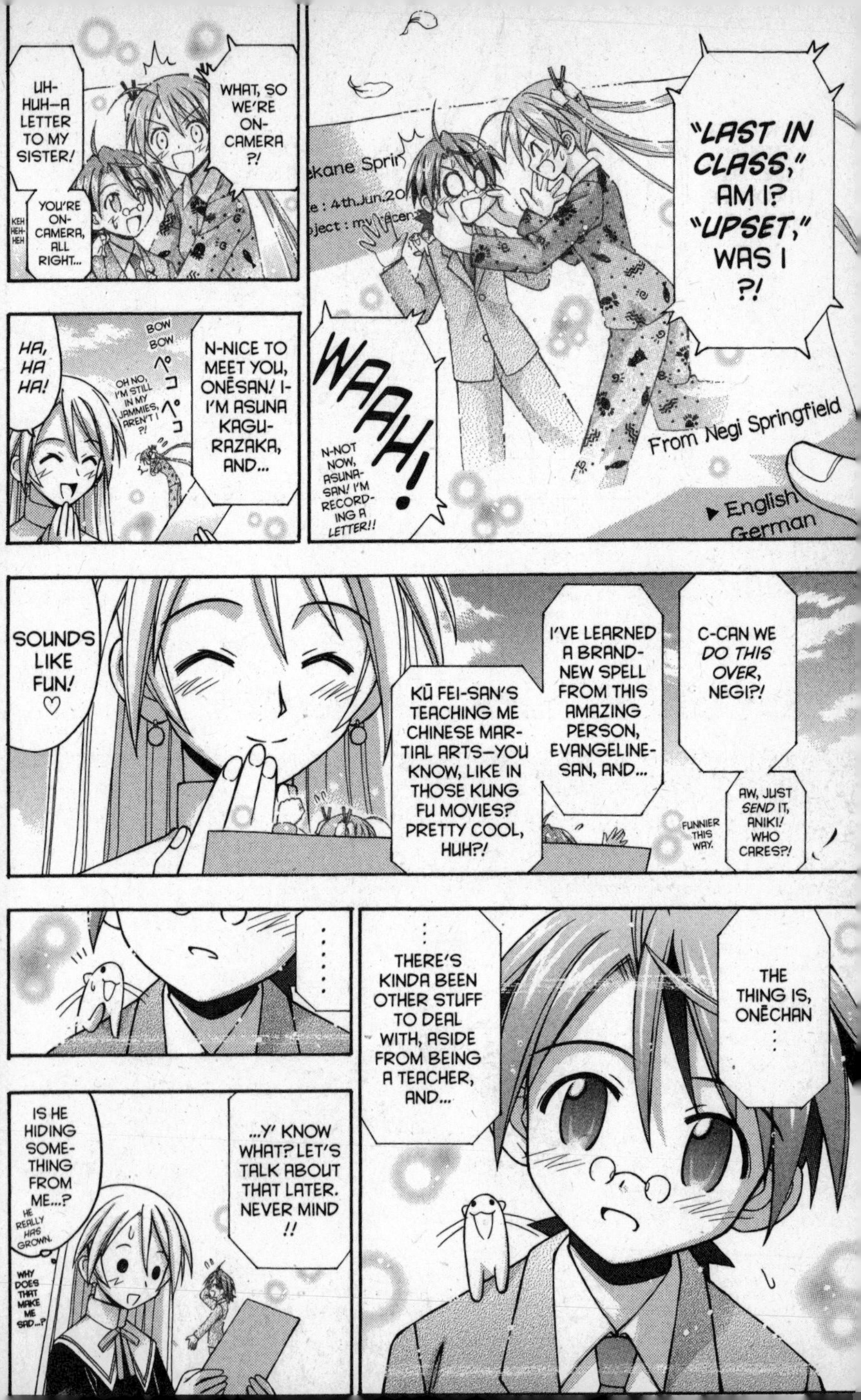
"LAST IN CLASS," AM I? "UPSET," WAS I ?!
From Negi Springfield
▶ English
German
WAAAH!
N-NOT NOW, ASUNA-SAN! I'M RECORDING A LETTER!!
WHAT, SO WE'RE ON-CAMERA ?!
UH-HUH—A LETTER TO MY SISTER!
YOU'RE ON-CAMERA, ALL RIGHT...
KEH HEH HEH
N-NICE TO MEET YOU, ONĒSAN! I-I'M ASUNA KAGURAZAKA, AND...
BOW BOW
へコ へコ
OH NO, I'M STILL IN MY JAMMIES, AREN'T I?
HA, HA HA!
C-CAN WE DO THIS OVER, NEGI?!
AW, JUST SEND IT, ANIKI! WHO CARES?!
FUNNIER THIS WAY.
I'VE LEARNED A BRAND-NEW SPELL FROM THIS AMAZING PERSON, EVANGELINE-SAN, AND...
KŪ FEI-SAN'S TEACHING ME CHINESE MARTIAL ARTS—YOU KNOW, LIKE IN THOSE KUNG FU MOVIES? PRETTY COOL, HUH?!
SOUNDS LIKE FUN! ♡
THE THING IS, ONĒCHAN ...
...THERE'S KINDA BEEN OTHER STUFF TO DEAL WITH, ASIDE FROM BEING A TEACHER, AND...
......
...Y' KNOW WHAT? LET'S TALK ABOUT THAT LATER. NEVER MIND !!
IS HE HIDING SOMETHING FROM ME...?
HE REALLY HAS GROWN.
WHY DOES THAT MAKE ME SAD...?

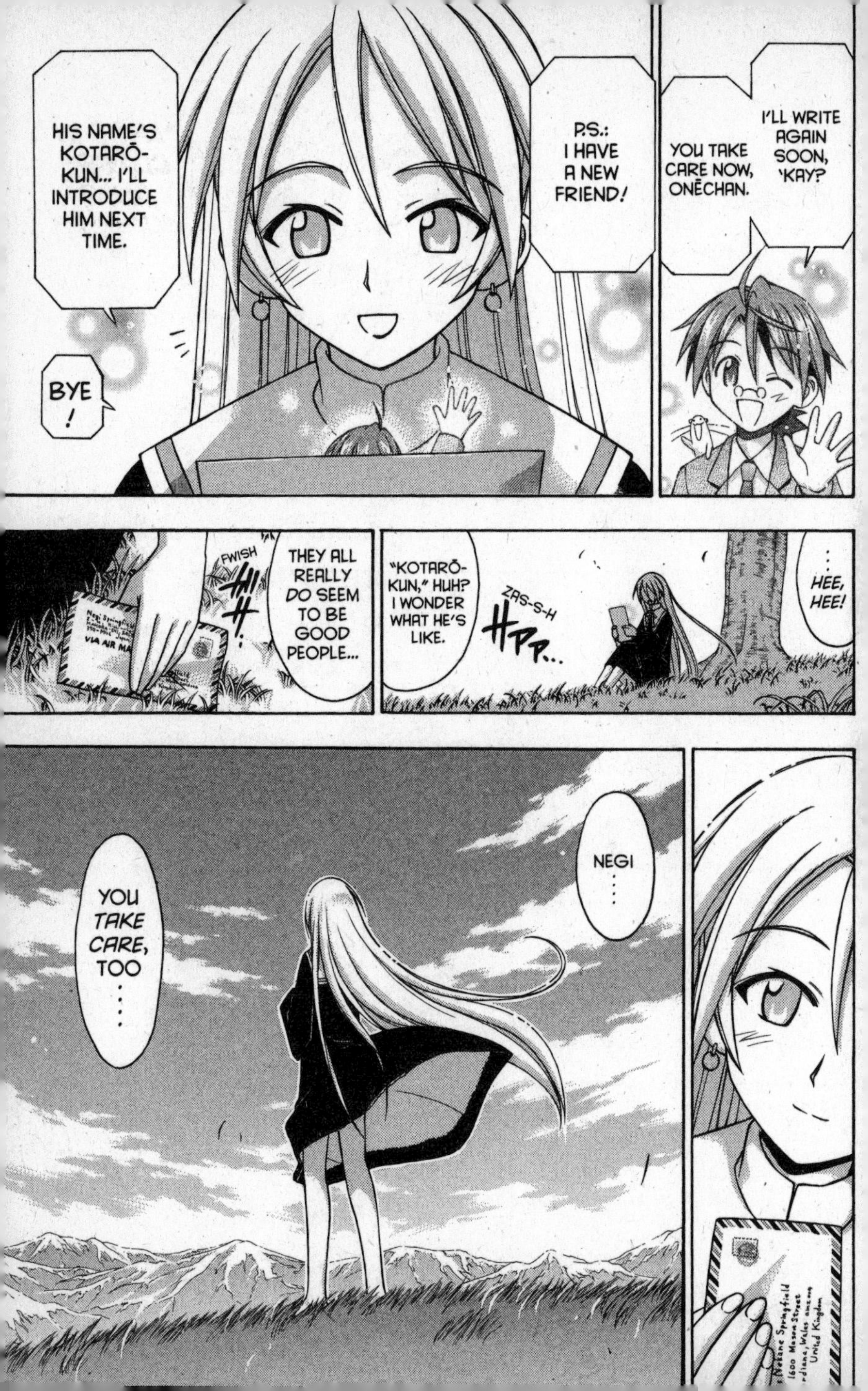

I'LL WRITE AGAIN SOON, 'KAY?
YOU TAKE CARE NOW, ONĒCHAN.
P.S.: I HAVE A NEW FRIEND!
HIS NAME'S KOTARŌ-KUN... I'LL INTRODUCE HIM NEXT TIME.
BYE!
...HEE, HEE!
ZAS-S-H
HPP...
"KOTARŌ-KUN," HUH? I WONDER WHAT HE'S LIKE.
FWISH
THEY ALL REALLY DO SEEM TO BE GOOD PEOPLE...
VIA AIR MAIL
NEGI....
YOU TAKE CARE, TOO....

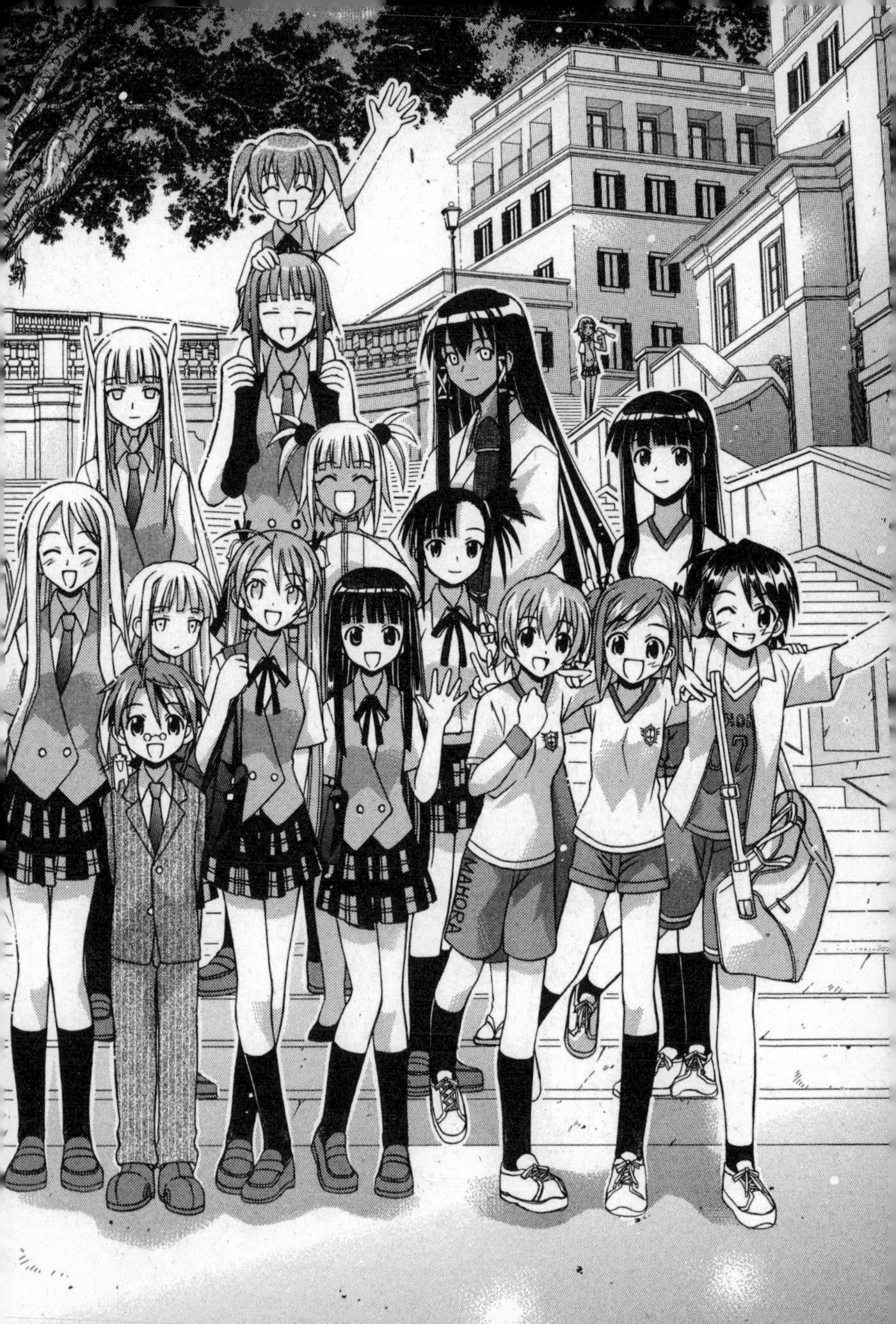
MAHORA

SEVENTY-SECOND PERIOD: THE MERRY MONTH OF MAIDS

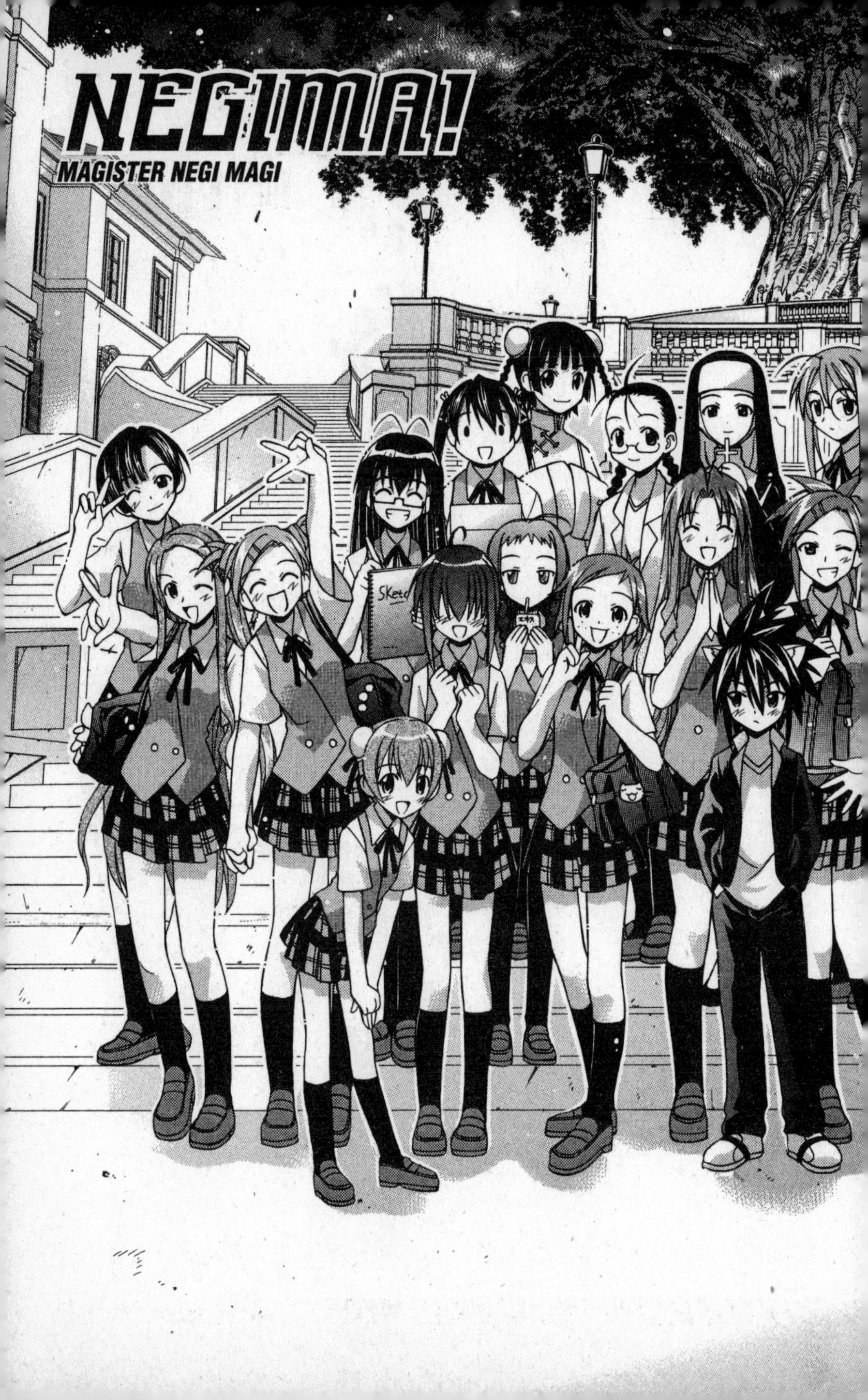
NEGIMA!
MAGISTER NEGI MAGI
Sketch

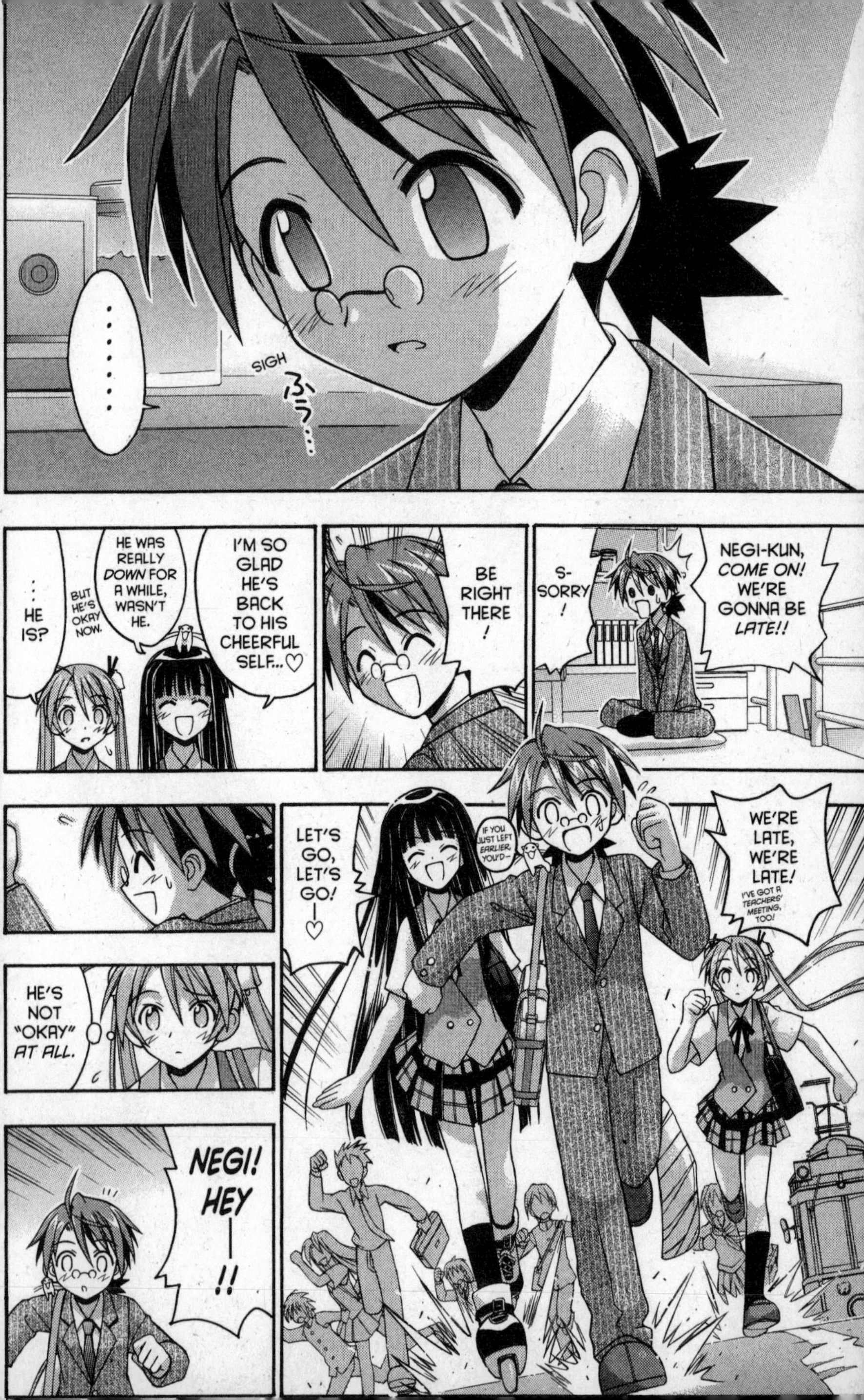
......
SIGH
ふぅ…
NEGI-KUN, COME ON! WE'RE GONNA BE LATE!!
S-SORRY!
BE RIGHT THERE!
I'M SO GLAD HE'S BACK TO HIS CHEERFUL SELF...♡
HE WAS REALLY DOWN FOR A WHILE, WASN'T HE.
BUT HE'S OKAY NOW.
...HE IS?
WE'RE LATE, WE'RE LATE!
I'VE GOT A TEACHERS' MEETING, TOO!
IF YOU JUST LEFT EARLIER, YOU'D—
LET'S GO, LET'S GO! ♡
HE'S NOT "OKAY" AT ALL.
NEGI! HEY—!!

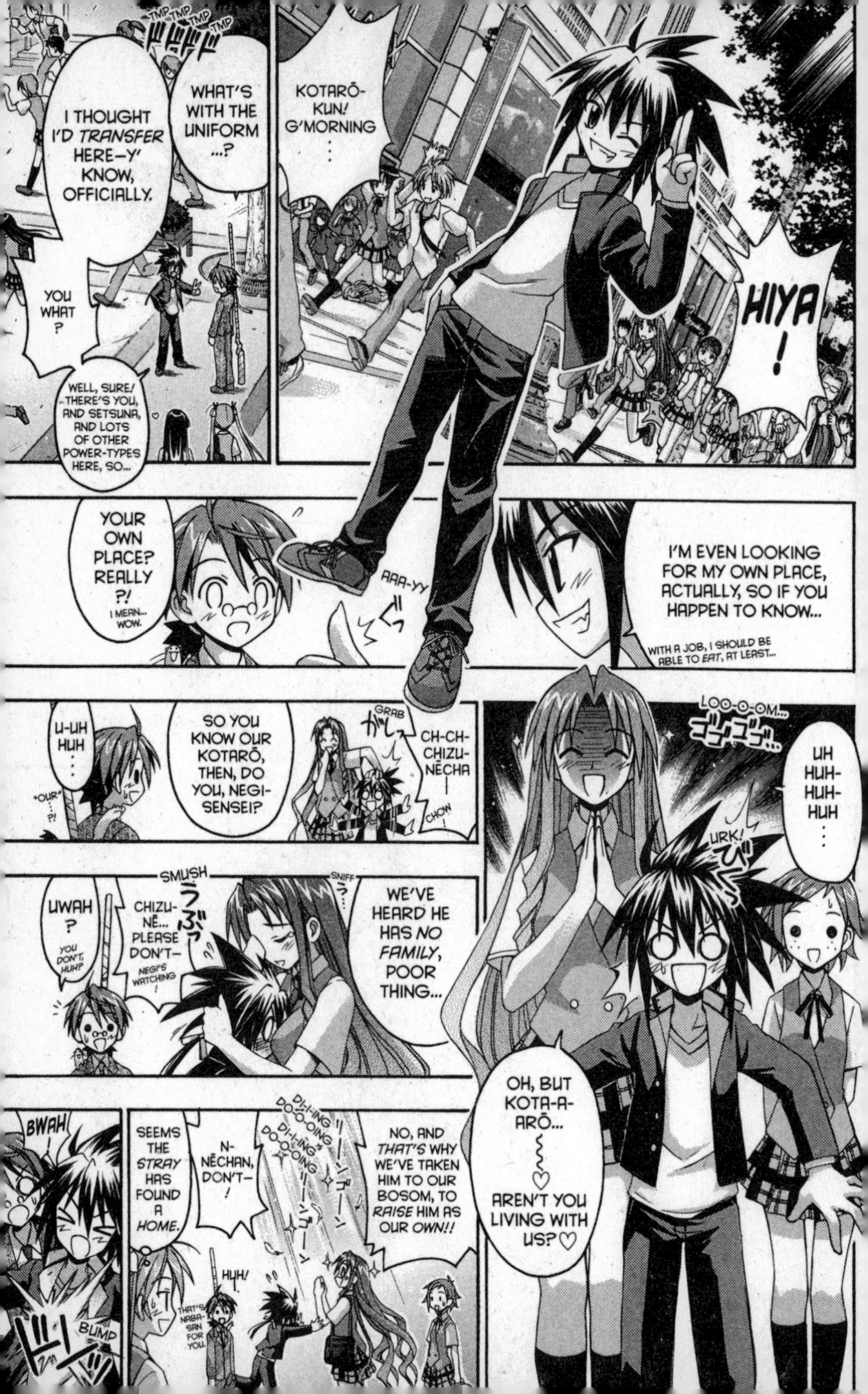
HIYA!
KOTARŌ-KUN! G'MORNING...
TMP TMP TMP TMP
WHAT'S WITH THE UNIFORM...?
I THOUGHT I'D *TRANSFER* HERE—Y' KNOW, OFFICIALLY.
YOU WHAT?
WELL, SURE! THERE'S YOU, AND SETSUNA, AND LOTS OF OTHER POWER-TYPES HERE, SO...
I'M EVEN LOOKING FOR MY OWN PLACE, ACTUALLY, SO IF YOU HAPPEN TO KNOW...
WITH A JOB, I SHOULD BE ABLE TO *EAT*, AT LEAST...
AAA-YY
YOUR OWN PLACE? REALLY?!
I MEAN... WOW.
LOO-O-OM...
UH HUH-HUH-HUH...
URK!
OH, BUT KOTA-A-ARŌ... AREN'T YOU LIVING WITH US?♡
CH-CH-CHIZU-NĒCHA!
CHOW!
GRAB
SO YOU KNOW OUR KOTARŌ, THEN, DO YOU, NEGI-SENSEI?
U-UH HUH...
"OUR"...?!
WE'VE HEARD HE HAS *NO FAMILY*, POOR THING...
SNIFF
SMUSH
CHIZU-NĒ... PLEASE DON'T—
NEGI'S WATCHING!
UWAH?
YOU DON'T, HUH?
NO, AND *THAT'S* WHY WE'VE TAKEN HIM TO OUR BOSOM, TO *RAISE* HIM AS OUR *OWN*!!
DI-I-ING DO-O-OING DI-I-ING DO-O-OING
N-NĒCHAN, DON'T—!
HUH!
SEEMS THE *STRAY* HAS FOUND A *HOME*.
THAT'S NABA-SAN FOR YOU.
BWAH!
BUMP

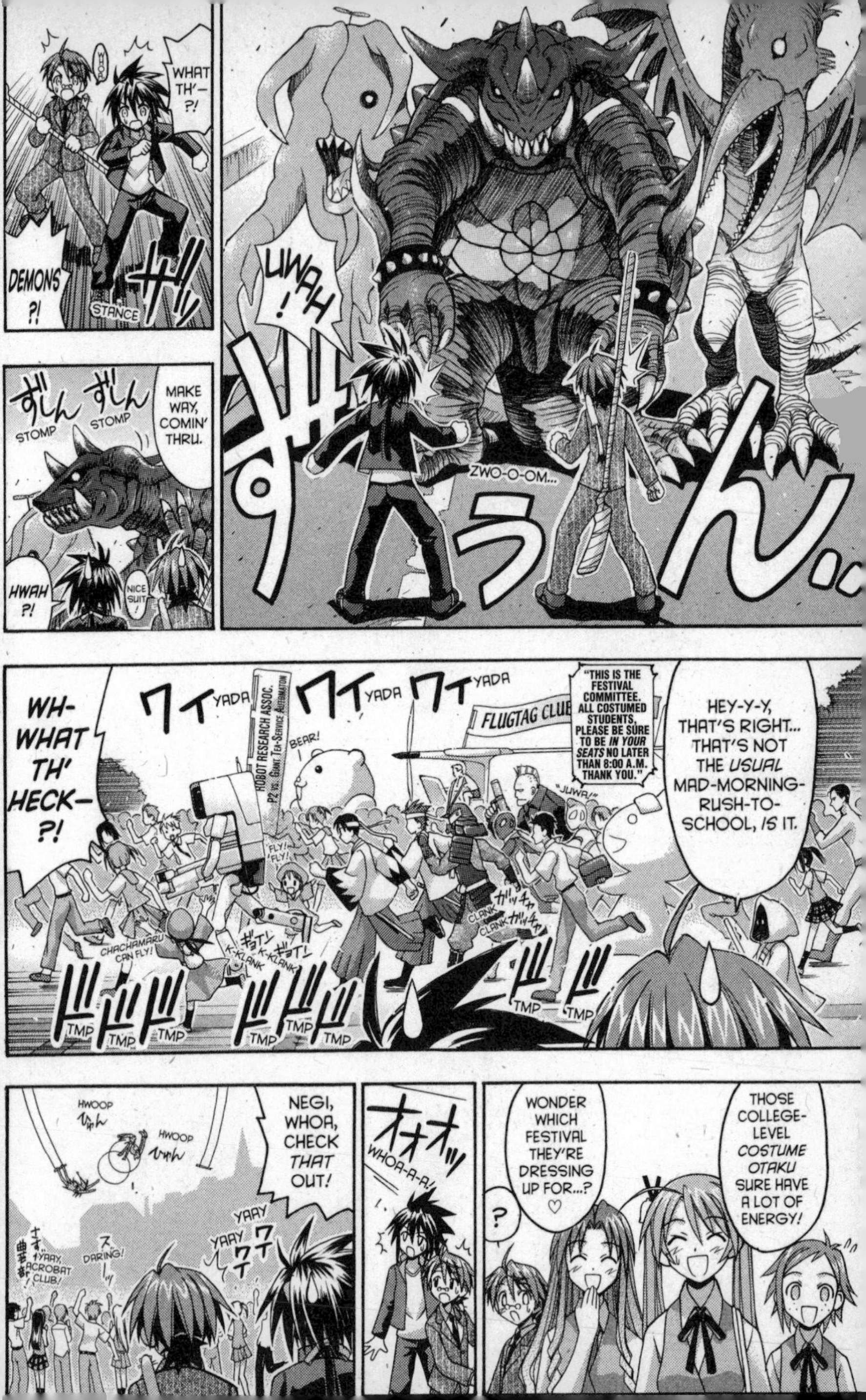
UWAH!
ZWO-O-OM...
ずうん..
WHOA
WHAT TH'—?!
DEMONS?!
ザッ
STANCE
ずしん ずしん
STOMP STOMP
MAKE WAY, COMIN' THRU.
NICE SUIT!
HWAH?!
HEY-Y-Y, THAT'S RIGHT... THAT'S NOT THE USUAL MAD-MORNING-RUSH-TO-SCHOOL, IS IT.
"THIS IS THE FESTIVAL COMMITTEE. ALL COSTUMED STUDENTS, PLEASE BE SURE TO BE IN YOUR SEATS NO LATER THAN 8:00 A.M. THANK YOU."
FLUGTAG CLUB
"JUWA!"
ワイ YADA ワイ YADA ワイ YADA
ROBOT RESEARCH ASSOC.
P2 vs. GIANT TEA-SERVICE AUTOMATION
BEAR!
FLY! FLY!
ガッチャ CLANK
ガッチャ CLANK
ギゴン K-KLANK
ギゴン K-KLANK
CHACHAMARU CAN FLY!
ドド TMP TMP
ドドド TMP TMP TMP
ドドド TMP TMP TMP
WH-WHAT TH' HECK—?!
THOSE COLLEGE-LEVEL COSTUME OTAKU SURE HAVE A LOT OF ENERGY!
WONDER WHICH FESTIVAL THEY'RE DRESSING UP FOR...? ♡
?
オオオッ
WHOA-A-A!
NEGI, WHOA, CHECK THAT OUT!
ひゅん HWOOP
ひゅん HWOOP
ワイ YAAY
ワイ YAAY
ス DARING!
すげー YAAY, ACROBAT CLUB!

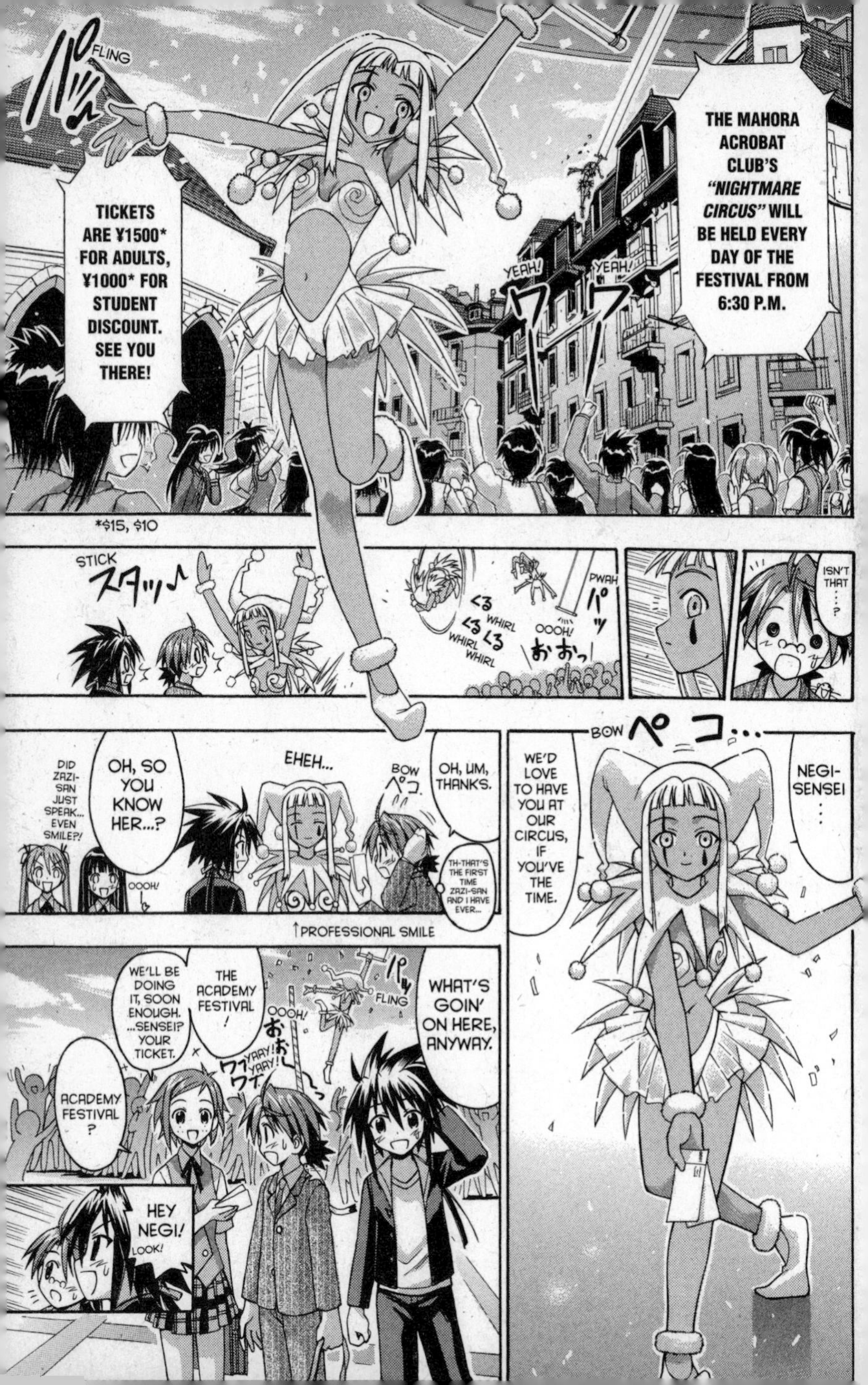

THE MAHORA ACROBAT CLUB'S *"NIGHTMARE CIRCUS"* WILL BE HELD EVERY DAY OF THE FESTIVAL FROM 6:30 P.M.
YEAH!
YEAH!
FLING
TICKETS ARE ¥1500* FOR ADULTS, ¥1000* FOR STUDENT DISCOUNT. SEE YOU THERE!
*$15, $10
ISN'T THAT...?
PWAH
OOOH!
WHIRL WHIRL WHIRL WHIRL
STICK
BOW
NEGI-SENSEI...
WE'D LOVE TO HAVE YOU AT OUR CIRCUS, IF YOU'VE THE TIME.
OH, UM, THANKS.
BOW
TH-THAT'S THE FIRST TIME ZAZI-SAN AND I HAVE EVER...
EHEH...
OH, SO YOU KNOW HER...?
DID ZAZI-SAN JUST SPEAK... EVEN SMILE?!
OOOH!
↑PROFESSIONAL SMILE
WHAT'S GOIN' ON HERE, ANYWAY.
FLING
OOOH!
YAAY! YAAY!
THE ACADEMY FESTIVAL!
WE'LL BE DOING IT, SOON ENOUGH. ...SENSEI? YOUR TICKET.
ACADEMY FESTIVAL?
HEY NEGI!
LOOK!

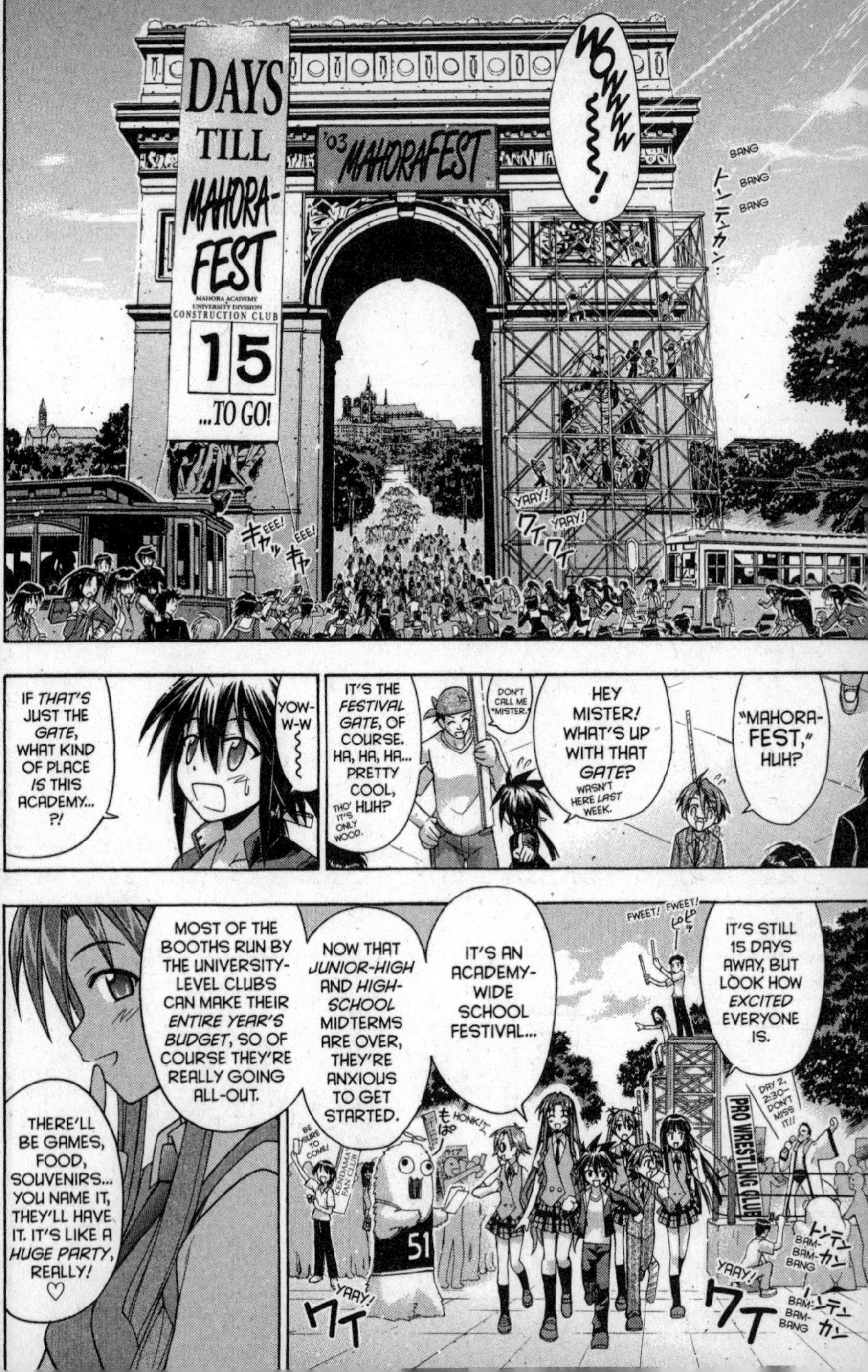
DAYS TILL MAHORA-FEST
MAHORA ACADEMY UNIVERSITY DIVISION CONSTRUCTION CLUB
15
...TO GO!
'03 MAHORAFEST
WOWWW~~~!
BANG BANG BANG
YAAY! YAAY!
EEE! EEE!
"MAHORA-FEST," HUH?
HEY MISTER! WHAT'S UP WITH THAT GATE?
WASN'T HERE LAST WEEK.
DON'T CALL ME "MISTER."
IT'S THE FESTIVAL GATE, OF COURSE. HA, HA, HA... PRETTY COOL, HUH?
THO' IT'S ONLY WOOD.
YOW-W-W~~~
IF THAT'S JUST THE GATE, WHAT KIND OF PLACE IS THIS ACADEMY...?!
FWEET! FWEET!
IT'S STILL 15 DAYS AWAY, BUT LOOK HOW EXCITED EVERYONE IS.
IT'S AN ACADEMY-WIDE SCHOOL FESTIVAL...
NOW THAT JUNIOR-HIGH AND HIGH-SCHOOL MIDTERMS ARE OVER, THEY'RE ANXIOUS TO GET STARTED.
MOST OF THE BOOTHS RUN BY THE UNIVERSITY-LEVEL CLUBS CAN MAKE THEIR ENTIRE YEAR'S BUDGET, SO OF COURSE THEY'RE REALLY GOING ALL-OUT.
THERE'LL BE GAMES, FOOD, SOUVENIRS... YOU NAME IT, THEY'LL HAVE IT. IT'S LIKE A HUGE PARTY, REALLY! ♡
DAY 2, 2:30— DON'T MISS IT!!
PRO WRESTLING CLUB
BAM-BAM-BANG
YAAY!
BAM-BAM-BANG
HONK!
BE SURE TO COME!
KENDAMA FAN CLUB
51
YAAY!

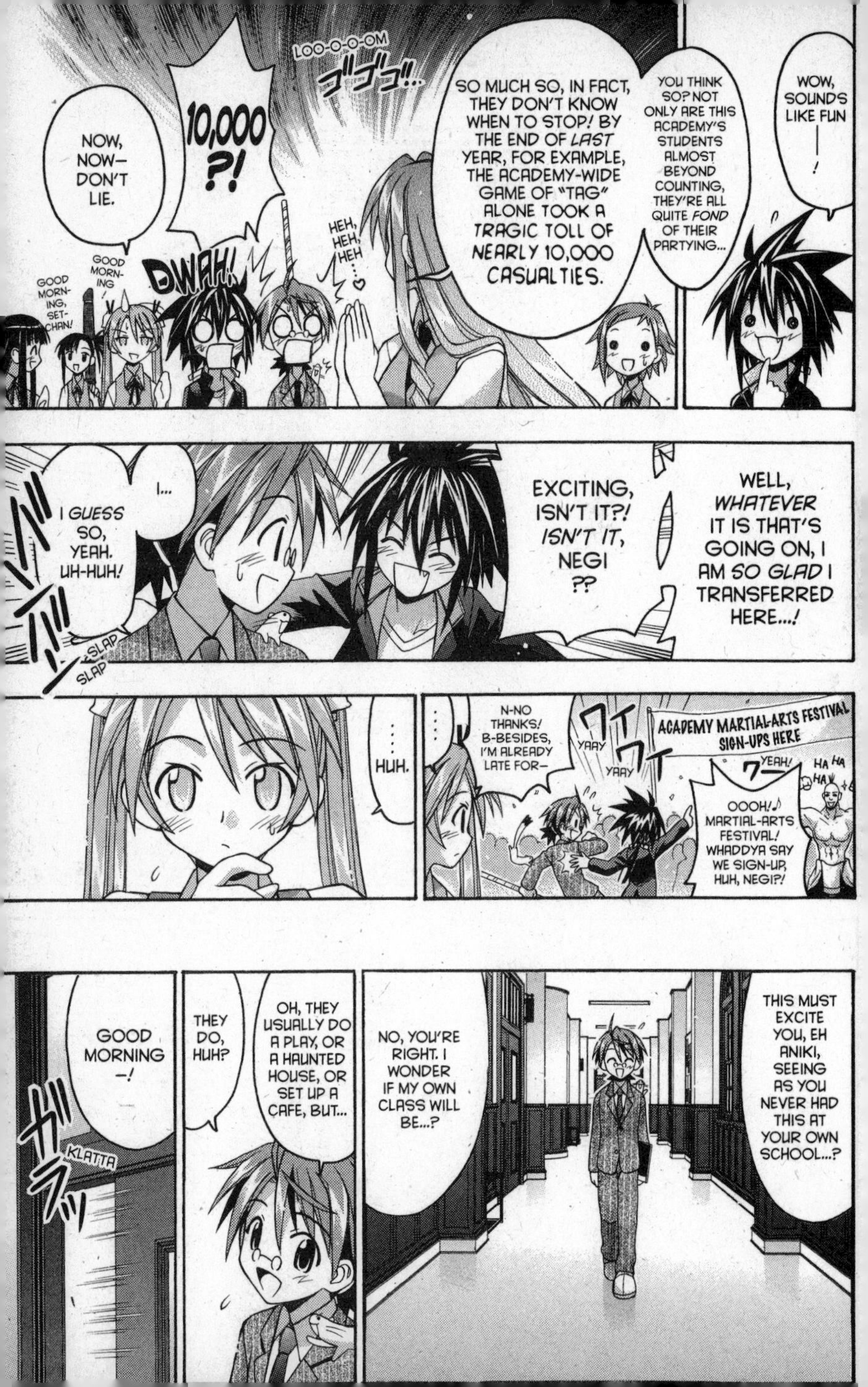
WOW, SOUNDS LIKE FUN—!
YOU THINK SO? NOT ONLY ARE THIS ACADEMY'S STUDENTS ALMOST BEYOND COUNTING, THEY'RE ALL QUITE *FOND* OF THEIR PARTYING...
SO MUCH SO, IN FACT, THEY DON'T KNOW WHEN TO STOP! BY THE END OF *LAST* YEAR, FOR EXAMPLE, THE ACADEMY-WIDE GAME OF "TAG" ALONE TOOK A *TRAGIC* TOLL OF *NEARLY* 10,000 CASUALTIES.
LOO-O-O-OM
HEH, HEH, HEH...♡
10,000?!
DWAH!
NOW, NOW—DON'T LIE.
GOOD MORNING!
GOOD MORNING, SET-CHAN!
WELL, *WHATEVER* IT IS THAT'S GOING ON, I AM *SO GLAD* I TRANSFERRED HERE...!
EXCITING, ISN'T IT?! *ISN'T IT*, NEGI??
I...
I *GUESS* SO, YEAH. UH-HUH!
SLAP
SLAP
SLAP
ACADEMY MARTIAL-ARTS FESTIVAL SIGN-UPS HERE
HA HA HA HA
YEAH!
OOOH!♪ MARTIAL-ARTS FESTIVAL! WHADDYA SAY WE SIGN-UP, HUH, NEGI?!
YAAY
YAAY
N-NO THANKS! B-BESIDES, I'M ALREADY LATE FOR—
....
... HUH.
THIS MUST EXCITE YOU, EH ANIKI, SEEING AS YOU NEVER HAD THIS AT YOUR OWN SCHOOL...?
NO, YOU'RE RIGHT. I WONDER IF MY OWN CLASS WILL BE...?
OH, THEY USUALLY DO A PLAY, OR A HAUNTED HOUSE, OR SET UP A CAFE, BUT...
THEY DO, HUH?
GOOD MORNING—!
KLATTA

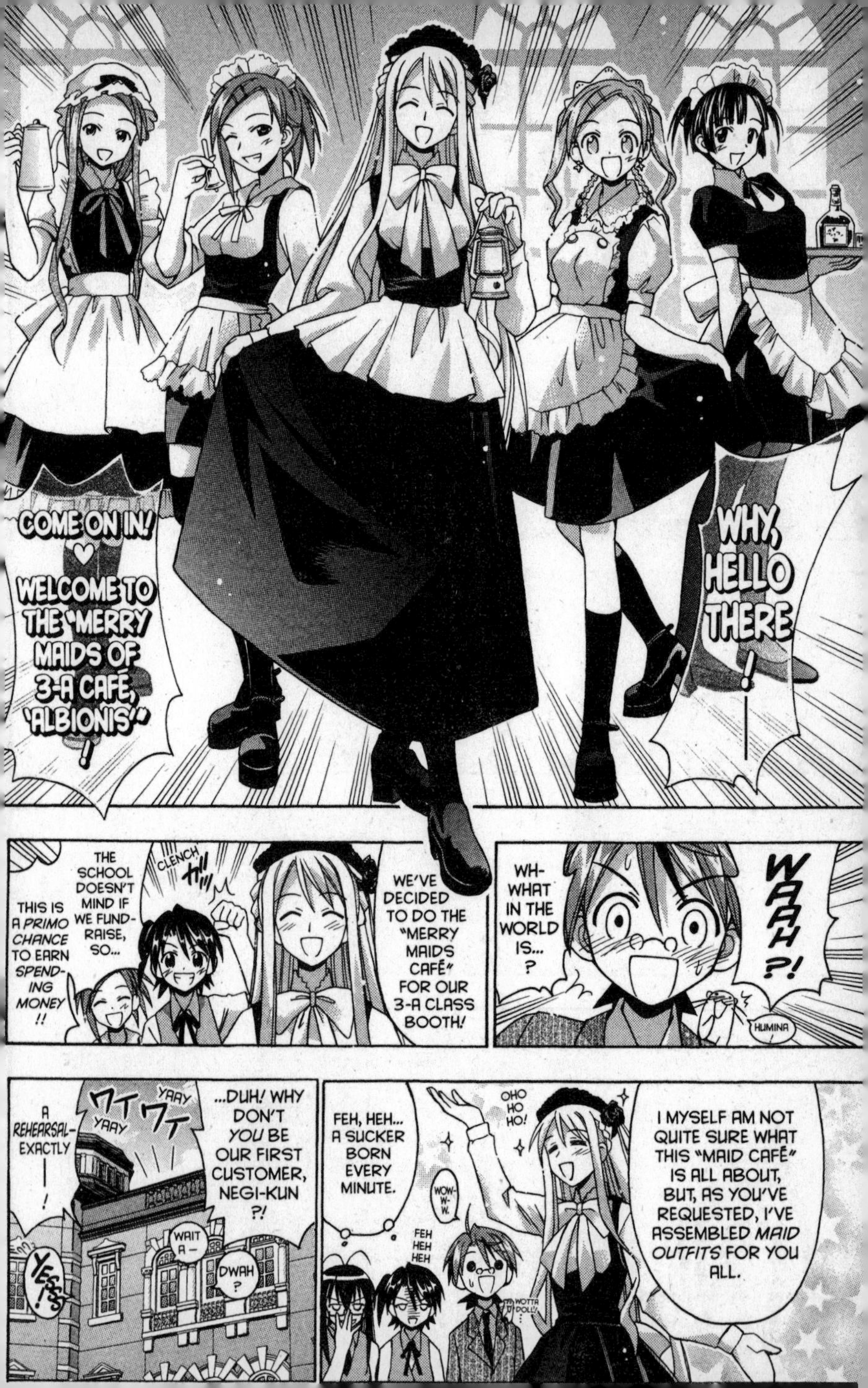
WHY, HELLO THERE!
COME ON IN! ♥ WELCOME TO THE "MERRY MAIDS OF 3-A CAFÉ, 'ALBIONIS'"!
WAAAH?!
WH-WHAT IN THE WORLD IS...?
HUMINA
WE'VE DECIDED TO DO THE "MERRY MAIDS CAFÉ" FOR OUR 3-A CLASS BOOTH!
CLENCH
THE SCHOOL DOESN'T MIND IF WE FUND-RAISE, SO...
THIS IS A *PRIMO* CHANCE TO EARN *SPENDING MONEY*!!
I MYSELF AM NOT QUITE SURE WHAT THIS "MAID CAFÉ" IS ALL ABOUT, BUT, AS YOU'VE REQUESTED, I'VE ASSEMBLED *MAID OUTFITS* FOR YOU ALL.
OHO HO HO!
FEH, HEH... A SUCKER BORN EVERY MINUTE.
WOW-W-W.
FEH HEH HEH
WOTTA DOLL!...
...DUH! WHY DON'T *YOU* BE OUR FIRST CUSTOMER, NEGI-KUN?!
YAAY
YAAY
A REHEARSAL-EXACTLY!
WAIT A—
DWAH?
YESSS!

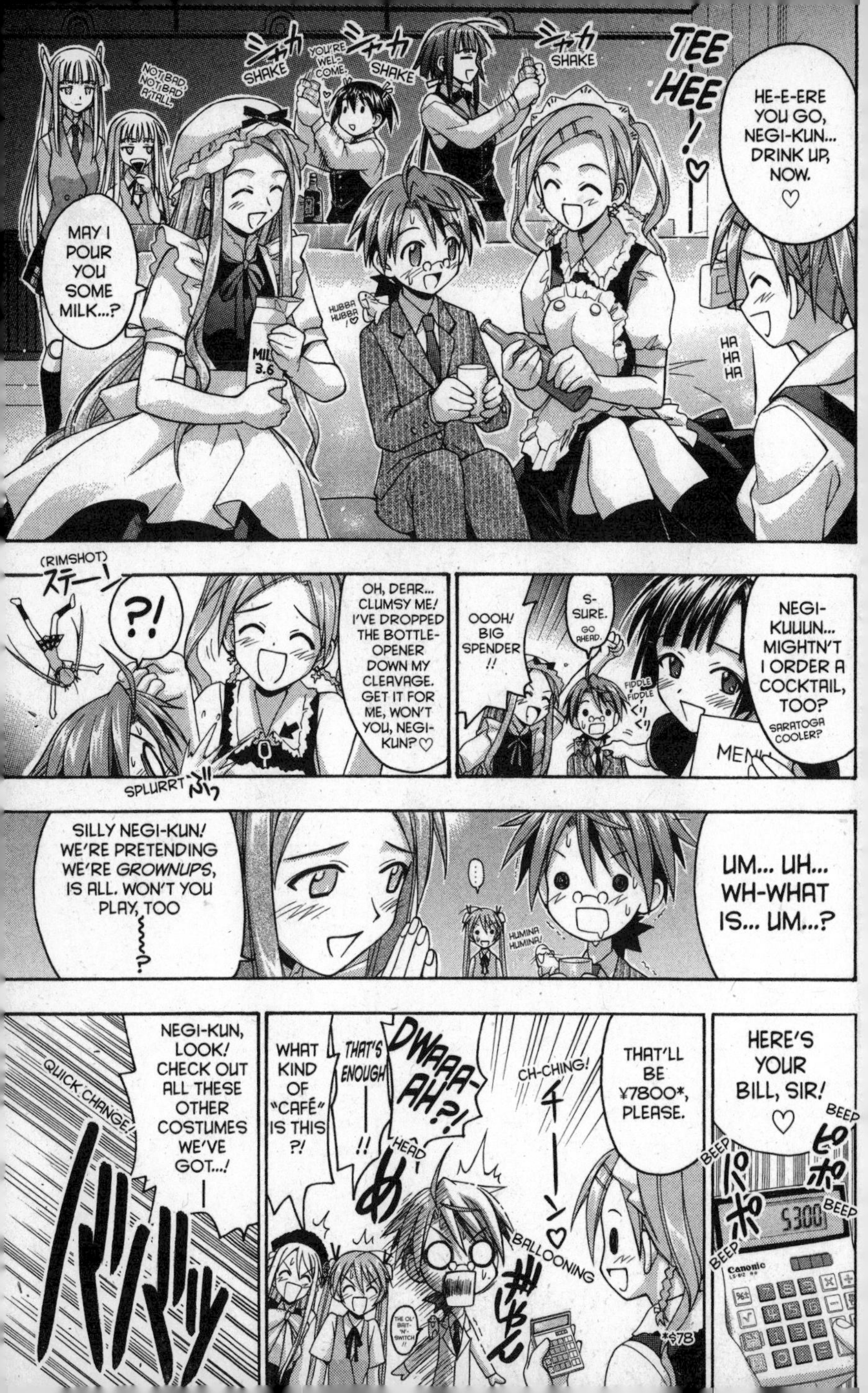
TEE HEE!♥
HE-E-ERE YOU GO, NEGI-KUN... DRINK UP, NOW. ♡
SHAKE
SHAKE
YOU'RE WEL-COME.
SHAKE
NOT BAD, NOT BAD AT ALL.
HA HA HA
HUBBA HUBBA!♡
MAY I POUR YOU SOME MILK...?
MILK 3.6
NEGI-KUUUN... MIGHTN'T I ORDER A COCKTAIL, TOO?
SARATOGA COOLER?
MENU
S-SURE.
GO AHEAD.
FIDDLE FIDDLE
OOOH! BIG SPENDER!!
OH, DEAR... CLUMSY ME! I'VE DROPPED THE BOTTLE-OPENER DOWN MY CLEAVAGE. GET IT FOR ME, WON'T YOU, NEGI-KUN?♡
?!
(RIMSHOT)
ステーン
SPLURRT
UM... UH... WH-WHAT IS... UM...?
HUMINA HUMINA!
...
SILLY NEGI-KUN! WE'RE PRETENDING WE'RE *GROWNUPS*, IS ALL. WON'T YOU PLAY, TOO?
HERE'S YOUR BILL, SIR! ♡
BEEP
BEEP
BEEP
BEEP
5300
THAT'LL BE ¥7800*, PLEASE.
CH-CHING!
チーン♡
BALLOONING
DWAAA-AH?!
HEAD
THAT'S ENOUGH!!
WHAT KIND OF "CAFÉ" IS THIS?!
THE OL' BAIT-'N'-SWITCH!!
*$78
NEGI-KUN, LOOK! CHECK OUT ALL THESE OTHER COSTUMES WE'VE GOT...!
QUICK CHANGE!

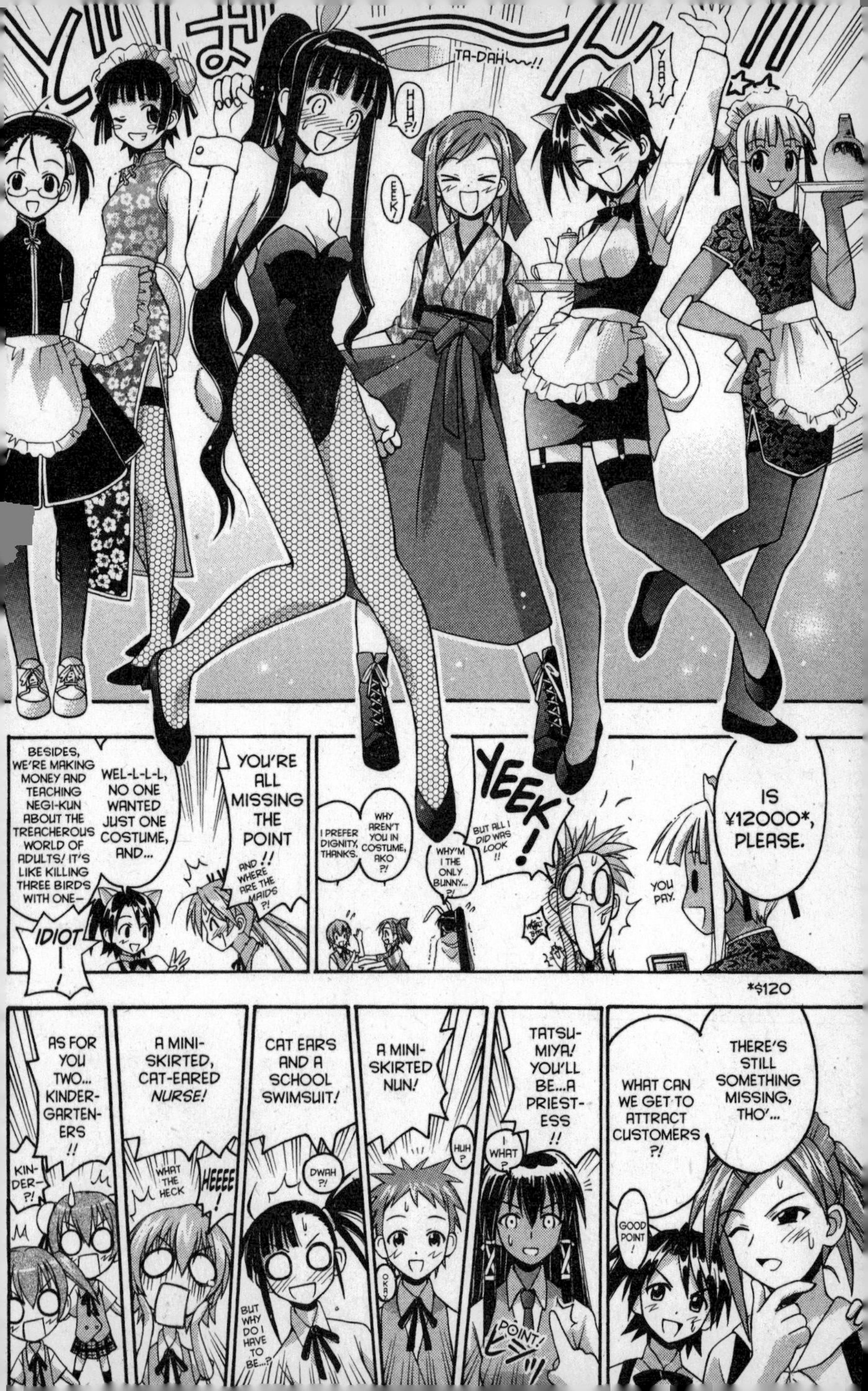
YAAY!
TA-DAH~~!!
HUH?!
EEK!
IS ¥12000*, PLEASE.
YOU PAY.
YEEK!
BUT ALL I DID WAS LOOK!!
WHY'M I THE ONLY BUNNY...?!
WHY AREN'T YOU IN COSTUME, AKO?!
I PREFER DIGNITY, THANKS.
YOU'RE ALL MISSING THE POINT!!
AND WHERE ARE THE MAIDS?!
WEL-L-L-L, NO ONE WANTED JUST ONE COSTUME, AND...
BESIDES, WE'RE MAKING MONEY AND TEACHING NEGI-KUN ABOUT THE TREACHEROUS WORLD OF ADULTS! IT'S LIKE KILLING THREE BIRDS WITH ONE—
IDIOT!
*$120
THERE'S STILL SOMETHING MISSING, THO'...
WHAT CAN WE GET TO ATTRACT CUSTOMERS?!
GOOD POINT!
TATSU-MIYA! YOU'LL BE...A PRIEST-ESS!!
I WHAT?
POINT!
A MINI-SKIRTED NUN!
HUH?
OKAY
BUT WHY DO I HAVE TO BE...?
CAT EARS AND A SCHOOL SWIMSUIT!
DWAH?!
A MINI-SKIRTED, CAT-EARED NURSE!
HEEEE!
WHAT THE HECK
AS FOR YOU TWO... KINDER-GARTEN-ERS!!
KINDER-?!

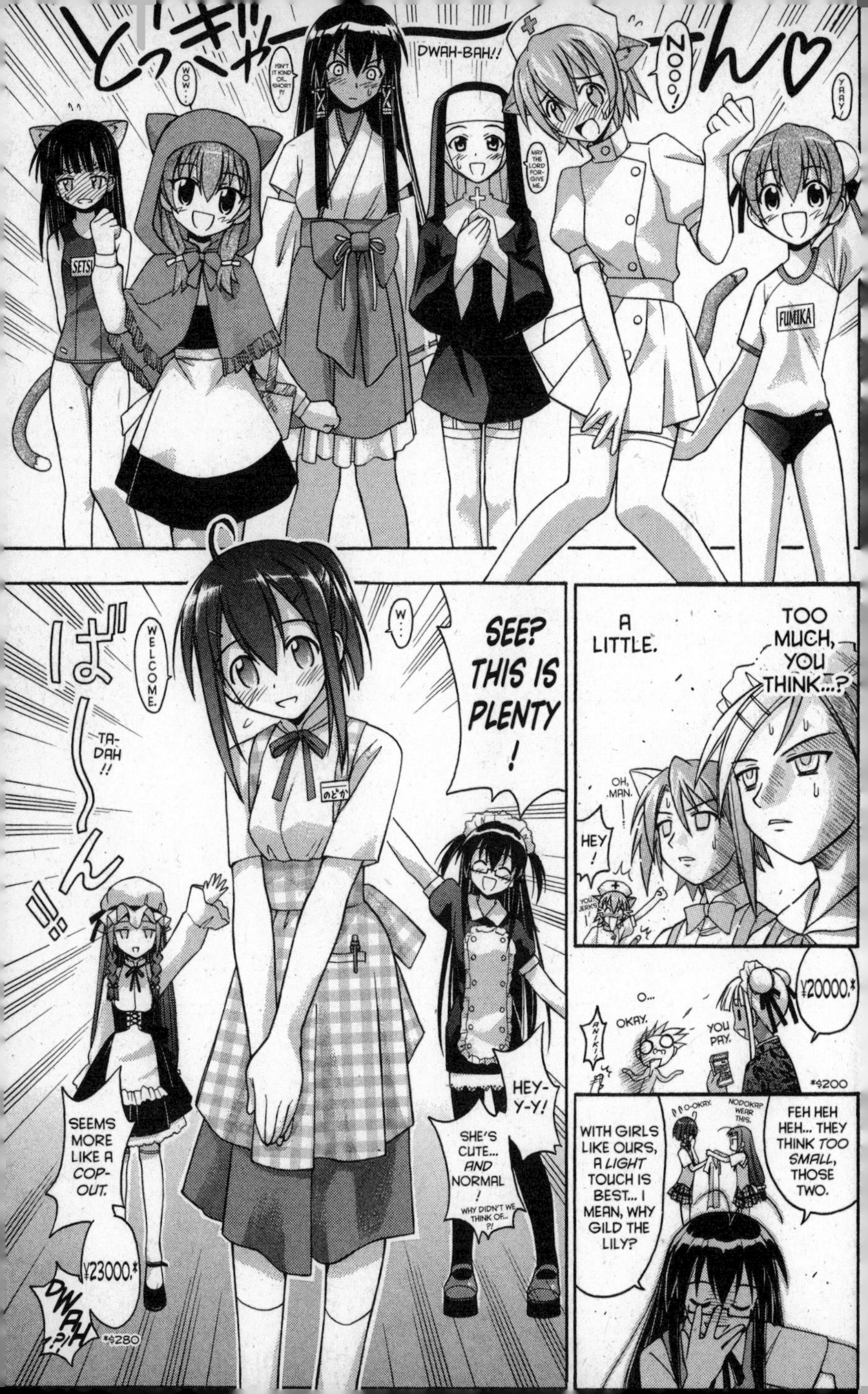
どっきゃーーーん♡
YAAY!
NOOO!
DWAH-BAH!!
MAY THE LORD FORGIVE ME.
ISN'T IT KIND OF... SHORT?!
WOW...
SETSU
FUMIKA
TOO MUCH, YOU THINK...?
A LITTLE.
OH, MAN.
HEY!
YOU JERKS!
¥20000.*
YOU PAY.
O... OKAY.
ANIKI!
*$200
FEH HEH HEH... THEY THINK *TOO SMALL*, THOSE TWO.
NODOKA? WEAR THIS.
O-OKAY.
WITH GIRLS LIKE OURS, A *LIGHT* TOUCH IS BEST... I MEAN, WHY GILD THE LILY?
SEE? THIS IS PLENTY!
W...
WELCOME.
ばーーん!!
TA-DAH!!
のどか
HEY-Y-Y!
SHE'S CUTE... *AND* NORMAL!
WHY DIDN'T WE THINK OF...?!
SEEMS MORE LIKE A *COP-OUT.*
¥23000.*
DWAH?!
*$280

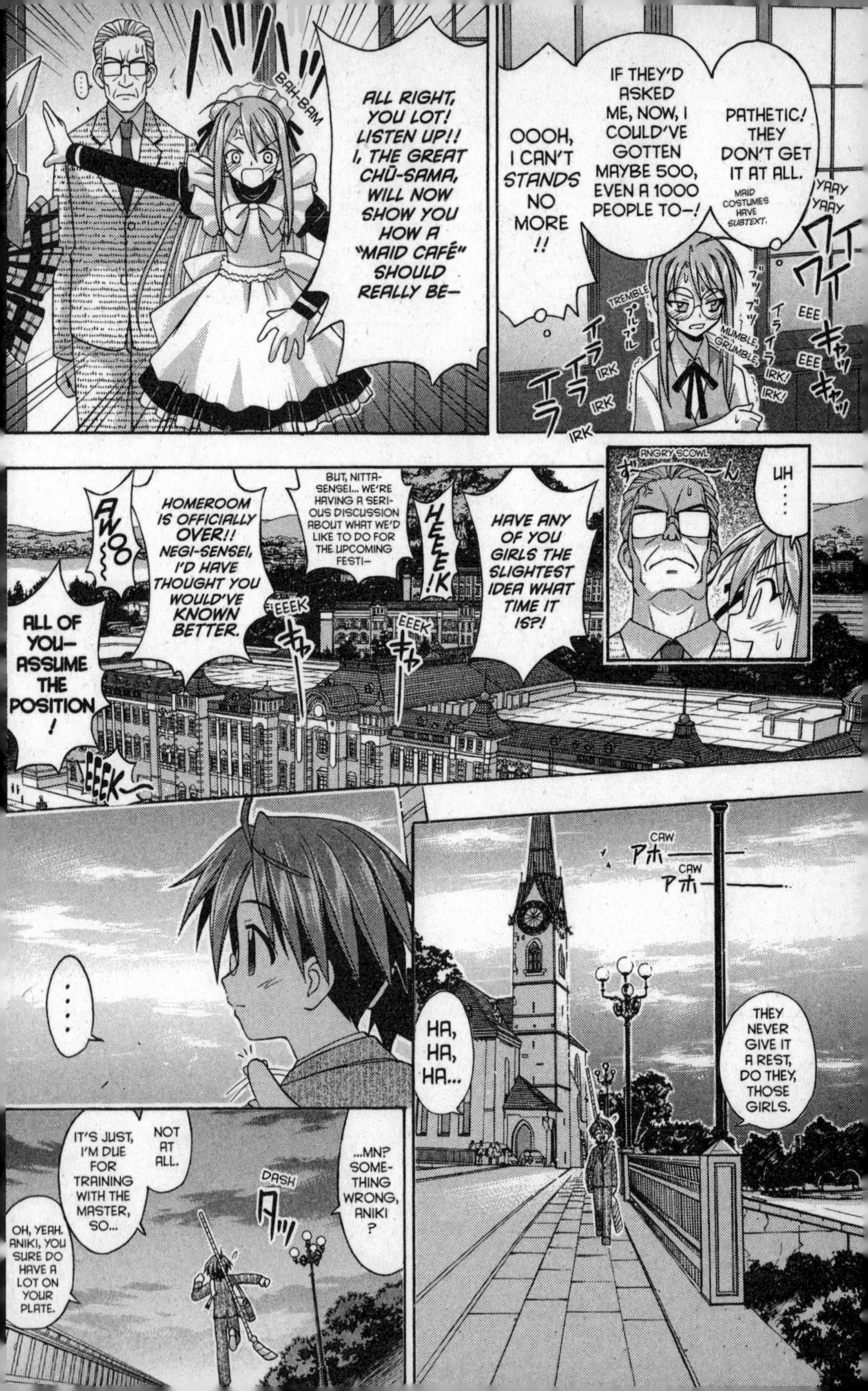
PATHETIC! THEY DON'T GET IT AT ALL.
MAID COSTUMES HAVE SUBTEXT.
YAAY YAAY
EEE EEE
IF THEY'D ASKED ME, NOW, I COULD'VE GOTTEN MAYBE 500, EVEN A 1000 PEOPLE TO—!
OOOH, I CAN'T STANDS NO MORE!!
TREMBLE
MUMBLE, GRUMBLE
IRK! IRK!
IRK IRK IRK
BAH-BAM
ALL RIGHT, YOU LOT! LISTEN UP!! I, THE GREAT CHŪ-SAMA, WILL NOW SHOW YOU HOW A "MAID CAFÉ" SHOULD REALLY BE—
...
ANGRY SCOWL
UH ....
HAVE ANY OF YOU GIRLS THE SLIGHTEST IDEA WHAT TIME IT IS?!
HEEEE!K
BUT, NITTA-SENSEI... WE'RE HAVING A SERIOUS DISCUSSION ABOUT WHAT WE'D LIKE TO DO FOR THE UPCOMING FESTI—
EEEK
EEEK
HOMEROOM IS OFFICIALLY OVER!! NEGI-SENSEI, I'D HAVE THOUGHT YOU WOULD'VE KNOWN BETTER.
AWOO~
ALL OF YOU—ASSUME THE POSITION!
EEEK~
CAW
CAW
THEY NEVER GIVE IT A REST, DO THEY, THOSE GIRLS.
HA, HA, HA...
....
...MN? SOMETHING WRONG, ANIKI?
NOT AT ALL.
IT'S JUST, I'M DUE FOR TRAINING WITH THE MASTER, SO...
DASH
OH, YEAH. ANIKI, YOU SURE DO HAVE A LOT ON YOUR PLATE.

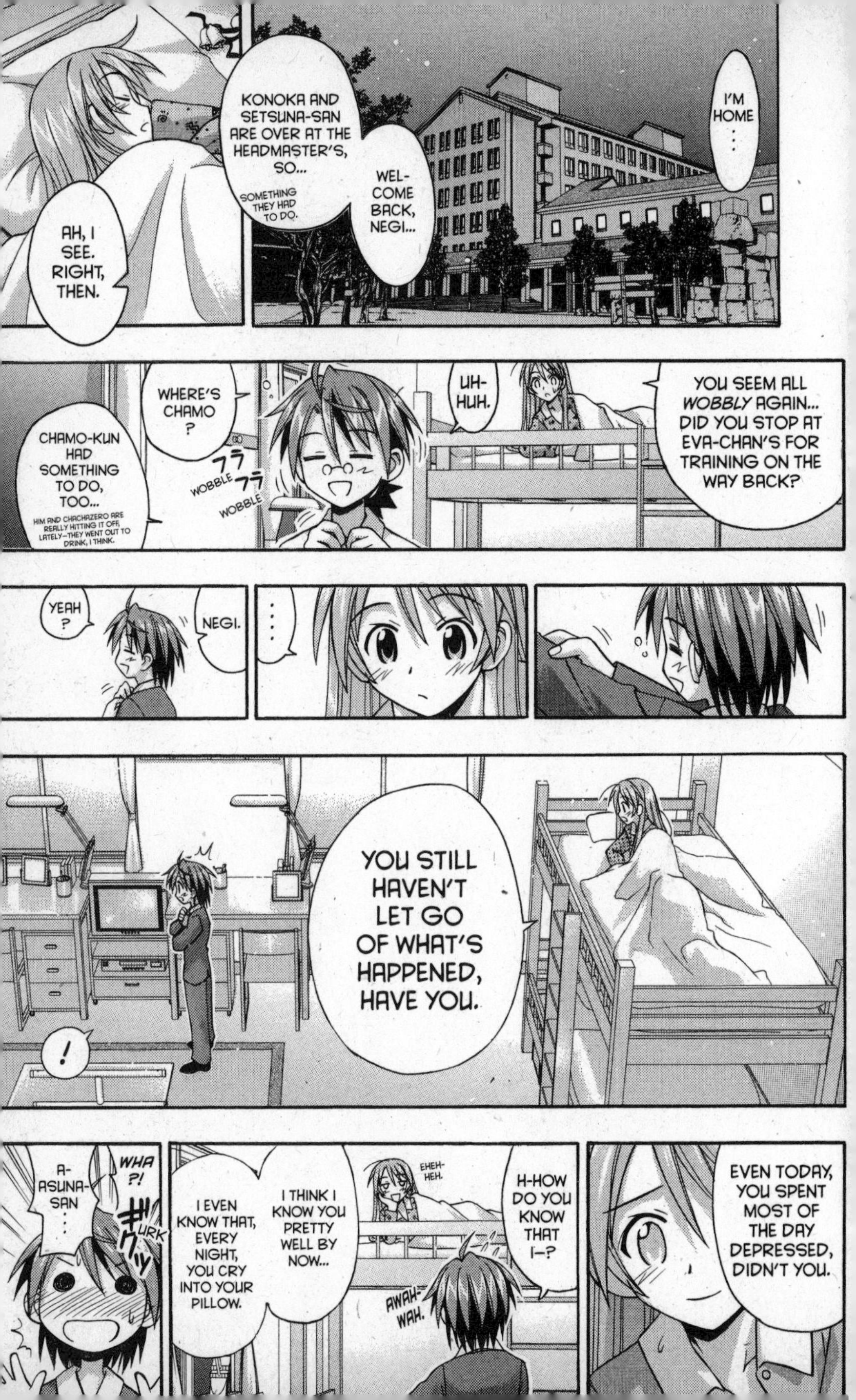
I'M HOME...
WELCOME BACK, NEGI...
KONOKA AND SETSUNA-SAN ARE OVER AT THE HEADMASTER'S, SO...
SOMETHING THEY HAD TO DO.
AH, I SEE. RIGHT, THEN.
YOU SEEM ALL *WOBBLY* AGAIN... DID YOU STOP AT EVA-CHAN'S FOR TRAINING ON THE WAY BACK?
UH-HUH.
フラ WOBBLE
フラ WOBBLE
WHERE'S CHAMO?
CHAMO-KUN HAD SOMETHING TO DO, TOO...
HIM AND CHACHAZERO ARE REALLY HITTING IT OFF, LATELY—THEY WENT OUT TO DRINK, I THINK.
....
NEGI.
YEAH?
YOU STILL HAVEN'T LET GO OF WHAT'S HAPPENED, HAVE YOU.
!
EVEN TODAY, YOU SPENT MOST OF THE DAY DEPRESSED, DIDN'T YOU.
H-HOW DO YOU KNOW THAT I—?
EHEH-HEH.
I THINK I KNOW YOU PRETTY WELL BY NOW...
AWAH-WAH.
I EVEN KNOW THAT, EVERY NIGHT, YOU CRY INTO YOUR PILLOW.
WHA?!
ギクッ URK
A-ASUNA-SAN...

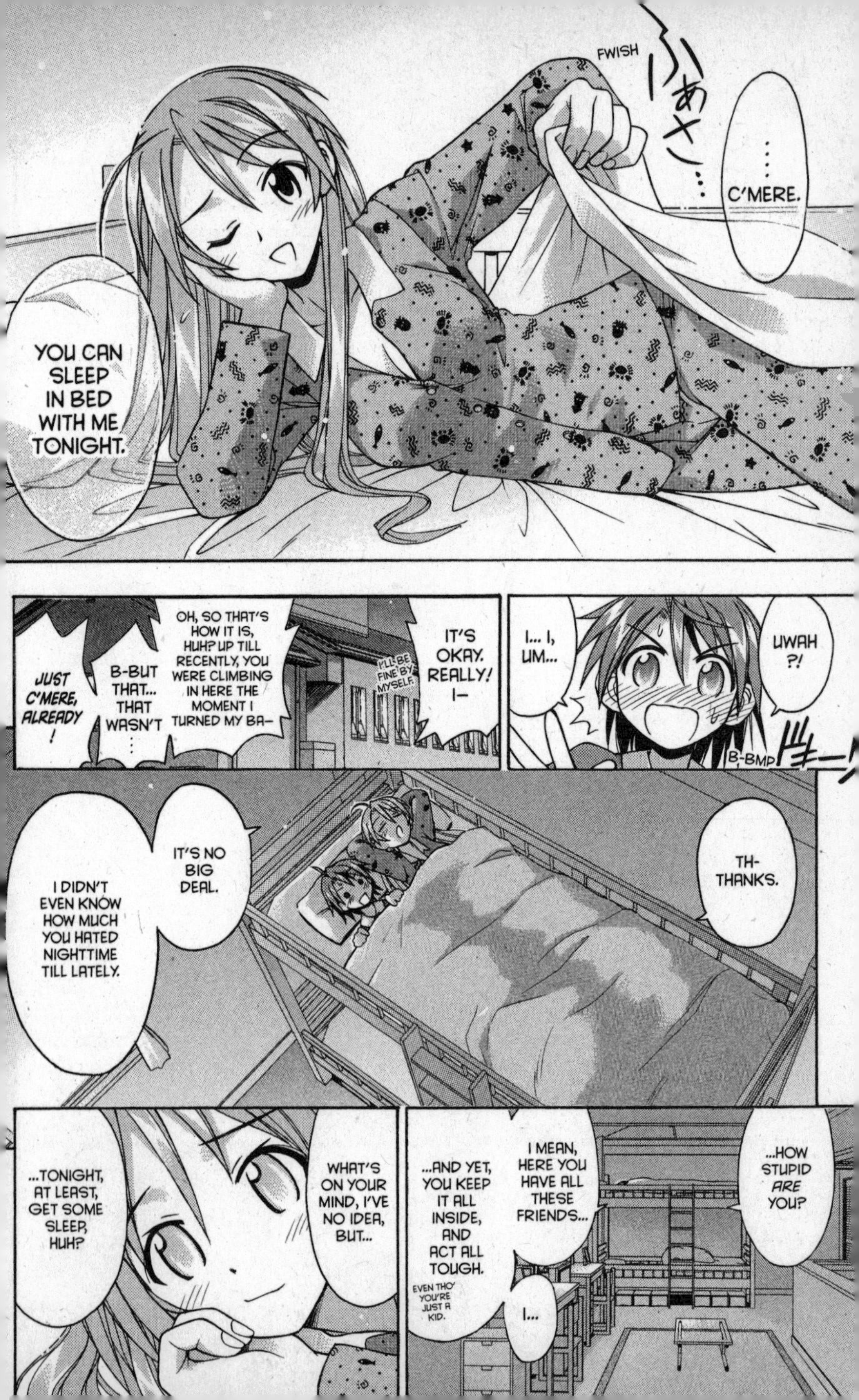
FWISH
ふあさ…
…… C'MERE.
YOU CAN SLEEP IN BED WITH ME TONIGHT.
UWAH?!
I… I, UM…
B-BMP
IT'S OKAY. REALLY! I—
I'LL BE FINE BY MYSELF.
OH, SO THAT'S HOW IT IS, HUH? UP TILL RECENTLY, YOU WERE CLIMBING IN HERE THE MOMENT I TURNED MY BA—
B-BUT THAT… THAT WASN'T …
JUST C'MERE, ALREADY!
TH-THANKS.
IT'S NO BIG DEAL.
I DIDN'T EVEN KNOW HOW MUCH YOU HATED NIGHTTIME TILL LATELY.
…HOW STUPID ARE YOU?
I MEAN, HERE YOU HAVE ALL THESE FRIENDS…
I…
…AND YET, YOU KEEP IT ALL INSIDE, AND ACT ALL TOUGH.
EVEN THO' YOU'RE JUST A KID.
WHAT'S ON YOUR MIND, I'VE NO IDEA, BUT…
…TONIGHT, AT LEAST, GET SOME SLEEP, HUH?

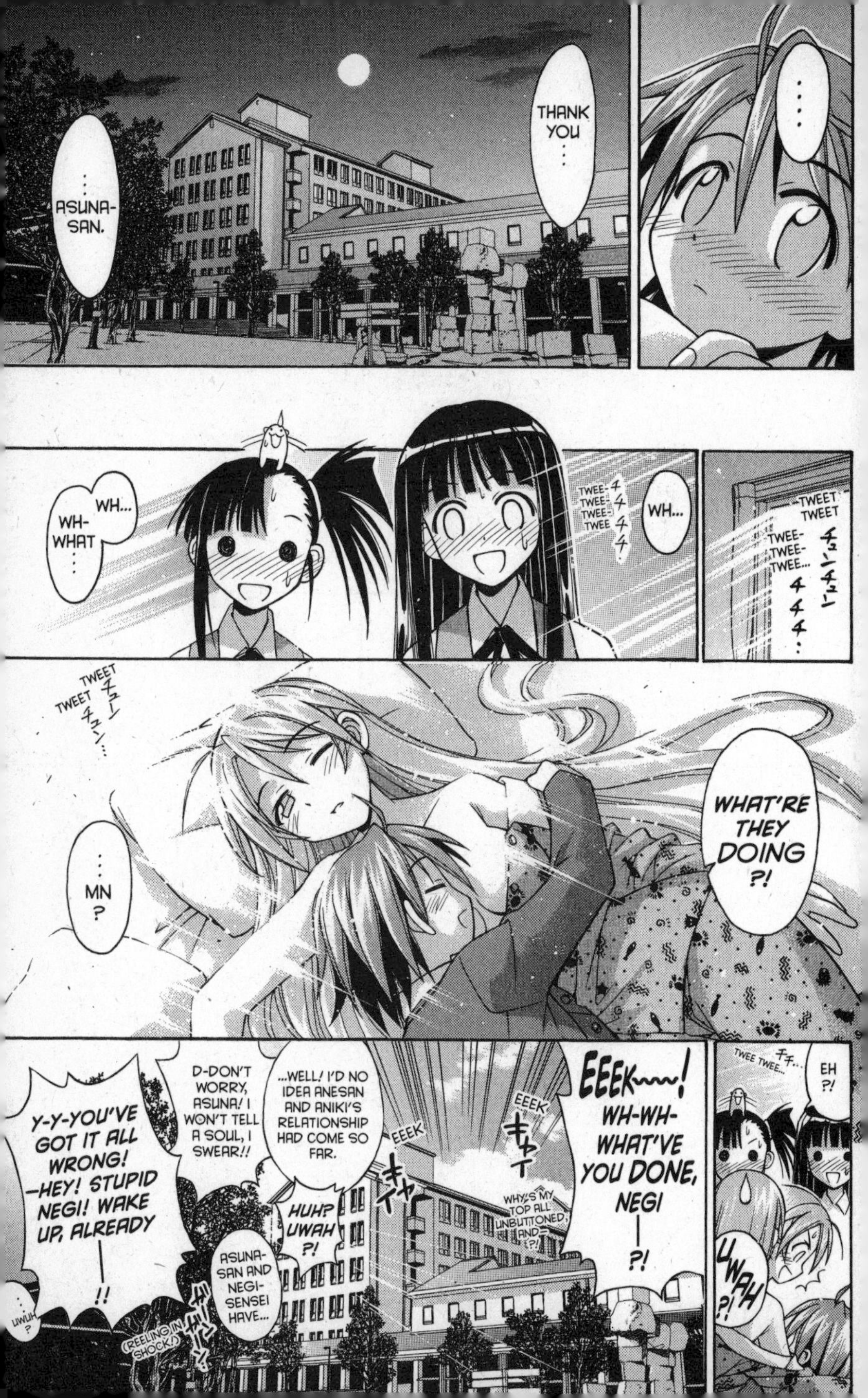
....
THANK YOU...
...ASUNA-SAN.
TWEET TWEET
TWEE- TWEE- TWEE...
チュンチュン
チチチ...
TWEE- TWEE- TWEE- TWEE
チチチチ.
WH...
WH... WH-WHAT...
WHAT'RE THEY DOING?!
...MN?
TWEET TWEET
チュンチュン...
EH?!
TWEE TWEE...
チチ...
UWAH?!
EEEK~~! WH-WH-WHAT'VE YOU DONE, NEGI—?!
EEEK
キャ
WHY'S MY TOP ALL UNBUTTONED, AND—?!
EEEK
キャ
...WELL! I'D NO IDEA ANESAN AND ANIKI'S RELATIONSHIP HAD COME SO FAR.
HUH? UWAH?!
D-DON'T WORRY, ASUNA! I WON'T TELL A SOUL, I SWEAR!!
ASUNA-SAN AND NEGI-SENSEI HAVE...
(REELING IN SHOCK!)
Y-Y-YOU'VE GOT IT ALL WRONG! —HEY! STUPID NEGI! WAKE UP, ALREADY—!!
...UWUH?

STUDENT NUMBER 30
YOTSUBA, SATSUKI

BORN: 12 MAY 1988
BLOODTYPE: A
LIKES: COOKING; HAVING OTHERS ENJOY MY COOKING; TAKING IT EASY
DISLIKES: NOTHING IN PARTICULAR... COMPETITION, MAYBE?
AFFILIATIONS: CHAIRMAN, "HOT LUNCH" COMMITTEE; MEMBER, COOKING RESEARCH CIRCLE

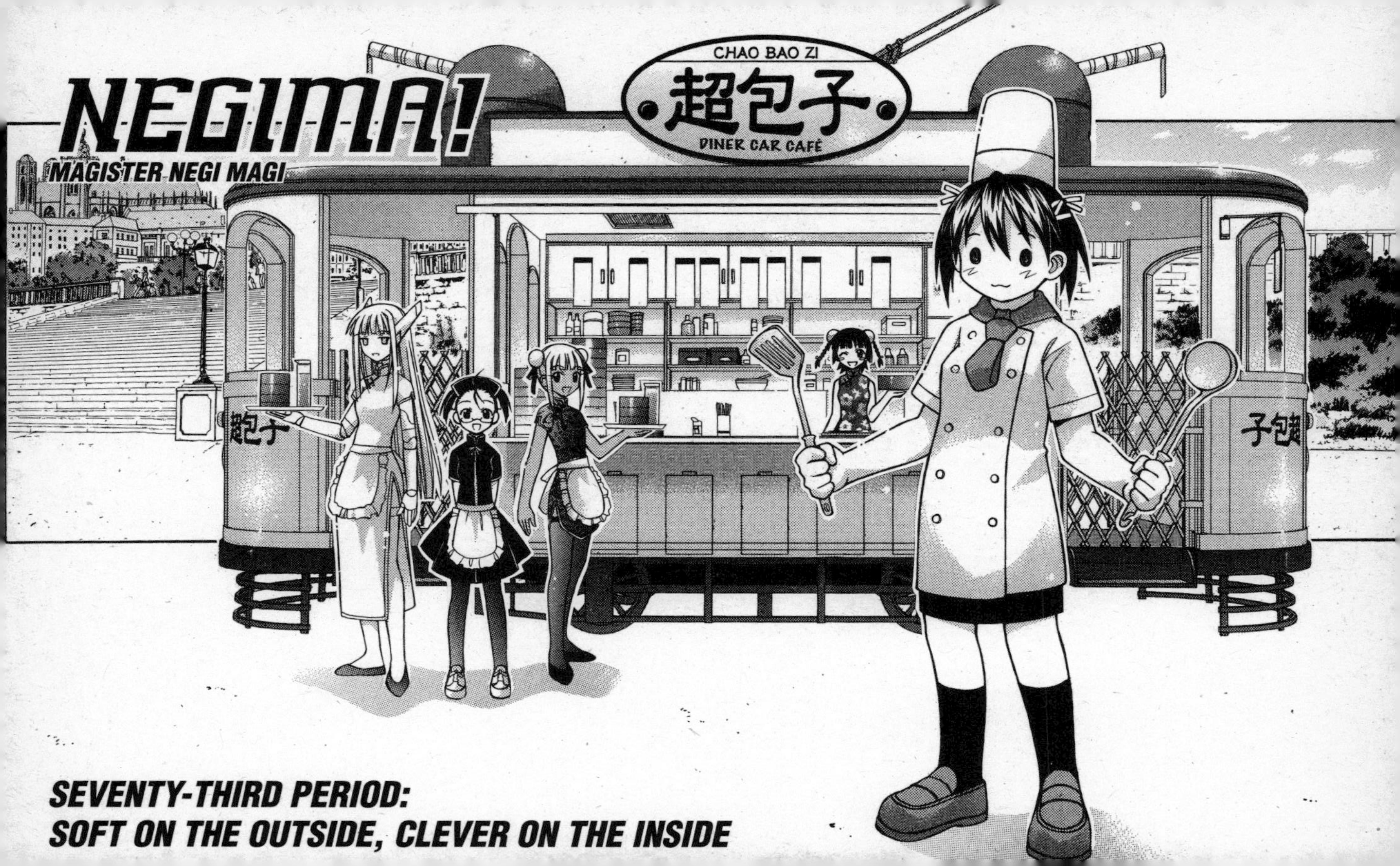
NEGIMA!
MAGISTER NEGI MAGI
CHAO BAO ZI
超包子
DINER CAR CAFÉ
超包子
超包子

SEVENTY-THIRD PERIOD:
SOFT ON THE OUTSIDE, CLEVER ON THE INSIDE

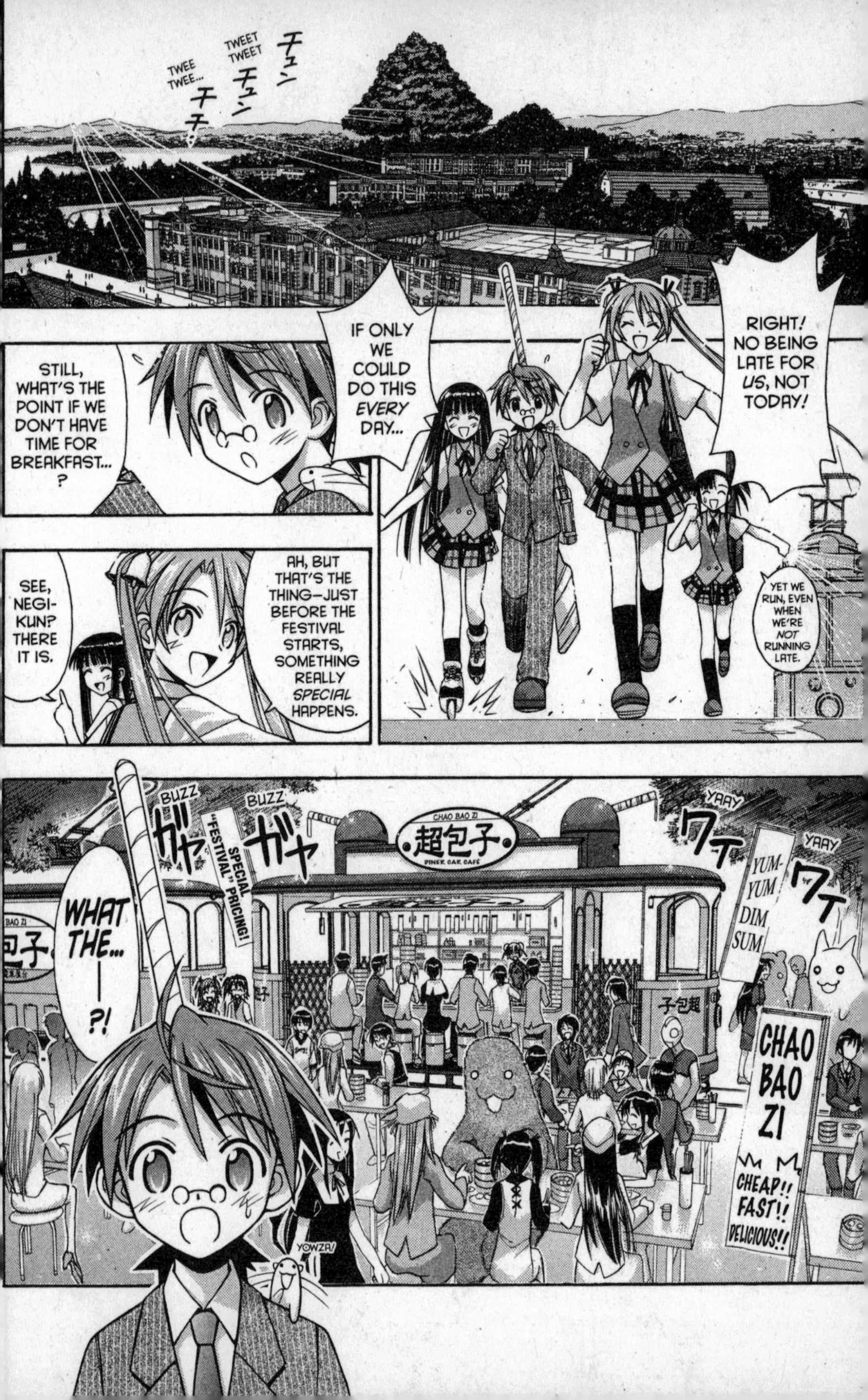
TWEET TWEET
チュン
チュン
TWEE TWEE...
チチ
RIGHT! NO BEING LATE FOR *US*, NOT TODAY!
IF ONLY WE COULD DO THIS *EVERY* DAY...
YET WE RUN, EVEN WHEN WE'RE *NOT* RUNNING LATE.
STILL, WHAT'S THE POINT IF WE DON'T HAVE TIME FOR BREAKFAST... ?
AH, BUT THAT'S THE THING—JUST BEFORE THE FESTIVAL STARTS, SOMETHING REALLY *SPECIAL* HAPPENS.
SEE, NEGI-KUN? THERE IT IS.
YAAY
ワイ
YAAY
ワイ
CHAO BAO ZI
超包子
DINER CAR CAFÉ
BUZZ
ガヤ
BUZZ
ガヤ
SPECIAL "FESTIVAL" PRICING!
YUM-YUM DIM SUM
CHAO BAO ZI
CHEAP!! FAST!! DELICIOUS!!
WHAT THE...—?!
YOWZA!

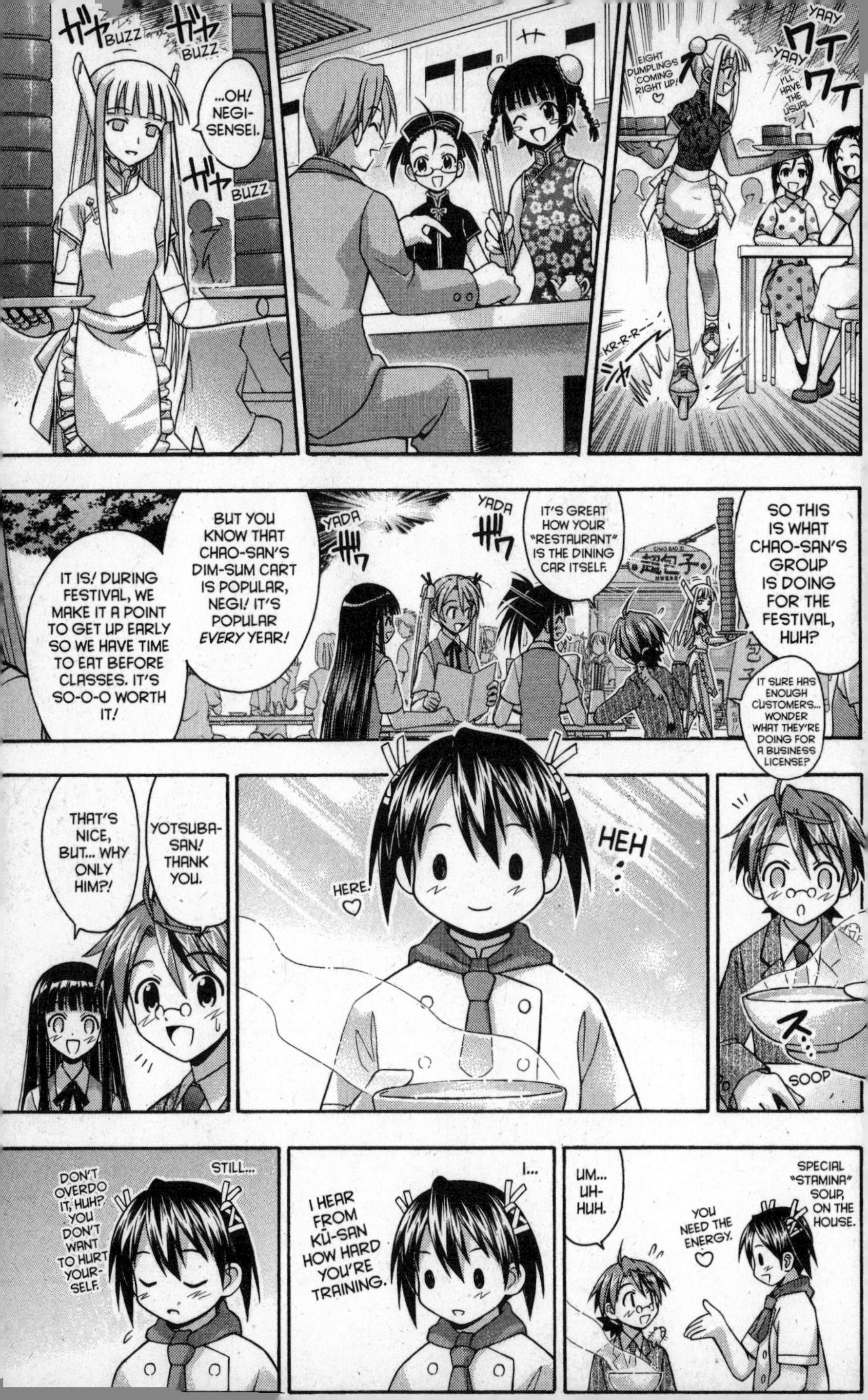
YAAY ワイ
YAAY ワイ
EIGHT DUMPLINGS COMING RIGHT UP! ♡
I'LL HAVE THE USUAL.
KR-R-R...
シャー
ガヤ BUZZ
ガヤ BUZZ
...OH! NEGI-SENSEI.
ガヤ BUZZ
SO THIS IS WHAT CHAO-SAN'S GROUP IS DOING FOR THE FESTIVAL, HUH?
IT SURE HAS ENOUGH CUSTOMERS... WONDER WHAT THEY'RE DOING FOR A BUSINESS LICENSE?
IT'S GREAT HOW YOUR "RESTAURANT" IS THE DINING CAR ITSELF.
超包子
YADA ガヤ
YADA ガヤ
BUT YOU KNOW THAT CHAO-SAN'S DIM-SUM CART IS POPULAR, NEGI! IT'S POPULAR EVERY YEAR!
IT IS! DURING FESTIVAL, WE MAKE IT A POINT TO GET UP EARLY SO WE HAVE TIME TO EAT BEFORE CLASSES. IT'S SO-O-O WORTH IT!
ス...
SOOP
HEH...
HERE. ♡
YOTSUBA-SAN! THANK YOU.
THAT'S NICE, BUT... WHY ONLY HIM?!
SPECIAL "STAMINA" SOUP, ON THE HOUSE.
YOU NEED THE ENERGY. ♡
UM... UH-HUH.
I...
I HEAR FROM KŪ-SAN HOW HARD YOU'RE TRAINING.
STILL...
DON'T OVERDO IT, HUH? YOU DON'T WANT TO HURT YOURSELF.

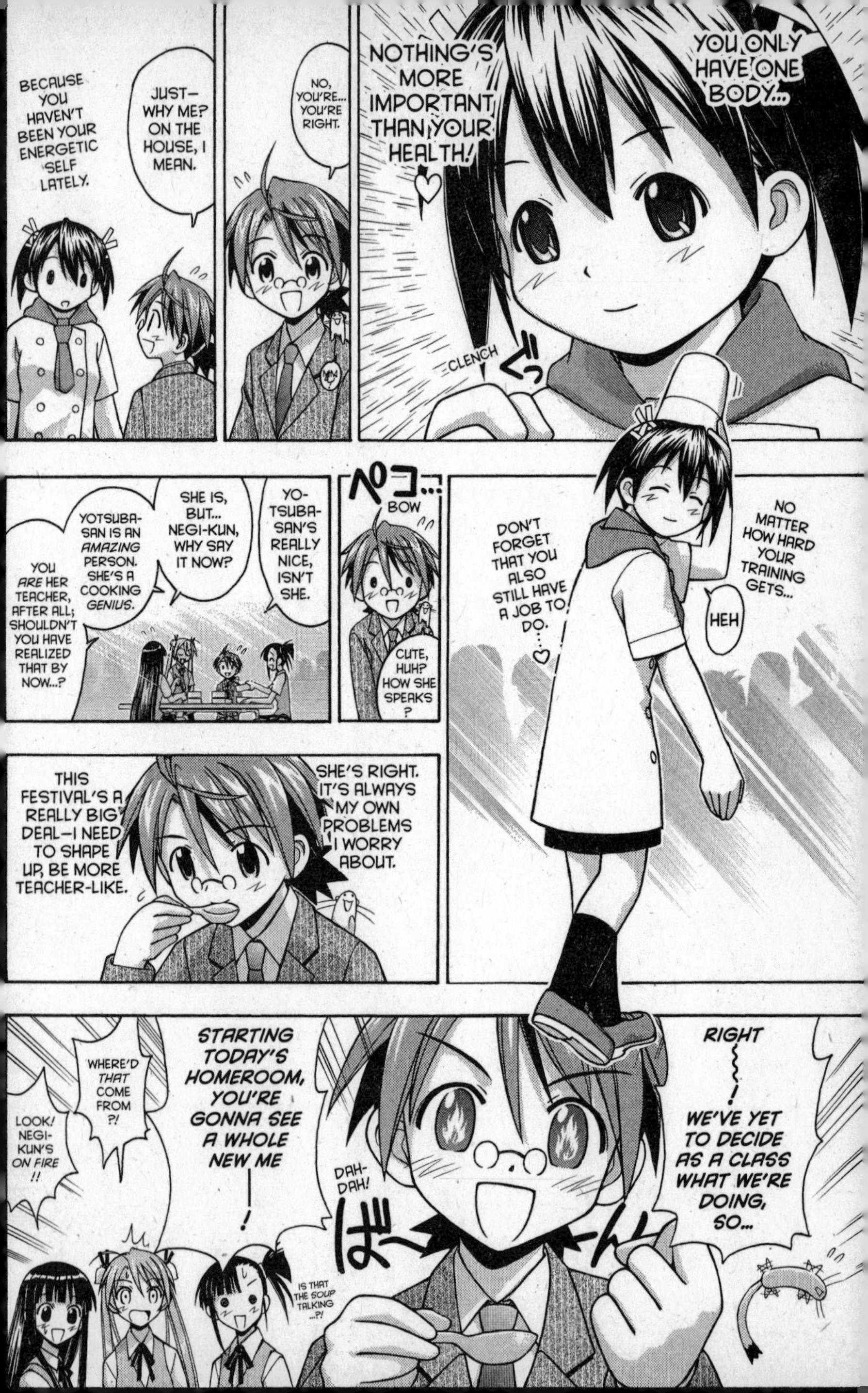
YOU ONLY HAVE ONE BODY...
NOTHING'S MORE IMPORTANT THAN YOUR HEALTH!
CLENCH
NO, YOU'RE... YOU'RE RIGHT.
JUST— WHY ME? ON THE HOUSE, I MEAN.
BECAUSE YOU HAVEN'T BEEN YOUR ENERGETIC SELF LATELY.
NO MATTER HOW HARD YOUR TRAINING GETS...
HEH
DON'T FORGET THAT YOU ALSO STILL HAVE A JOB TO DO...
ペコ…
BOW
YO-TSUBA-SAN'S REALLY NICE, ISN'T SHE.
CUTE, HUH? HOW SHE SPEAKS?
SHE IS, BUT... NEGI-KUN, WHY SAY IT NOW?
YOTSUBA-SAN IS AN *AMAZING* PERSON. SHE'S A COOKING *GENIUS*.
YOU *ARE* HER TEACHER, AFTER ALL; SHOULDN'T YOU HAVE REALIZED THAT BY NOW...?
SHE'S RIGHT. IT'S ALWAYS MY OWN PROBLEMS I WORRY ABOUT.
THIS FESTIVAL'S A REALLY BIG DEAL—I NEED TO SHAPE UP, BE MORE TEACHER-LIKE.
RIGHT~~~! WE'VE YET TO DECIDE AS A CLASS WHAT WE'RE DOING, SO...
STARTING TODAY'S HOMEROOM, YOU'RE GONNA SEE A WHOLE NEW ME!
DAH-DAH!
IS THAT THE *SOUP* TALKING...?!
WHERE'D *THAT* COME FROM?!
LOOK! NEGI-KUN'S *ON FIRE*!!

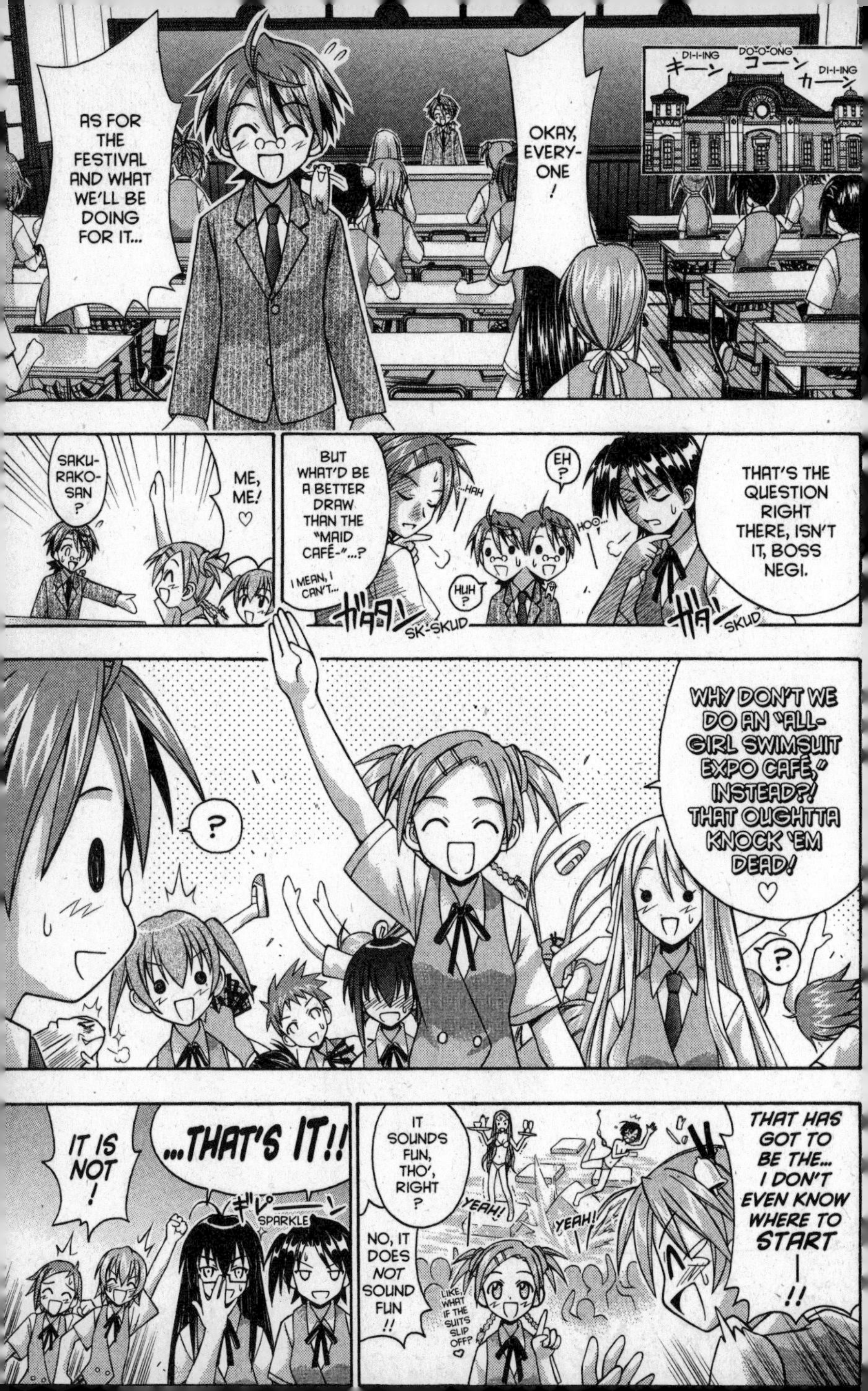

DI-I-ING
キーン
DO-O-ONG
コーン
DI-I-ING
カーン
OKAY, EVERY-ONE!
AS FOR THE FESTIVAL AND WHAT WE'LL BE DOING FOR IT...
THAT'S THE QUESTION RIGHT THERE, ISN'T IT, BOSS NEGI.
HOO...
SKUD
EH?
HUH?
BUT WHAT'D BE A BETTER DRAW THAN THE "MAID CAFÉ-"...?
...HAH
I MEAN, I CAN'T...
SK-SKUD
ME, ME! ♡
SAKU-RAKO-SAN?
WHY DON'T WE DO AN "ALL-GIRL SWIMSUIT EXPO CAFÉ," INSTEAD?! THAT OUGHTTA KNOCK 'EM DEAD! ♡
?
?
THAT HAS GOT TO BE THE... I DON'T EVEN KNOW WHERE TO START!!
IT SOUNDS FUN, THO', RIGHT?
YEAH!
YEAH!
NO, IT DOES NOT SOUND FUN!!
LIKE, WHAT IF THE SUITS SLIP OFF? ♡
...THAT'S IT!!
SPARKLE
IT IS NOT!

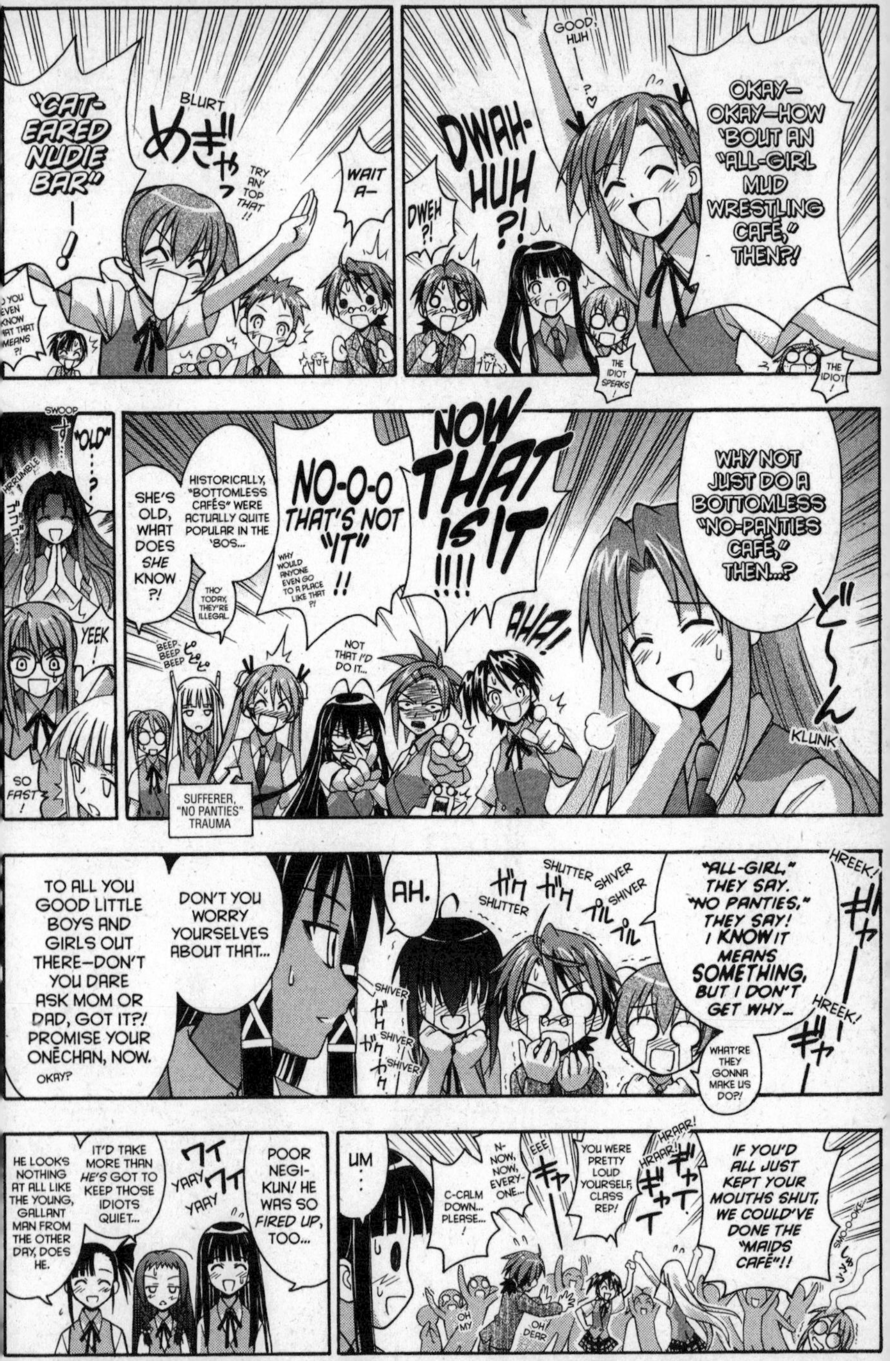
GOOD, HUH ?♡
OKAY—OKAY—HOW 'BOUT AN "ALL-GIRL MUD WRESTLING CAFÉ," THEN?!
DWAH-HUH ?!
DWEH ?!
THE IDIOT SPEAKS !
THE IDIOT !
WAIT A—
TRY AN' TOP THAT !!
BLURT
めぎゃっ
"CAT-EARED NUDIE BAR" — !
D YOU EVEN KNOW HAT THAT MEANS ?!
WHY NOT JUST DO A BOTTOMLESS "NO-PANTIES CAFÉ," THEN...?
ど~ん
KLUNK
AHA!
NOW THAT IS IT !!!!
NO-O-O THAT'S NOT "IT" !!
WHY WOULD ANYONE EVEN GO TO A PLACE LIKE THAT ?!
NOT THAT I'D DO IT...
HISTORICALLY, "BOTTOMLESS CAFÉS" WERE ACTUALLY QUITE POPULAR IN THE '80S...
THO' TODAY, THEY'RE ILLEGAL.
SHE'S OLD, WHAT DOES SHE KNOW ?!
BEEP BEEP BEEP ピピピ
SUFFERER, "NO PANTIES" TRAUMA
SWOOP
す
"OLD" ...?
HRRUMBLE ゴゴゴ...
YEEK !
SO FAST !
HREEK! ギャー!
HREEK! ギャ
"ALL-GIRL," THEY SAY. "NO PANTIES," THEY SAY! I KNOW IT MEANS SOMETHING, BUT I DON'T GET WHY...
WHAT'RE THEY GONNA MAKE US DO?!
SHUTTER ガクガク SHUTTER SHIVER SHIVER プルプル
SHIVER ガク SHIVER ガク SHIVER
AH.
DON'T YOU WORRY YOURSELVES ABOUT THAT...
TO ALL YOU GOOD LITTLE BOYS AND GIRLS OUT THERE—DON'T YOU DARE ASK MOM OR DAD, GOT IT?! PROMISE YOUR ONĒCHAN, NOW.
OKAY?
IF YOU'D ALL JUST KEPT YOUR MOUTHS SHUT, WE COULD'VE DONE THE "MAIDS CAFÉ"!!
SMO-O-OKE
HRAAR! ギャー HRAAR! ギャー
YOU WERE PRETTY LOUD YOURSELF, CLASS REP!
EEE キャー
N-NOW, NOW, EVERY-ONE...
C-CALM DOWN... PLEASE...!
OH MY
OH DEAR
UM ...
POOR NEGI-KUN! HE WAS SO FIRED UP, TOO...
YAAY ワイ YAAY ワイ
IT'D TAKE MORE THAN HE'S GOT TO KEEP THOSE IDIOTS QUIET...
HE LOOKS NOTHING AT ALL LIKE THE YOUNG, GALLANT MAN FROM THE OTHER DAY, DOES HE.

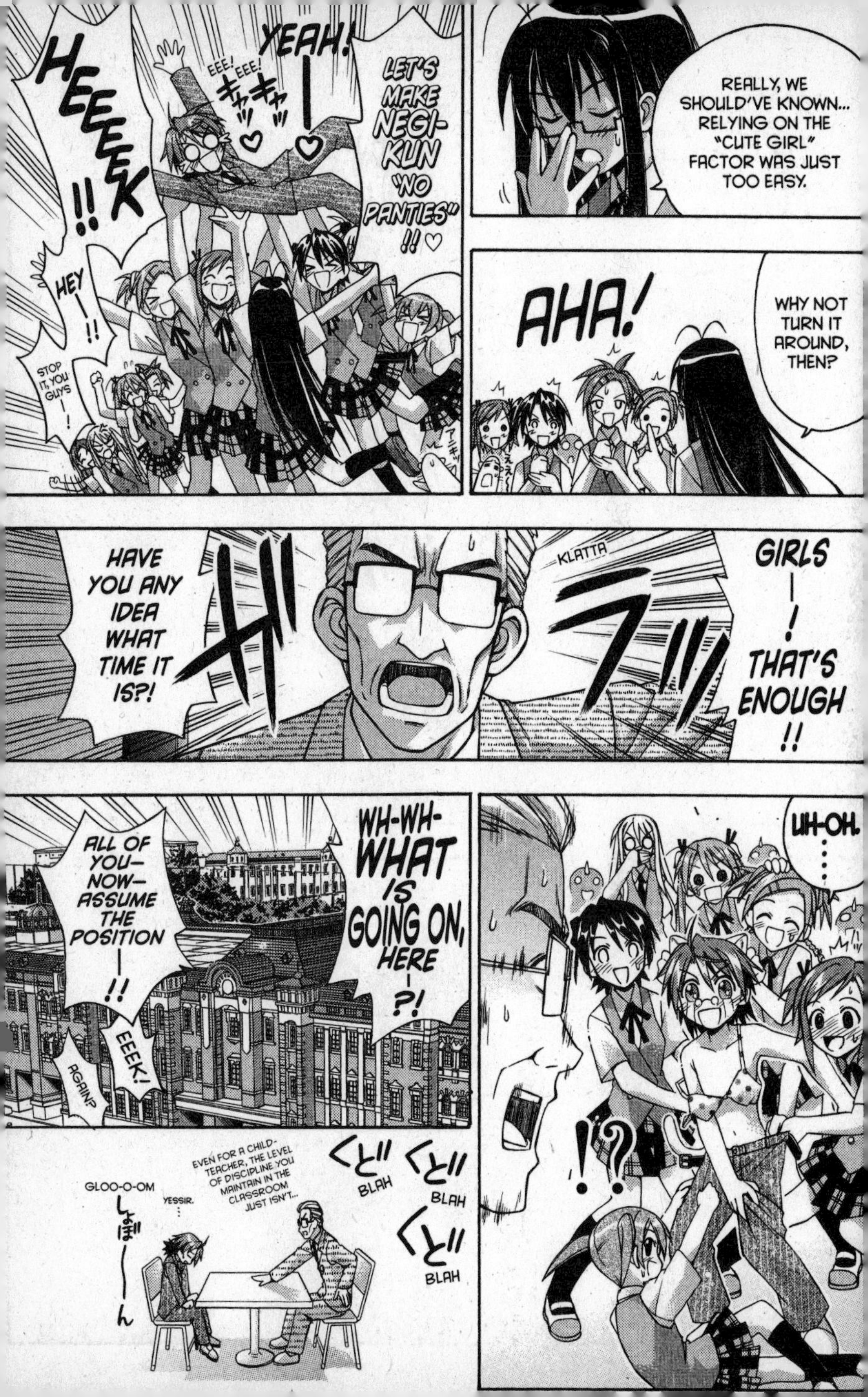

REALLY, WE SHOULD'VE KNOWN... RELYING ON THE "CUTE GIRL" FACTOR WAS JUST TOO EASY.
AHA!
WHY NOT TURN IT AROUND, THEN?
YEAH!—♥
EEE! EEE!
キャッ キャッ ♥
LET'S MAKE NEGI-KUN "NO PANTIES"!! ♡
HEEEEEK!!
HEY—!!
STOP IT, YOU GUYS—!
GIRLS—! THAT'S ENOUGH!!
KLATTA
HAVE YOU ANY IDEA WHAT TIME IT IS?!
UH-OH....
!?
WH-WH-WHAT IS GOING ON, HERE—?!
ALL OF YOU—NOW—ASSUME THE POSITION—!!
EEEK!
AGAIN?
くど BLAH
くど BLAH
くど BLAH
EVEN FOR A CHILD-TEACHER, THE LEVEL OF DISCIPLINE YOU MAINTAIN IN THE CLASSROOM JUST ISN'T...
YESSIR. ...
GLOO-O-OM
しょぼーーん

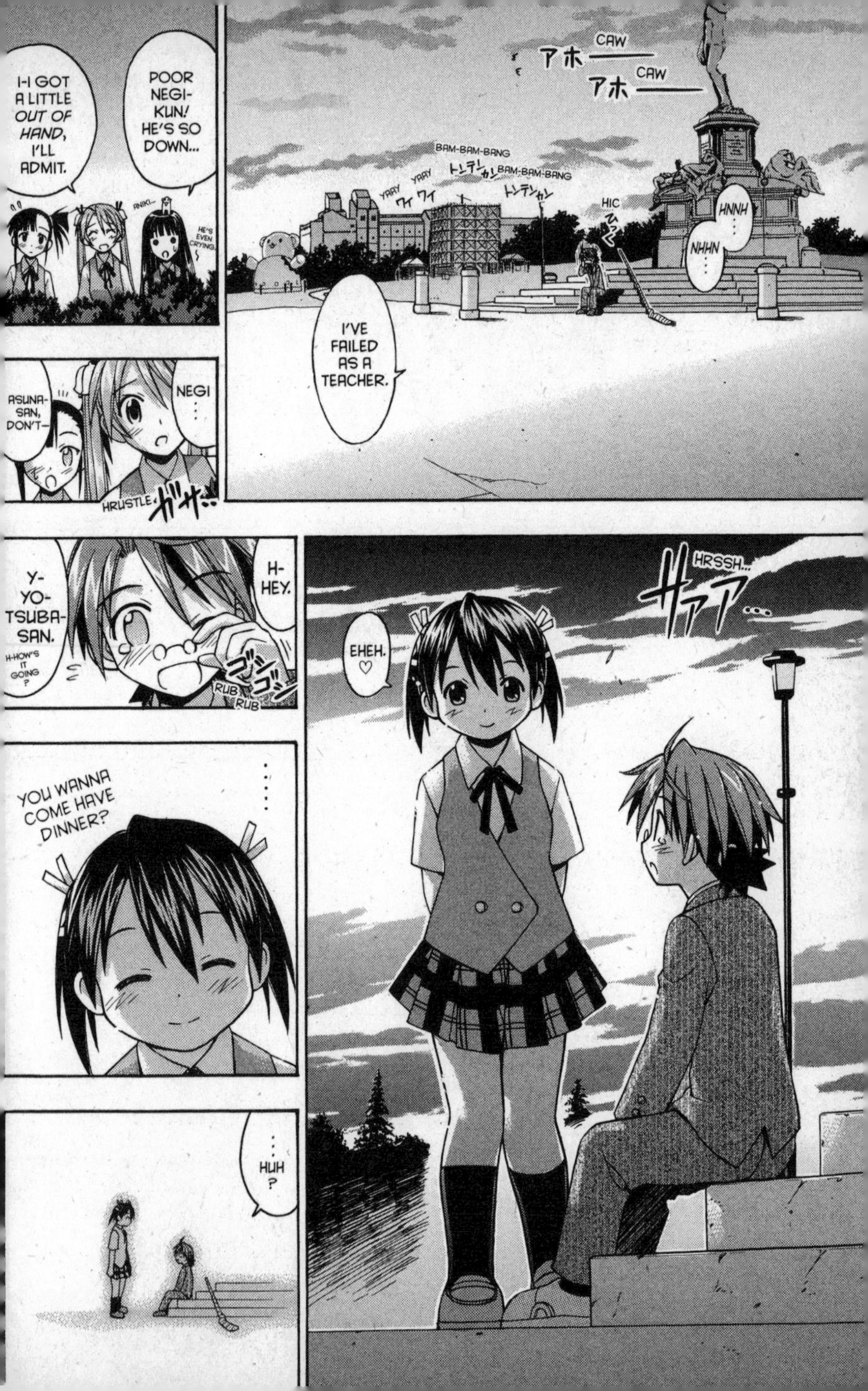
アホー CAW
アホー CAW
BAM-BAM-BANG トンテンカン
BAM-BAM-BANG トンテンカン
YAAY YAAY ワイワイ
HIC ひっく
HNNH...
NHHN...
I'VE FAILED AS A TEACHER.
POOR NEGI-KUN! HE'S SO DOWN...
I-I GOT A LITTLE *OUT OF HAND*, I'LL ADMIT.
ANIKI...
HE'S EVEN CRYING.
NEGI...
ASUNA-SAN, DON'T—
HRUSTLE ガサ
HRSSH... サァア
EHEH. ♡
H-HEY.
Y-YOTSUBA-SAN.
H-HOW'S IT GOING?
RUB RUB ゴシゴシ
.....
YOU WANNA COME HAVE DINNER?
...HUH?

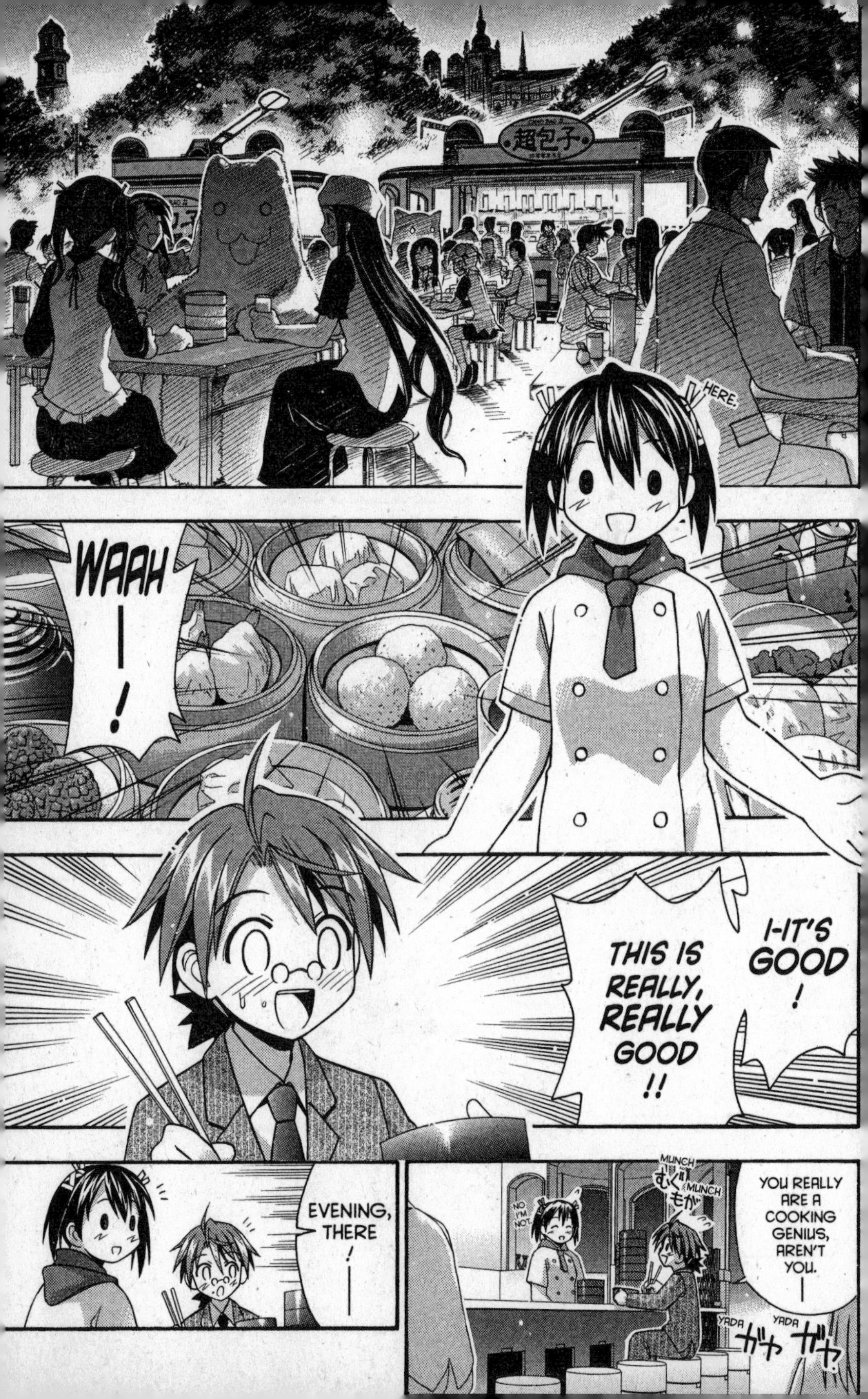
超包子
HERE.
WAAH—!
I-IT'S GOOD!
THIS IS REALLY, REALLY GOOD!!
YOU REALLY ARE A COOKING GENIUS, AREN'T YOU.
むぐ MUNCH
もが MUNCH
NO I'M NOT
ガヤ YADA
ガヤ YADA
EVENING, THERE!

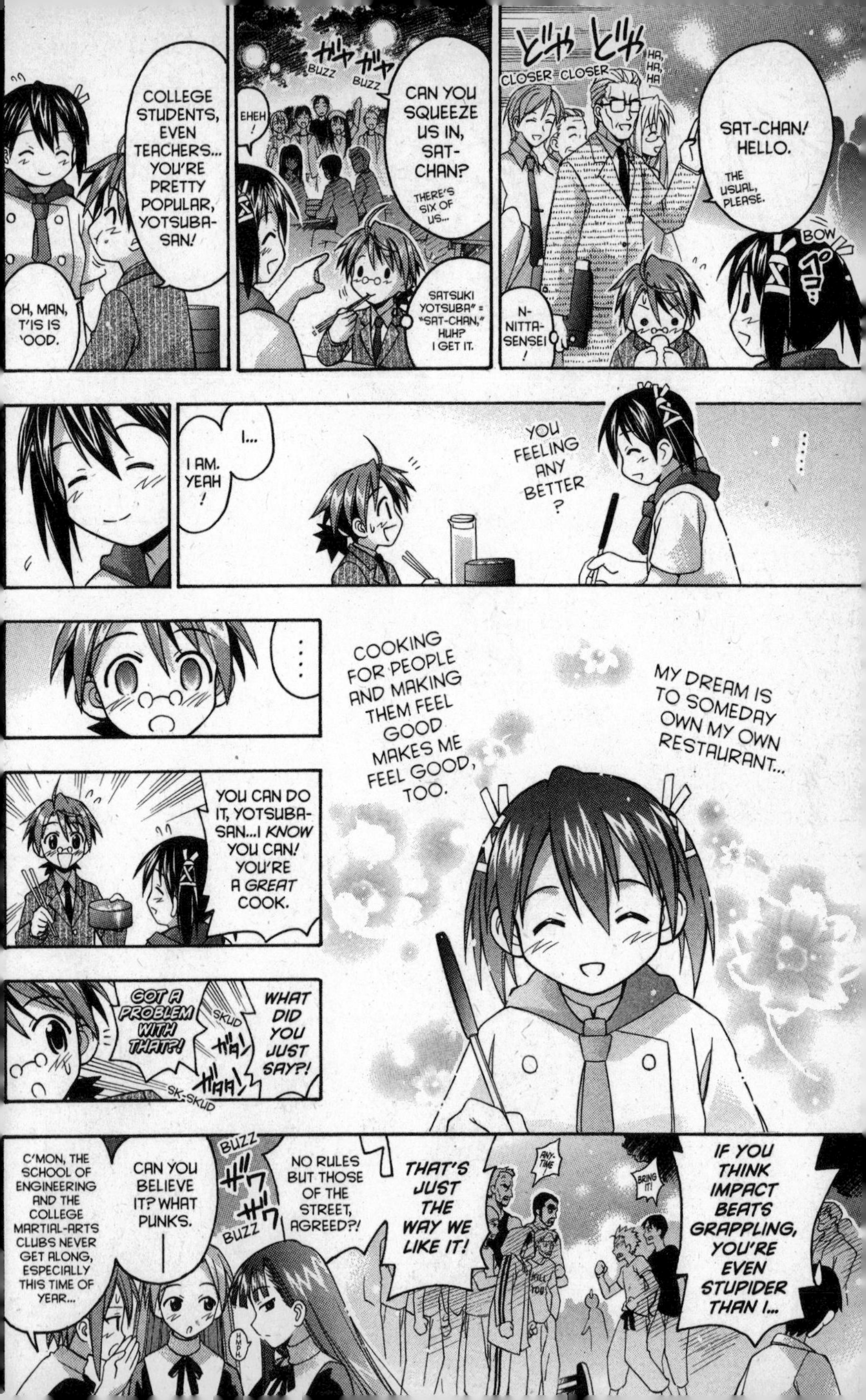
どや どや
CLOSER CLOSER
HA, HA, HA
SAT-CHAN! HELLO.
THE USUAL, PLEASE.
BOW
N-NITTA-SENSEI!
ガヤ ガヤ
BUZZ BUZZ
CAN YOU SQUEEZE US IN, SAT-CHAN?
THERE'S SIX OF US...
EHEH!
SATSUKI YOTSUBA" = "SAT-CHAN," HUH? I GET IT.
COLLEGE STUDENTS, EVEN TEACHERS... YOU'RE PRETTY POPULAR, YOTSUBA-SAN!
OH, MAN, T'IS IS 'OOD.
....
YOU FEELING ANY BETTER?
I...
I AM. YEAH!
MY DREAM IS TO SOMEDAY OWN MY OWN RESTAURANT...
COOKING FOR PEOPLE AND MAKING THEM FEEL GOOD MAKES ME FEEL GOOD, TOO.
....
YOU CAN DO IT, YOTSUBA-SAN...I KNOW YOU CAN! YOU'RE A GREAT COOK.
WHAT DID YOU JUST SAY?!
GOT A PROBLEM WITH THAT?!
SKUD
ガタ!
ガタタ!
SK-SKUD
IF YOU THINK IMPACT BEATS GRAPPLING, YOU'RE EVEN STUPIDER THAN I...
BRING IT!
ANY-TIME
THAT'S JUST THE WAY WE LIKE IT!
NO RULES BUT THOSE OF THE STREET, AGREED?!
BUZZ
ザワ ザワ
BUZZ
CAN YOU BELIEVE IT? WHAT PUNKS.
C'MON, THE SCHOOL OF ENGINEERING AND THE COLLEGE MARTIAL-ARTS CLUBS NEVER GET ALONG, ESPECIALLY THIS TIME OF YEAR...
HMPH.

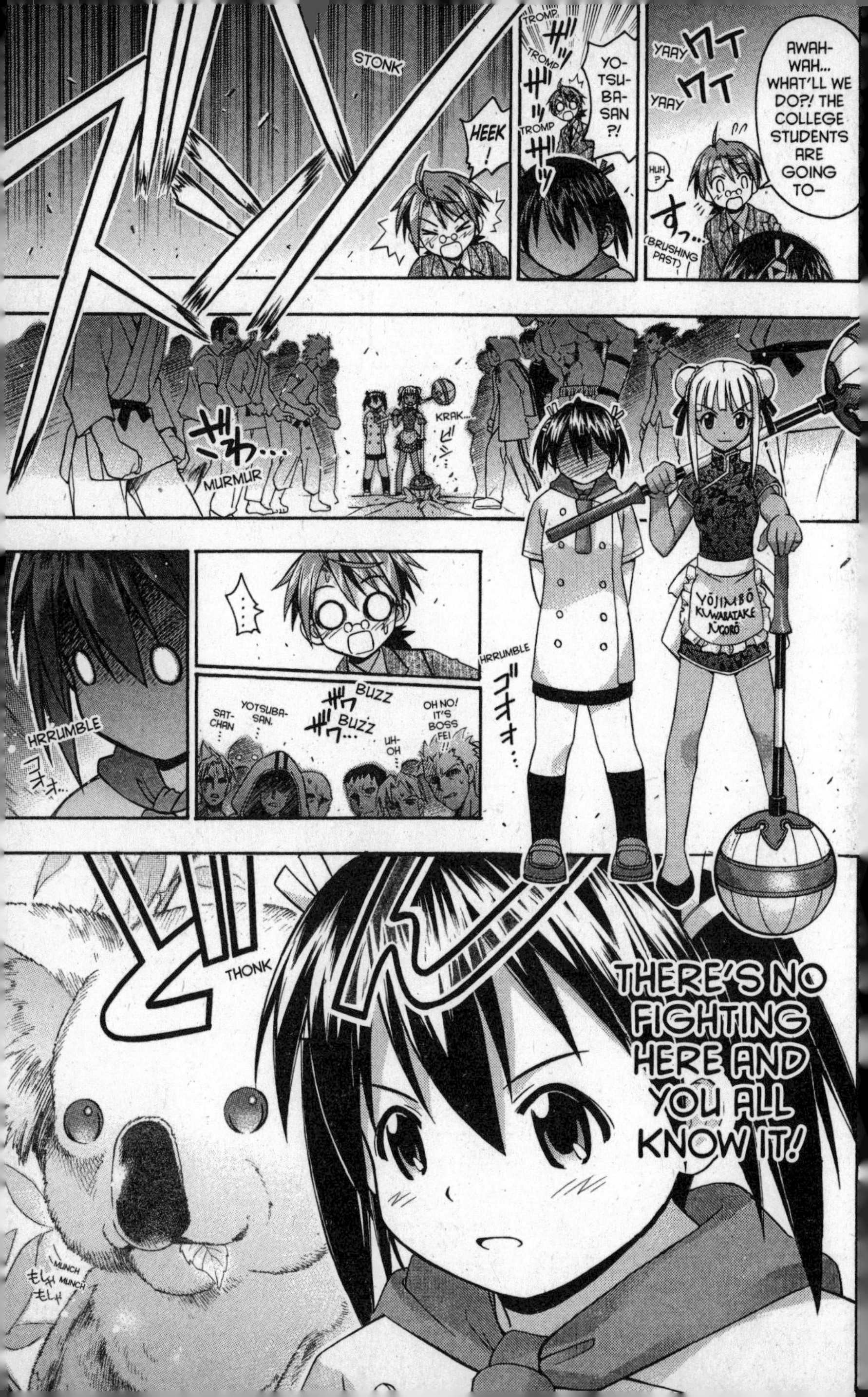

AWAH-WAH... WHAT'LL WE DO?! THE COLLEGE STUDENTS ARE GOING TO—
YAAY
YAAY
HUH?
(BRUSHING PAST)
TROMP
TROMP
TROMP
YO-TSU-BA-SAN?!
STONK
HEEK!
KRAK...
MURMUR
HRRUMBLE
YŌJIMBŌ KUWABATAKE JŪGORŌ
...
OH NO! IT'S BOSS FEI!!
BUZZ
BUZZ
UH-OH...
YOTSUBA-SAN...
SAT-CHAN...
HRRUMBLE
THERE'S NO FIGHTING HERE AND YOU ALL KNOW IT!
THONK
MUNCH
MUNCH

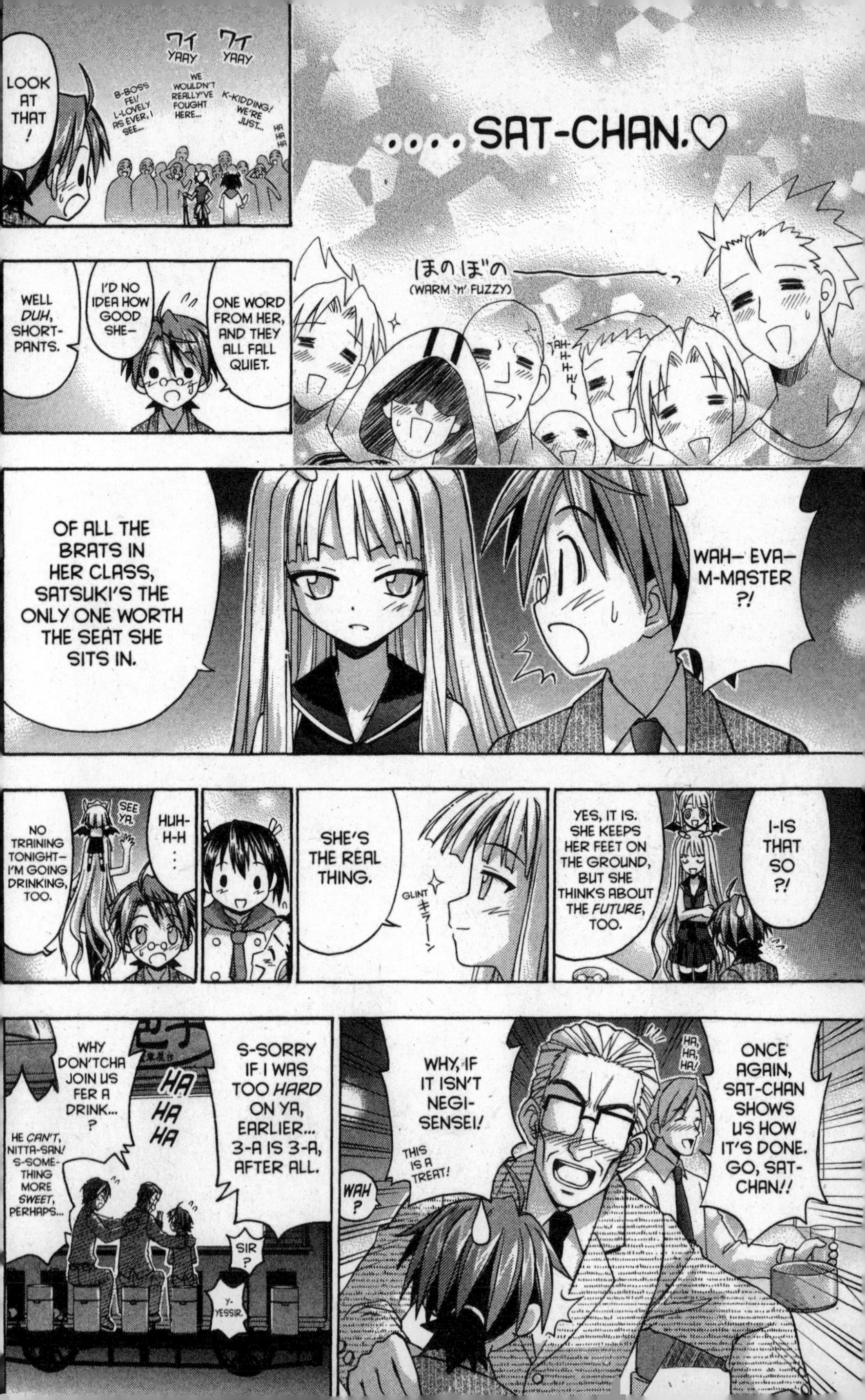
....SAT-CHAN.♡
ほのぼの——
(WARM 'N' FUZZY)
AH-H-H-H!
LOOK AT THAT!
ワイ YAAY ワイ YAAY
B-BOSS FEI! L-LOVELY AS EVER, I SEE...
WE WOULDN'T REALLY'VE FOUGHT HERE...
K-KIDDING! WE'RE JUST...
HA HA HA
ONE WORD FROM HER, AND THEY ALL FALL QUIET.
I'D NO IDEA HOW GOOD SHE—
WELL DUH, SHORT-PANTS.
WAH— EVA— M-MASTER?!
OF ALL THE BRATS IN HER CLASS, SATSUKI'S THE ONLY ONE WORTH THE SEAT SHE SITS IN.
I-IS THAT SO?!
YES, IT IS. SHE KEEPS HER FEET ON THE GROUND, BUT SHE THINKS ABOUT THE FUTURE, TOO.
SHE'S THE REAL THING.
GLINT キラーン
HUH-H-H...
SEE YA.
NO TRAINING TONIGHT— I'M GOING DRINKING, TOO.
ONCE AGAIN, SAT-CHAN SHOWS US HOW IT'S DONE. GO, SAT-CHAN!!
HA, HA, HA!
WHY, IF IT ISN'T NEGI-SENSEI!
THIS IS A TREAT!
WAH?
S-SORRY IF I WAS TOO HARD ON YA, EARLIER... 3-A IS 3-A, AFTER ALL.
HA HA HA
WHY DON'TCHA JOIN US FER A DRINK...?
HE CAN'T, NITTA-SAN! S-SOMETHING MORE SWEET, PERHAPS...
SIR?
Y-YESSIR.

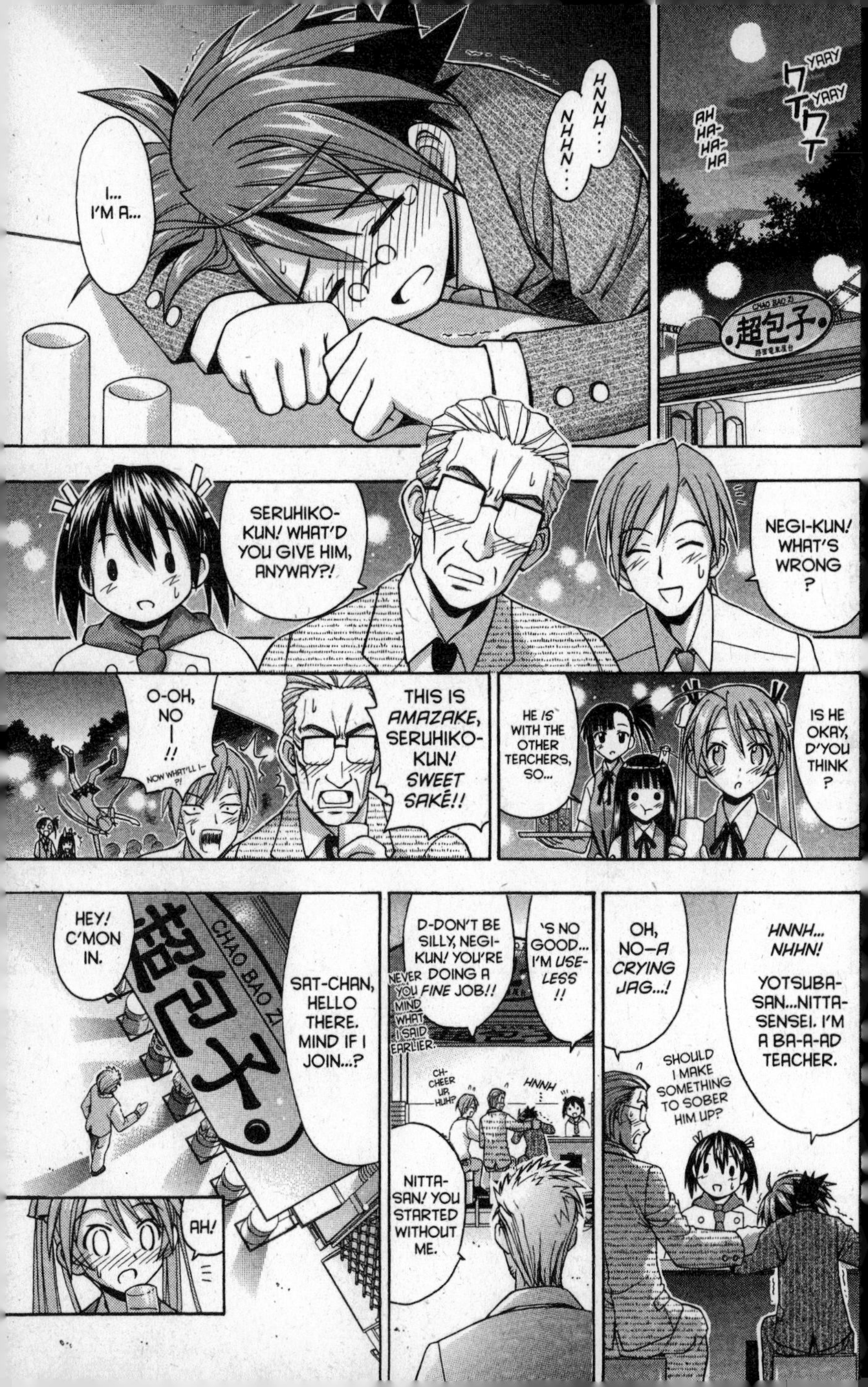
YAAY
YAAY
AH HA-HA-HA
CHAO BAO ZI
超包子
HNNH... NHHN...
I... I'M A...
NEGI-KUN! WHAT'S WRONG?
SERUHIKO-KUN! WHAT'D YOU GIVE HIM, ANYWAY?!
IS HE OKAY, D'YOU THINK?
HE *IS* WITH THE OTHER TEACHERS, SO...
THIS IS *AMAZAKE*, SERUHIKO-KUN! *SWEET SAKÉ*!!
O-OH, NO-!!
NOW WHAT'LL I-?!
HNNH... NHHN!
YOTSUBA-SAN...NITTA-SENSEI. I'M A BA-A-AD TEACHER.
OH, NO—A CRYING JAG...!
SHOULD I MAKE SOMETHING TO SOBER HIM UP?
'S NO GOOD... I'M *USELESS*!!
D-DON'T BE SILLY, NEGI-KUN! YOU'RE DOING A *FINE* JOB!!
NEVER YOU MIND WHAT I SAID EARLIER.
HNNH
CH-CHEER UP, HUH?
NITTA-SAN! YOU STARTED WITHOUT ME.
SAT-CHAN, HELLO THERE. MIND IF I JOIN...?
HEY! C'MON IN.
CHAO BAO ZI
AH!

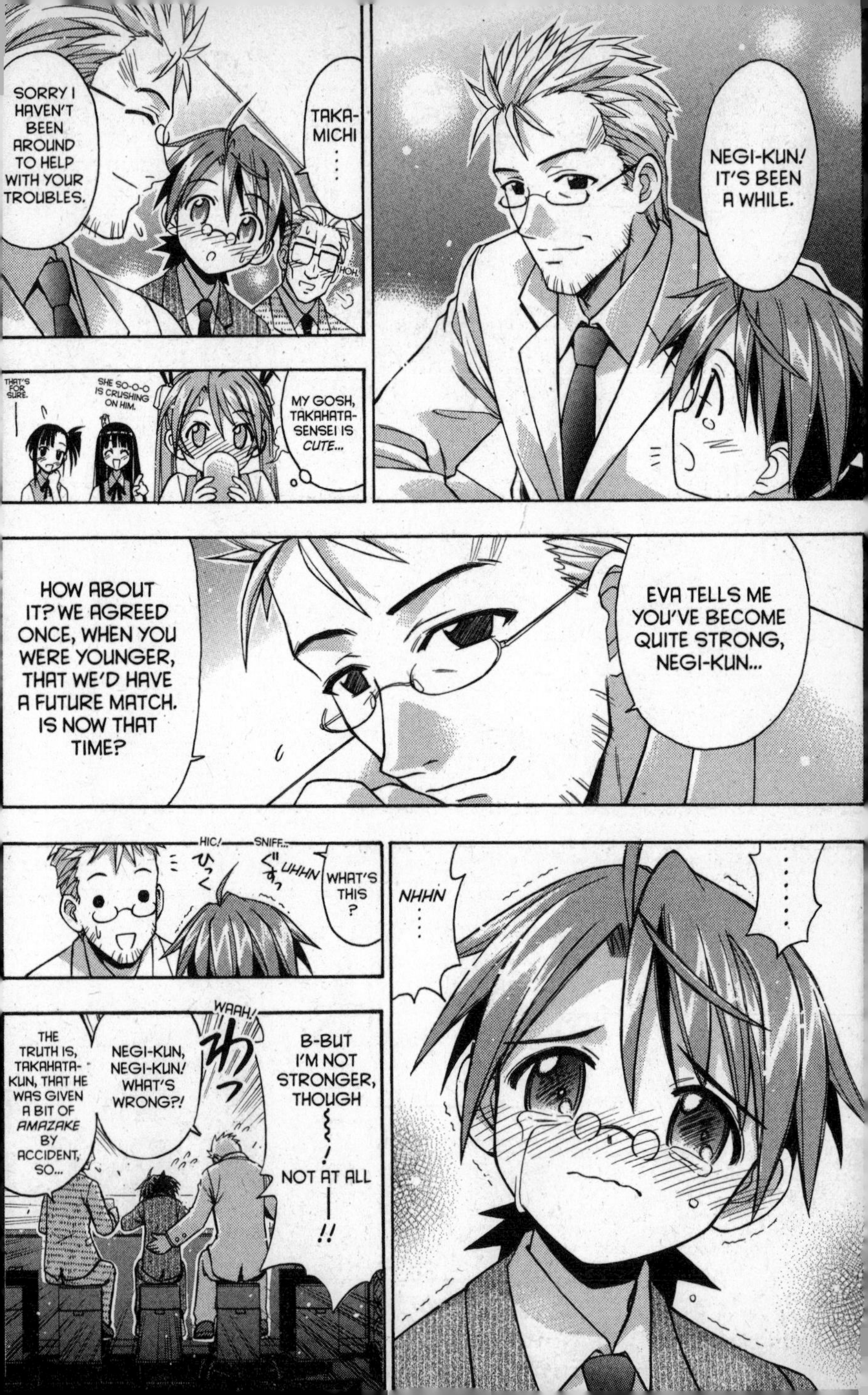
NEGI-KUN! IT'S BEEN A WHILE.
TAKA-MICHI ...
SORRY I HAVEN'T BEEN AROUND TO HELP WITH YOUR TROUBLES.
HOH.
MY GOSH, TAKAHATA-SENSEI IS CUTE...
SHE SO-O-O IS CRUSHING ON HIM.
THAT'S FOR SURE.
EVA TELLS ME YOU'VE BECOME QUITE STRONG, NEGI-KUN...
HOW ABOUT IT? WE AGREED ONCE, WHEN YOU WERE YOUNGER, THAT WE'D HAVE A FUTURE MATCH. IS NOW THAT TIME?
......
NHHN ....
WHAT'S THIS ?
UHHN
ぐすっ
SNIFF...
ひっく
HIC!
B-BUT I'M NOT STRONGER, THOUGH ~~! NOT AT ALL —!!
わっ
WAAH!
NEGI-KUN, NEGI-KUN! WHAT'S WRONG?!
THE TRUTH IS, TAKAHATA-KUN, THAT HE WAS GIVEN A BIT OF AMAZAKE BY ACCIDENT, SO...

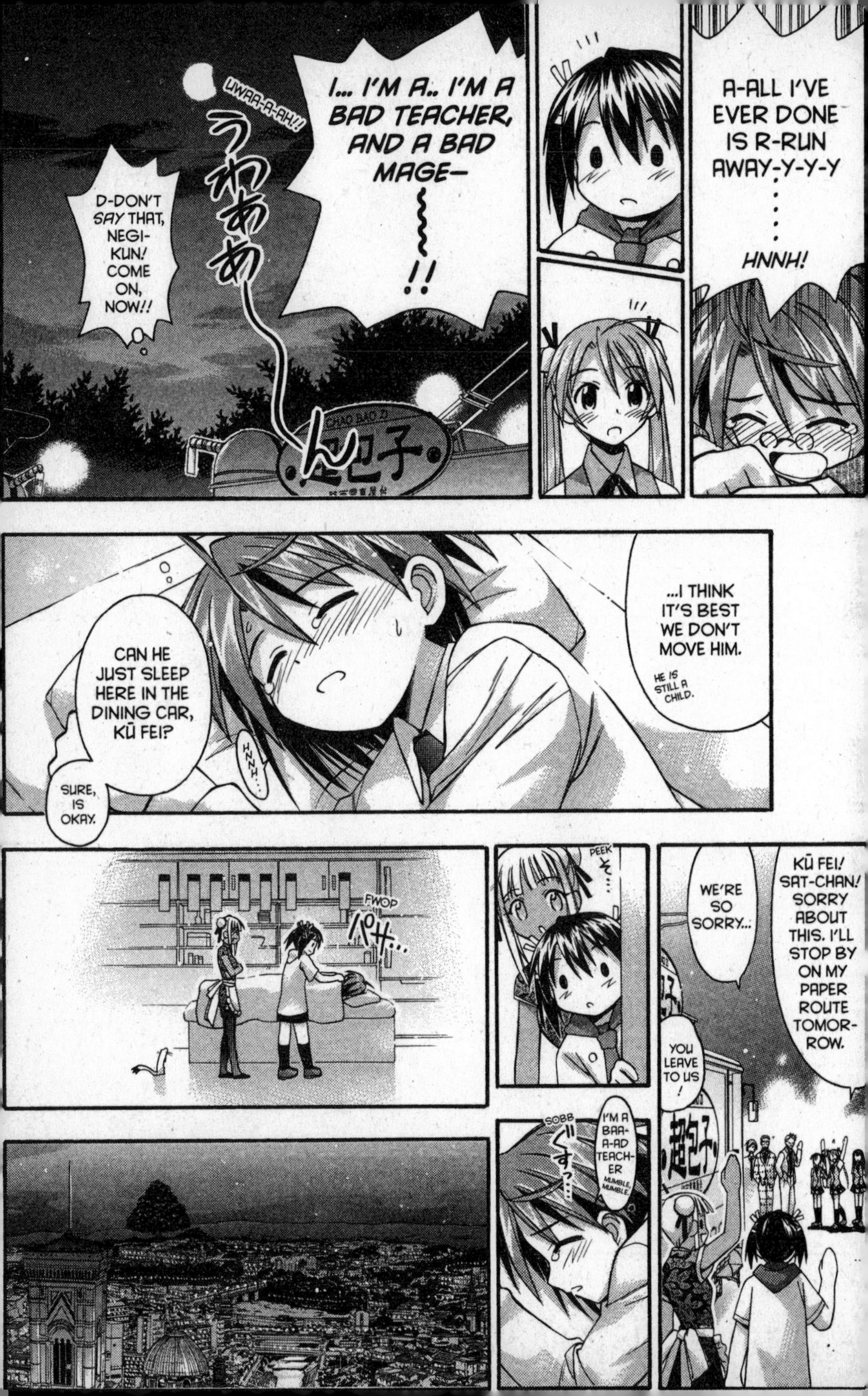
A-ALL I'VE EVER DONE IS R-RUN AWAY-Y-Y-Y .....
HNNH!
I... I'M A.. I'M A BAD TEACHER, AND A BAD MAGE— ~~~ !!
UWAA-A-AH!!
うわあああん
D-DON'T SAY THAT, NEGI-KUN! COME ON, NOW!!
CHAO BAO ZI
超包子
...I THINK IT'S BEST WE DON'T MOVE HIM.
HE IS STILL A CHILD.
CAN HE JUST SLEEP HERE IN THE DINING CAR, KŪ FEI?
HNNH...
SURE, IS OKAY.
KŪ FEI! SAT-CHAN! SORRY ABOUT THIS. I'LL STOP BY ON MY PAPER ROUTE TOMORROW.
WE'RE SO SORRY...
YOU LEAVE TO US!
超包子
PEEK
そ…
SOBB
ぐすっ…
I'M A BAA-A-AD TEACHER
MUMBLE, MUMBLE.
FWOP
パサ…

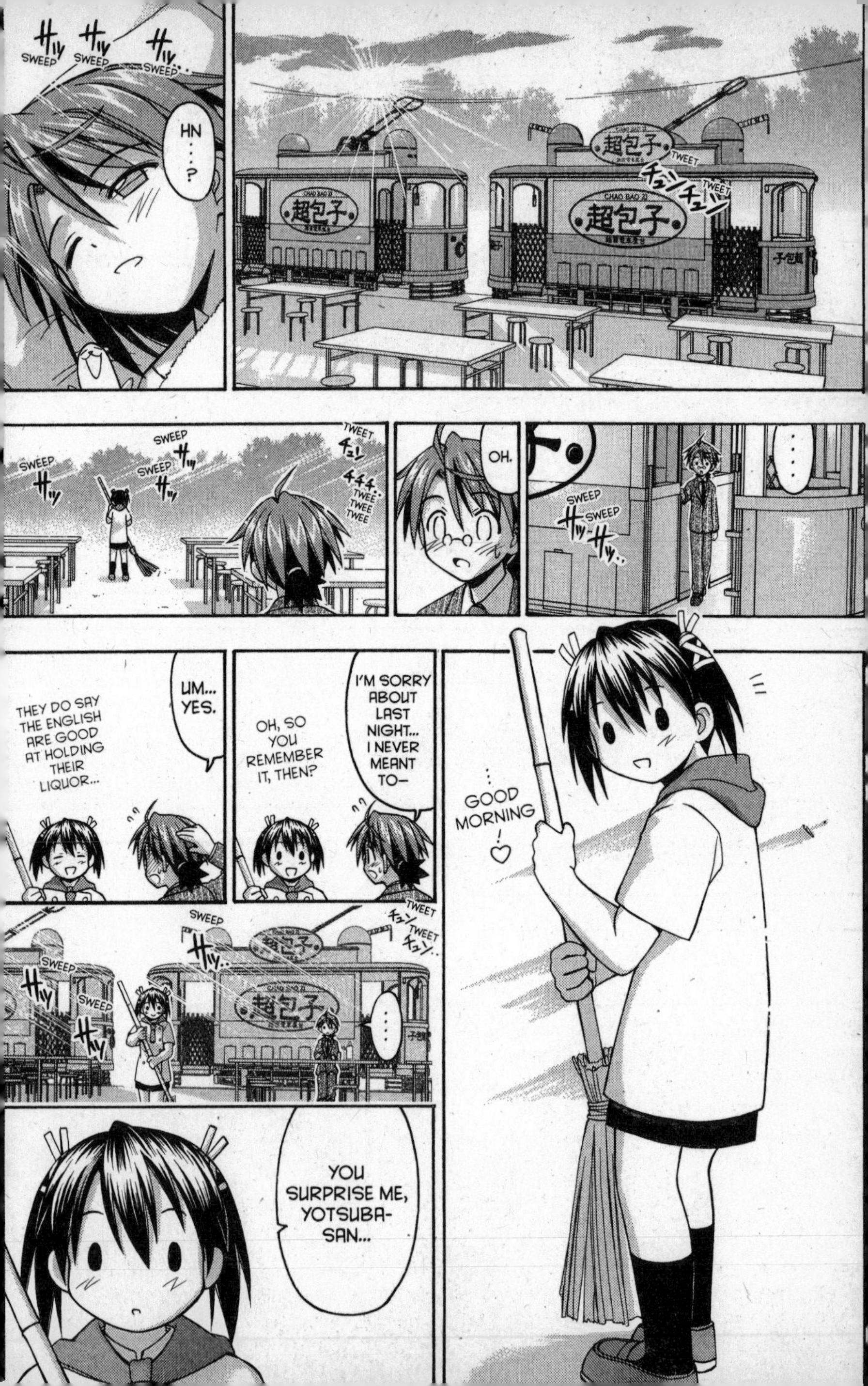
超包子
CHAO BAO ZI
超包子
TWEET
TWEET
SWEEP
SWEEP
SWEEP
HN . . . ?
. . . .
SWEEP
SWEEP
OH.
TWEET
TWEE
TWEE
TWEE
SWEEP
SWEEP
SWEEP
. . . GOOD MORNING! ♡
I'M SORRY ABOUT LAST NIGHT... I NEVER MEANT TO–
OH, SO YOU REMEMBER IT, THEN?
UM... YES.
THEY DO SAY THE ENGLISH ARE GOOD AT HOLDING THEIR LIQUOR...
TWEET
TWEET
SWEEP
SWEEP
SWEEP
. . . . .
YOU SURPRISE ME, YOTSUBA-SAN...

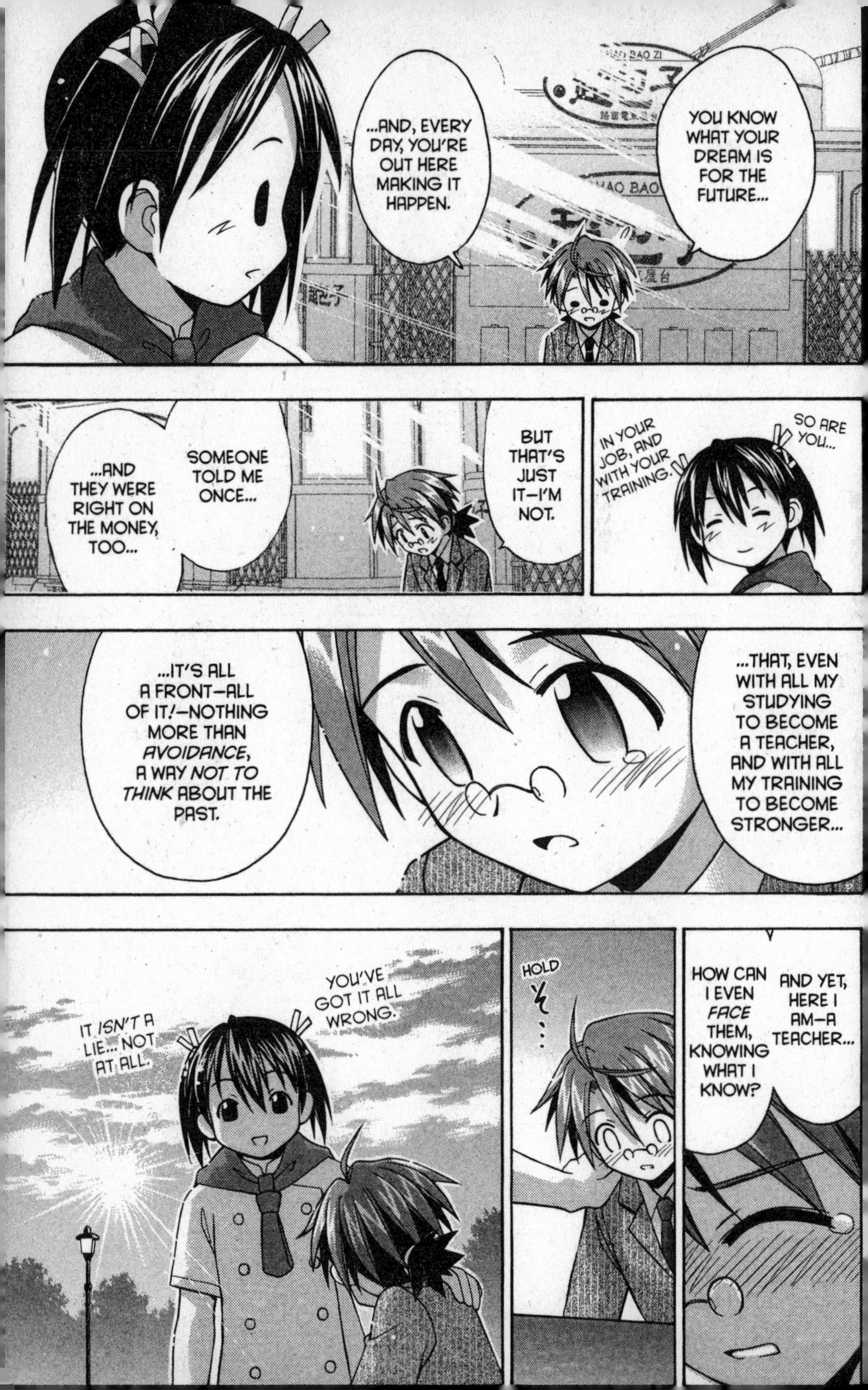
YOU KNOW WHAT YOUR DREAM IS FOR THE FUTURE...
...AND, EVERY DAY, YOU'RE OUT HERE MAKING IT HAPPEN.
SO ARE YOU...
IN YOUR JOB, AND WITH YOUR TRAINING.
BUT THAT'S JUST IT—I'M NOT.
SOMEONE TOLD ME ONCE...
...AND THEY WERE RIGHT ON THE MONEY, TOO...
...THAT, EVEN WITH ALL MY STUDYING TO BECOME A TEACHER, AND WITH ALL MY TRAINING TO BECOME STRONGER...
...IT'S ALL A FRONT—ALL OF IT!—NOTHING MORE THAN *AVOIDANCE*, A WAY *NOT TO THINK* ABOUT THE PAST.
AND YET, HERE I AM—A TEACHER...
HOW CAN I EVEN *FACE* THEM, KNOWING WHAT I KNOW?
HOLD
...
YOU'VE GOT IT ALL WRONG.
IT *ISN'T* A LIE... NOT AT ALL.

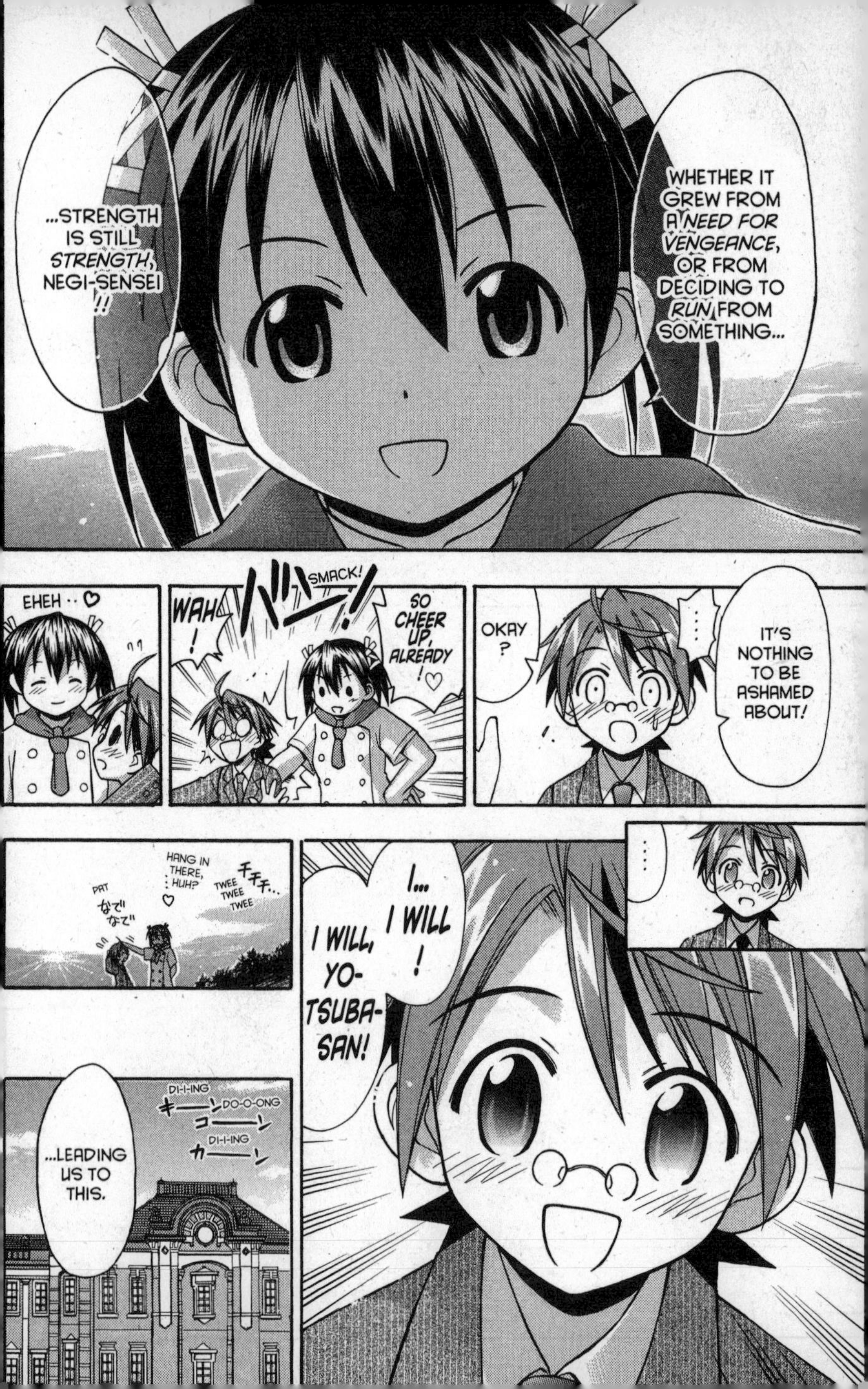
WHETHER IT GREW FROM A NEED FOR VENGEANCE, OR FROM DECIDING TO RUN FROM SOMETHING...
...STRENGTH IS STILL STRENGTH, NEGI-SENSEI!!
IT'S NOTHING TO BE ASHAMED ABOUT!
...
OKAY?
SO CHEER UP, ALREADY! ♡
SMACK!
WAH!
EHEH.. ♡
...
I... I WILL!
I WILL, YO-TSUBA-SAN!
HANG IN THERE, HUH? ♡
PAT
なでなで
TWEE TWEE TWEE
チチチ...
DI-I-ING
キーン
DO-O-ONG
コーン
DI-I-ING
カーン
...LEADING US TO THIS.

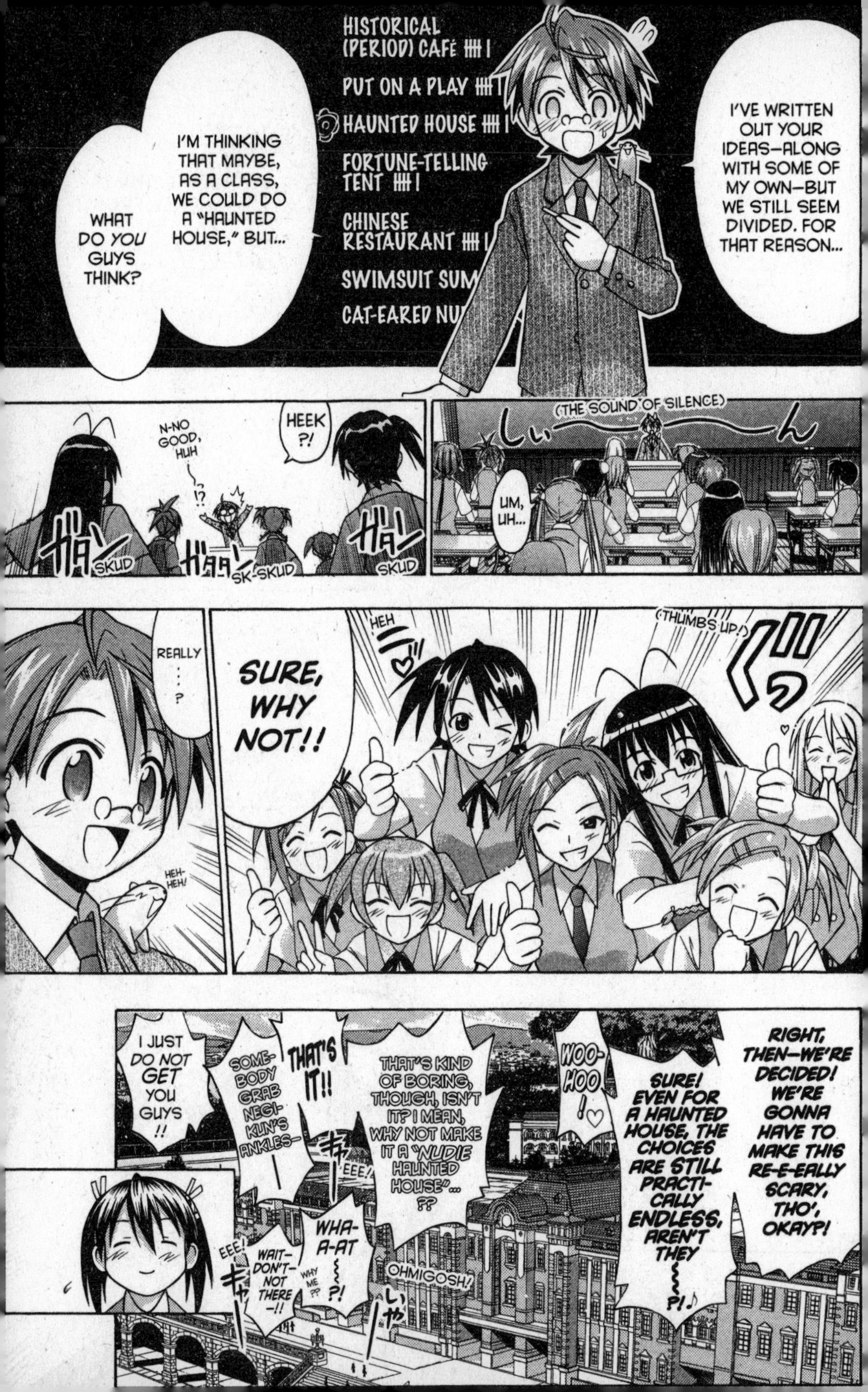
I'VE WRITTEN OUT YOUR IDEAS—ALONG WITH SOME OF MY OWN—BUT WE STILL SEEM DIVIDED. FOR THAT REASON...
HISTORICAL (PERIOD) CAFÉ
PUT ON A PLAY
HAUNTED HOUSE
FORTUNE-TELLING TENT
CHINESE RESTAURANT
SWIMSUIT SUM
CAT-EARED NU
I'M THINKING THAT MAYBE, AS A CLASS, WE COULD DO A "HAUNTED HOUSE," BUT...
WHAT DO YOU GUYS THINK?
(THE SOUND OF SILENCE)
しぃーーん
UM, UH...
HEEK ?!
N-NO GOOD, HUH !?
SKUD
SK-SKUD
SKUD
(THUMBS UP!)
HEH
SURE, WHY NOT!!
REALLY...?
HEH-HEH!
RIGHT, THEN—WE'RE DECIDED! WE'RE GONNA HAVE TO MAKE THIS RE-E-EALLY SCARY, THO', OKAY?!
SURE! EVEN FOR A HAUNTED HOUSE, THE CHOICES ARE STILL PRACTICALLY ENDLESS, AREN'T THEY~?!♪
WOO-HOO!♡
THAT'S KIND OF BORING, THOUGH, ISN'T IT? I MEAN, WHY NOT MAKE IT A "NUDIE HAUNTED HOUSE"...??
THAT'S IT!!
SOMEBODY GRAB NEGI-KUN'S ANKLES—
I JUST DO NOT GET YOU GUYS!!
EEE!
OHMIGOSH!
WHA-A-AT~?!
WHY ME??
WAIT—DON'T—NOT THERE—!!
EEE!

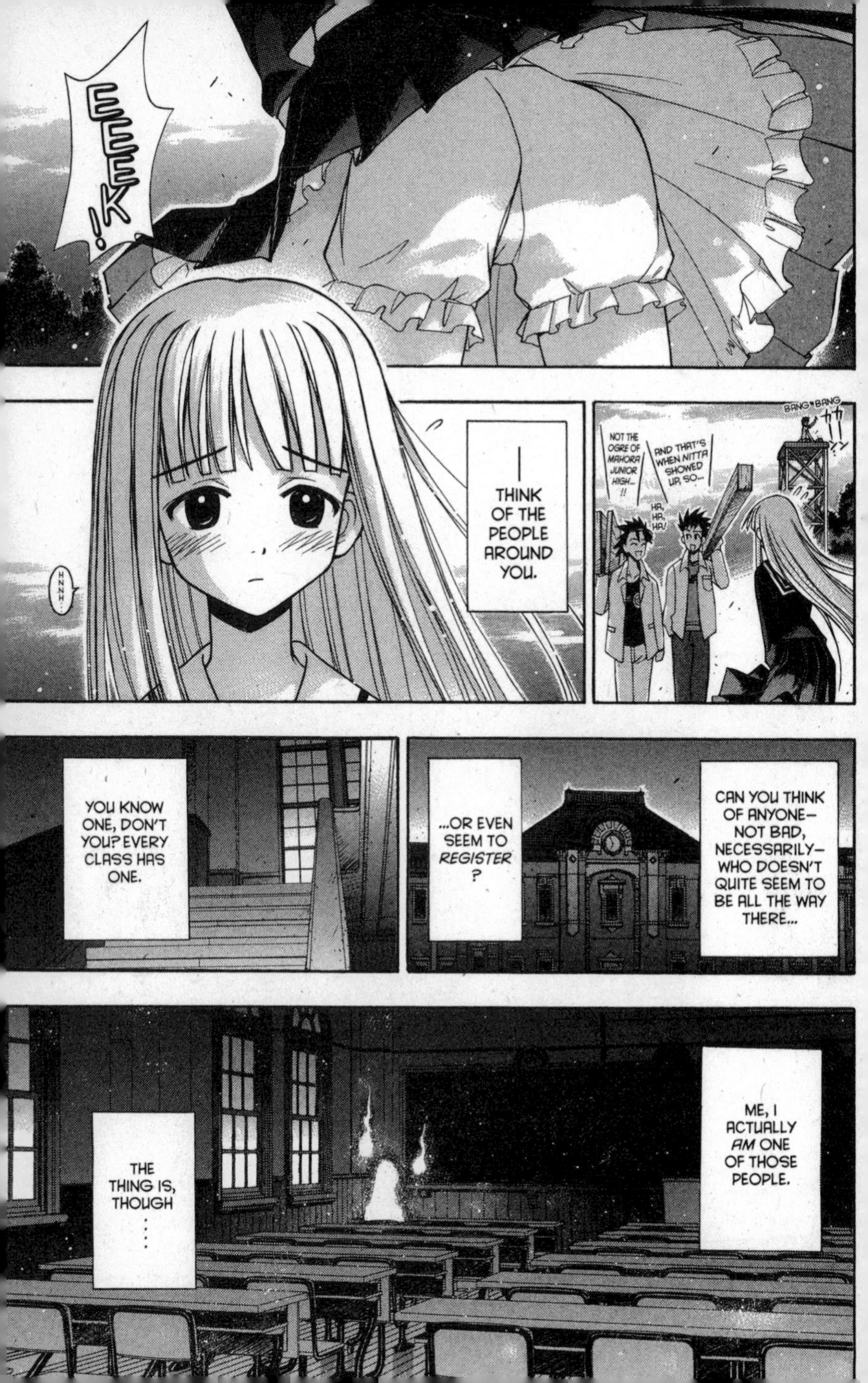
EEEEK!
BANG BANG
AND THAT'S WHEN NITTA SHOWED UP, SO...
NOT THE OGRE OF MAHORA JUNIOR HIGH...!!
HA, HA, HA!
I THINK OF THE PEOPLE AROUND YOU.
HNNH...
CAN YOU THINK OF ANYONE— NOT BAD, NECESSARILY— WHO DOESN'T QUITE SEEM TO BE ALL THE WAY THERE...
...OR EVEN SEEM TO *REGISTER*?
YOU KNOW ONE, DON'T YOU? EVERY CLASS HAS ONE.
ME, I ACTUALLY *AM* ONE OF THOSE PEOPLE.
THE THING IS, THOUGH....

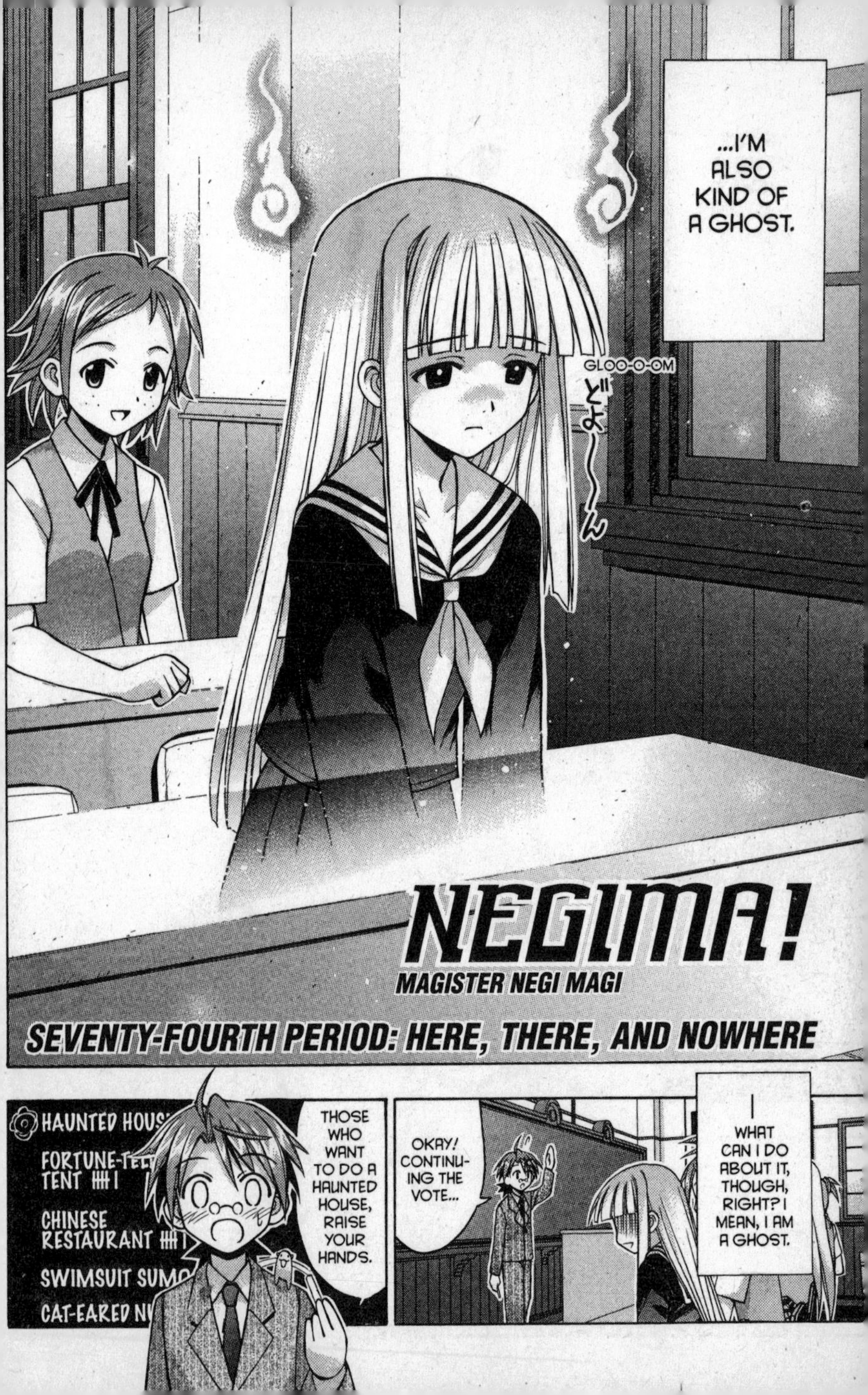
...I'M ALSO KIND OF A GHOST.
GLOO-O-OM
どよ～～ん
NEGIMA!
MAGISTER NEGI MAGI
SEVENTY-FOURTH PERIOD: HERE, THERE, AND NOWHERE
I WHAT CAN I DO ABOUT IT, THOUGH, RIGHT? I MEAN, I AM A GHOST.
OKAY! CONTINUING THE VOTE...
THOSE WHO WANT TO DO A HAUNTED HOUSE, RAISE YOUR HANDS.
HAUNTED HOUS
FORTUNE-TEL TENT
CHINESE RESTAURANT
SWIMSUIT SUM
CAT-EARED N

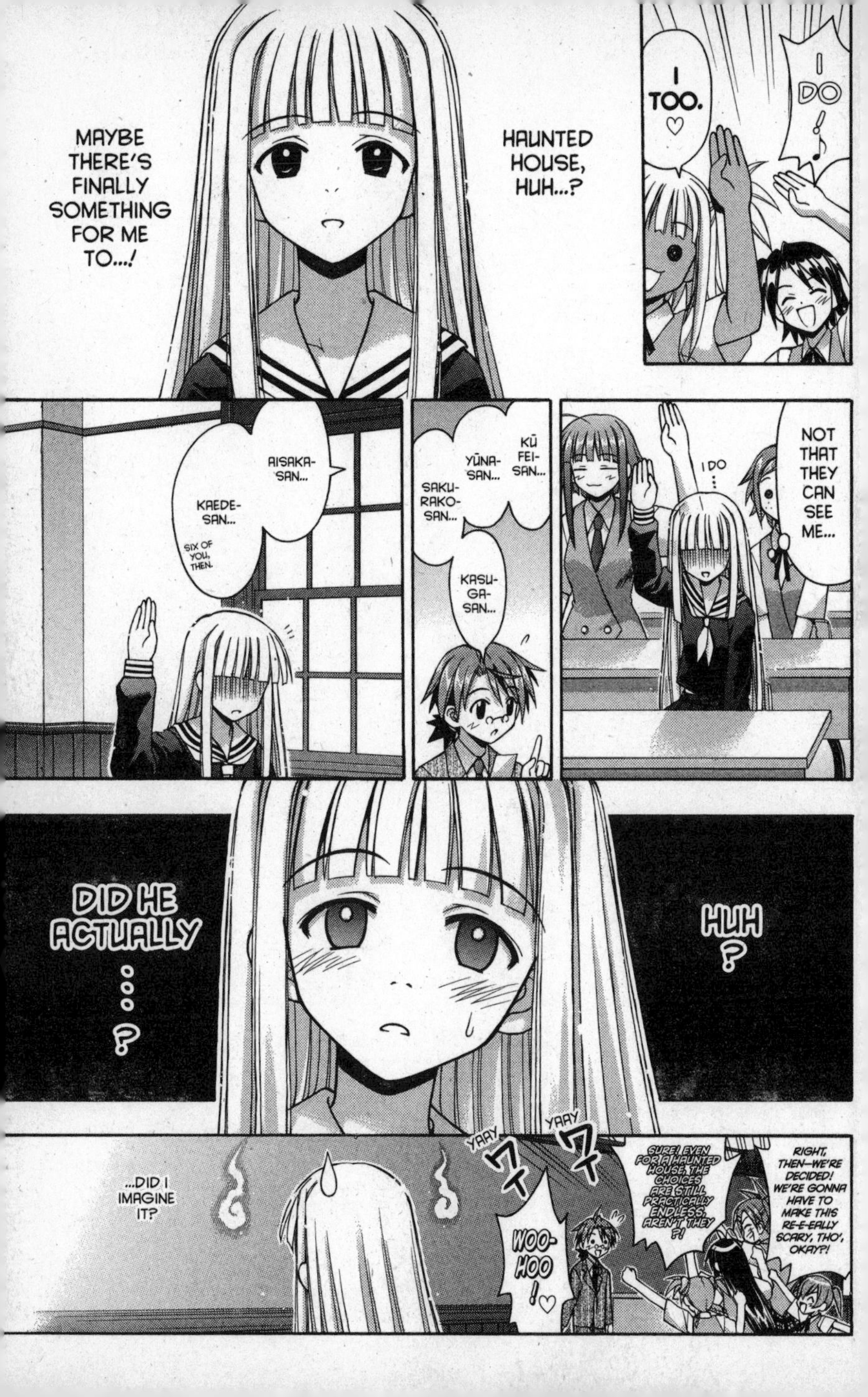
I DO!♪
I TOO.♡
HAUNTED HOUSE, HUH...?
MAYBE THERE'S FINALLY SOMETHING FOR ME TO...!
NOT THAT THEY CAN SEE ME...
I DO...
KŪ FEI-SAN...
YŪNA-SAN...
SAKURAKO-SAN...
KASUGA-SAN...
AISAKA-SAN...
KAEDE-SAN...
SIX OF YOU, THEN.
HUH?
DID HE ACTUALLY...?
RIGHT, THEN—WE'RE DECIDED! WE'RE GONNA HAVE TO MAKE THIS RE-E-EALLY SCARY, THO', OKAY?!
SURE! EVEN FOR A HAUNTED HOUSE, THE CHOICES ARE STILL PRACTICALLY ENDLESS, AREN'T THEY?!
YAAY
YAAY
WOO-HOO!♡
...DID I IMAGINE IT?

AHA, HA, HA...

CATCH YOU LATER!

SEE YOU!

YAAY YAAY

7T 7T

DO-O-ONG DI-I-ING

キーンコーン

MY NAME IS SAYO AISAKA...

...AND I'VE BEEN A GHOST SIXTY YEARS, NOW.

...SO, BEFORE I KNEW IT, IT KIND OF BECAME PERMANENTLY EMPTY.

PEOPLE SAY THEY FEEL A "CHILL" WHEN THEY SIT THERE...

MAHORA JUNIOR HIGH, THIRD FLOOR, CLASS-ROOM "A"... THE WINDOW-MOST SEAT IN THE VERY FRONT ROW IS MINE.

(SOUND OF SILENCE)

I MAY AS WELL NOT EVEN BE HERE.

EEE! EEE!

...IN THAT THEY HARDLY EVEN SEEM TO NOTICE ME.

"BOO-O-O..."

UM "BOO..."

Y'KNOW?

BLAH, BLAH...

I'M NOT A VERY LIKELY CANDIDATE FOR A GHOST, I KNOW...

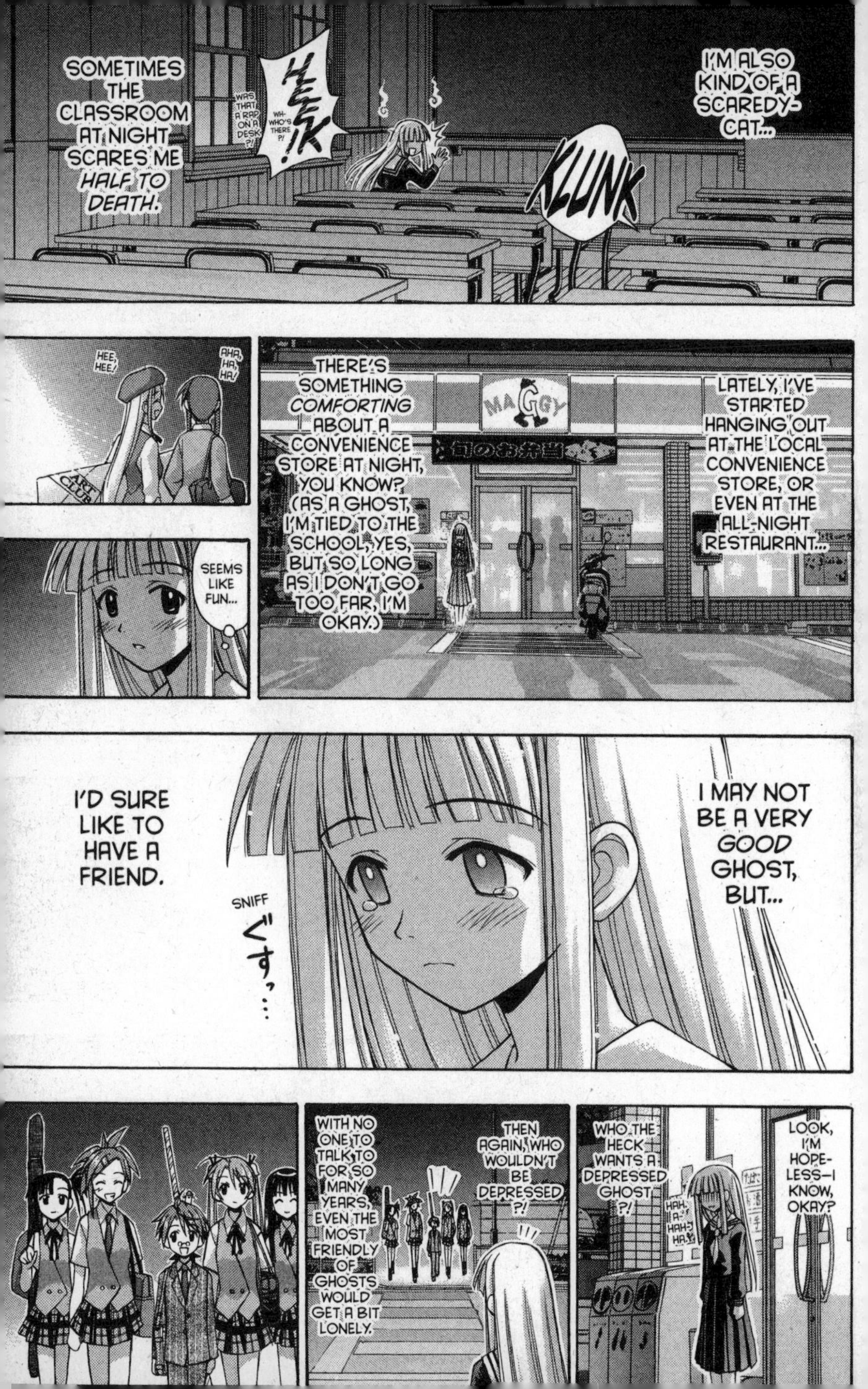
I'M ALSO KIND OF A SCAREDY-CAT...
KLUNK
HEEK!
WH-WHO'S THERE?!
WAS THAT A RAP ON A DESK?!
SOMETIMES THE CLASSROOM AT NIGHT SCARES ME *HALF TO DEATH.*
LATELY, I'VE STARTED HANGING OUT AT THE LOCAL CONVENIENCE STORE, OR EVEN AT THE ALL-NIGHT RESTAURANT...
MAGGY
旬のお弁当
THERE'S SOMETHING *COMFORTING* ABOUT A CONVENIENCE STORE AT NIGHT, YOU KNOW? (AS A GHOST, I'M TIED TO THE SCHOOL, YES, BUT SO LONG AS I DON'T GO TOO FAR, I'M OKAY.)
AHA, HA, HA!
HEE, HEE!
ART CLUB
SEEMS LIKE FUN...
I MAY NOT BE A VERY *GOOD* GHOST, BUT...
I'D SURE LIKE TO HAVE A FRIEND.
SNIFF
ぐすっ…
LOOK, I'M HOPELESS—I KNOW, OKAY?
WHO THE HECK WANTS A DEPRESSED GHOST?!
HAH, A-HAH-HA.
THEN AGAIN, WHO WOULDN'T BE DEPRESSED?!
WITH NO ONE TO TALK TO FOR SO MANY YEARS, EVEN THE MOST FRIENDLY OF GHOSTS WOULD GET A BIT LONELY.
!!!

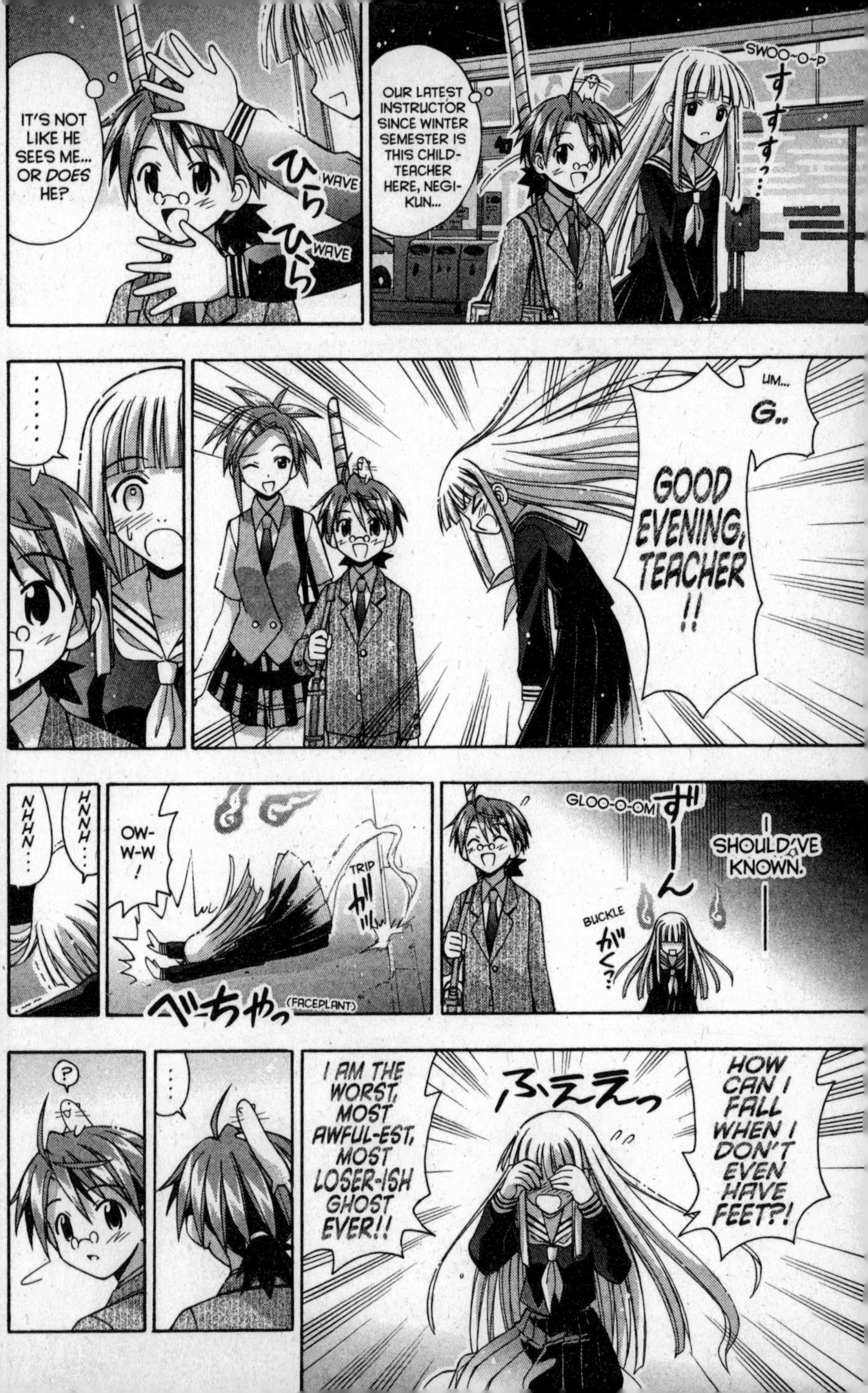
SWOO~O~P
すすすっ…
OUR LATEST INSTRUCTOR SINCE WINTER SEMESTER IS THIS CHILD-TEACHER HERE, NEGI-KUN...
ひら WAVE
ひら WAVE
IT'S NOT LIKE HE SEES ME... OR DOES HE?
UM... G..
GOOD EVENING, TEACHER!!
......
GLOO-O-OM
ずーん
I SHOULD'VE KNOWN.
BUCKLE
がくっ
OW-W-W!
TRIP
ガッ
べちゃっ (FACEPLANT)
HNNH...
NHHN...
HOW CAN I FALL WHEN I DON'T EVEN HAVE FEET?!
ふええっ
I AM THE WORST, MOST AWFUL-EST, MOST LOSER-ISH GHOST EVER!!
....
?

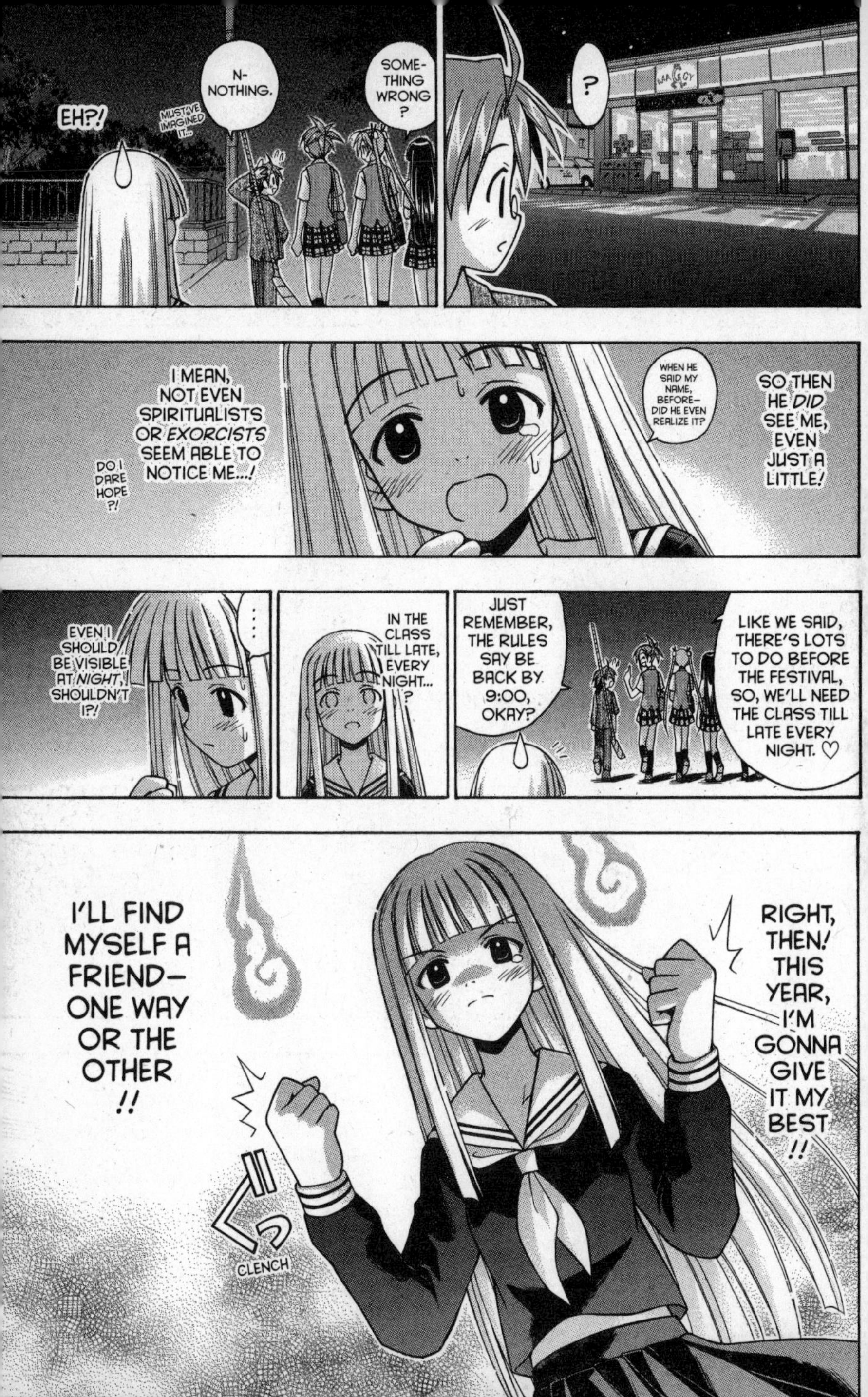
?
SOME-THING WRONG?
N-NOTHING.
MUST'VE IMAGINED IT...
EH?!
SO THEN HE *DID* SEE ME, EVEN JUST A LITTLE!
WHEN HE SAID MY NAME, BEFORE—DID HE EVEN REALIZE IT?
I MEAN, NOT EVEN SPIRITUALISTS OR *EXORCISTS* SEEM ABLE TO NOTICE ME...!
DO I DARE HOPE?!
LIKE WE SAID, THERE'S LOTS TO DO BEFORE THE FESTIVAL, SO, WE'LL NEED THE CLASS TILL LATE EVERY NIGHT. ♡
JUST REMEMBER, THE RULES SAY BE BACK BY 9:00, OKAY?
IN THE CLASS TILL LATE, EVERY NIGHT...?
...
EVEN I SHOULD BE VISIBLE AT *NIGHT*, SHOULDN'T I?!
RIGHT, THEN! THIS YEAR, I'M GONNA GIVE IT MY BEST!!
I'LL FIND MYSELF A FRIEND—ONE WAY OR THE OTHER!!
CLENCH

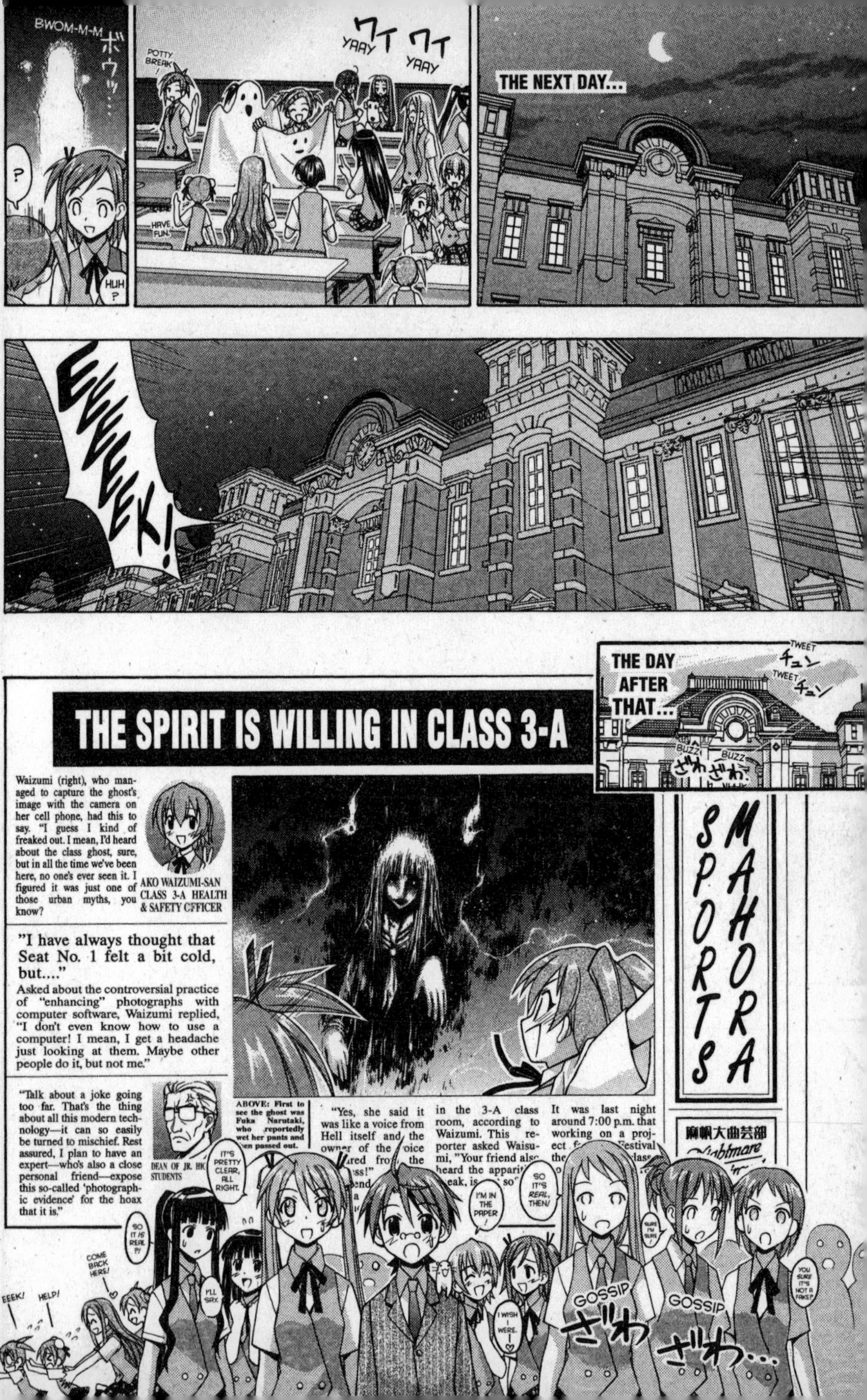
THE NEXT DAY...
ワイ
YAAY
ワイ
YAAY
POTTY BREAK!
HAVE FUN.
BWOM-M-M
ボウッ
?
HUH?
EEEEEEK!
THE DAY AFTER THAT...
TWEET
チュン
TWEET
チュン
BUZZ
BUZZ
ざわ ざわ
MAHORA SPORTS
THE SPIRIT IS WILLING IN CLASS 3-A
Waizumi (right), who managed to capture the ghost's image with the camera on her cell phone, had this to say. "I guess I kind of freaked out. I mean, I'd heard about the class ghost, sure, but in all the time we've been here, no one's ever seen it. I figured it was just one of those urban myths, you know?
AKO WAIZUMI-SAN CLASS 3-A HEALTH & SAFETY OFFICER
"I have always thought that Seat No. 1 felt a bit cold, but...."
Asked about the controversial practice of "enhancing" photographs with computer software, Waizumi replied, "I don't even know how to use a computer! I mean, I get a headache just looking at them. Maybe other people do it, but not me."
"Talk about a joke going too far. That's the thing about all this modern technology—it can so easily be turned to mischief. Rest assured, I plan to have an expert—who's also a close personal friend—expose this so-called 'photographic evidence' for the hoax that it is."
DEAN OF JR. HIGH STUDENTS
ABOVE: First to see the ghost was Fuka Narutaki, who reportedly wet her pants and then passed out.
"Yes, she said it was like a voice from Hell itself and the owner of the voice
in the 3-A class room, according to Waizumi. This reporter asked Waisumi, "Your friend also heard the apparit
It was last night around 7:00 p.m. that working on a project
麻帆大曲芸部
SO IT'S REAL, THEN!
SURE I'M SURE!
YOU SURE IT'S NOT A FAKE!?
I'M IN THE PAPER!
IT'S PRETTY CLEAR, ALL RIGHT.
SO IT IS REAL!?
I'LL SAY.
I WISH I WERE.
COME BACK HERE!
HELP!
EEEK!
GOSSIP
ざわ
GOSSIP
ざわ...

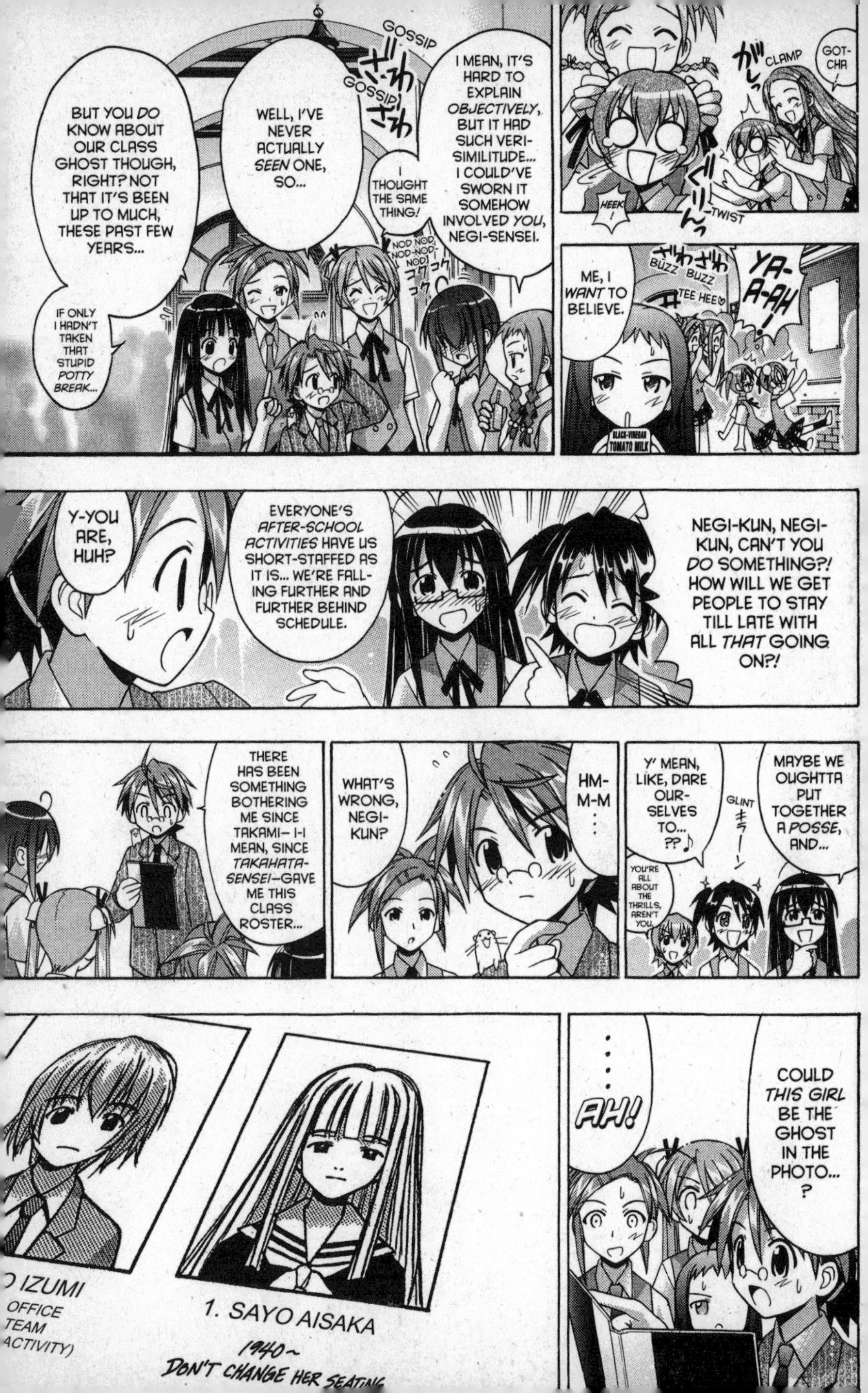
GOT-CHA
CLAMP
HEEK!
TWIST
YA-A-AH!
BUZZ BUZZ
TEE HEE♥
ME, I WANT TO BELIEVE.
BLACK-VINEGAR TOMATO MILK
GOSSIP
GOSSIP
I MEAN, IT'S HARD TO EXPLAIN OBJECTIVELY, BUT IT HAD SUCH VERI-SIMILITUDE... I COULD'VE SWORN IT SOMEHOW INVOLVED YOU, NEGI-SENSEI.
I THOUGHT THE SAME THING!
NOD NOD NOD-NOD NOD
WELL, I'VE NEVER ACTUALLY SEEN ONE, SO...
BUT YOU DO KNOW ABOUT OUR CLASS GHOST THOUGH, RIGHT? NOT THAT IT'S BEEN UP TO MUCH, THESE PAST FEW YEARS...
IF ONLY I HADN'T TAKEN THAT STUPID POTTY BREAK...
NEGI-KUN, NEGI-KUN, CAN'T YOU DO SOMETHING?! HOW WILL WE GET PEOPLE TO STAY TILL LATE WITH ALL THAT GOING ON?!
EVERYONE'S AFTER-SCHOOL ACTIVITIES HAVE US SHORT-STAFFED AS IT IS... WE'RE FALLING FURTHER AND FURTHER BEHIND SCHEDULE.
Y-YOU ARE, HUH?
MAYBE WE OUGHTTA PUT TOGETHER A POSSE, AND...
GLINT
Y' MEAN, LIKE, DARE OURSELVES TO... ??♪
YOU'RE ALL ABOUT THE THRILLS, AREN'T YOU.
HM-M-M...
WHAT'S WRONG, NEGI-KUN?
THERE HAS BEEN SOMETHING BOTHERING ME SINCE TAKAMI— I-I MEAN, SINCE TAKAHATA-SENSEI—GAVE ME THIS CLASS ROSTER...
COULD THIS GIRL BE THE GHOST IN THE PHOTO...?
...
AH!
1. SAYO AISAKA
1940~
DON'T CHANGE HER SEATING
IZUMI
OFFICE
TEAM
ACTIVITY)

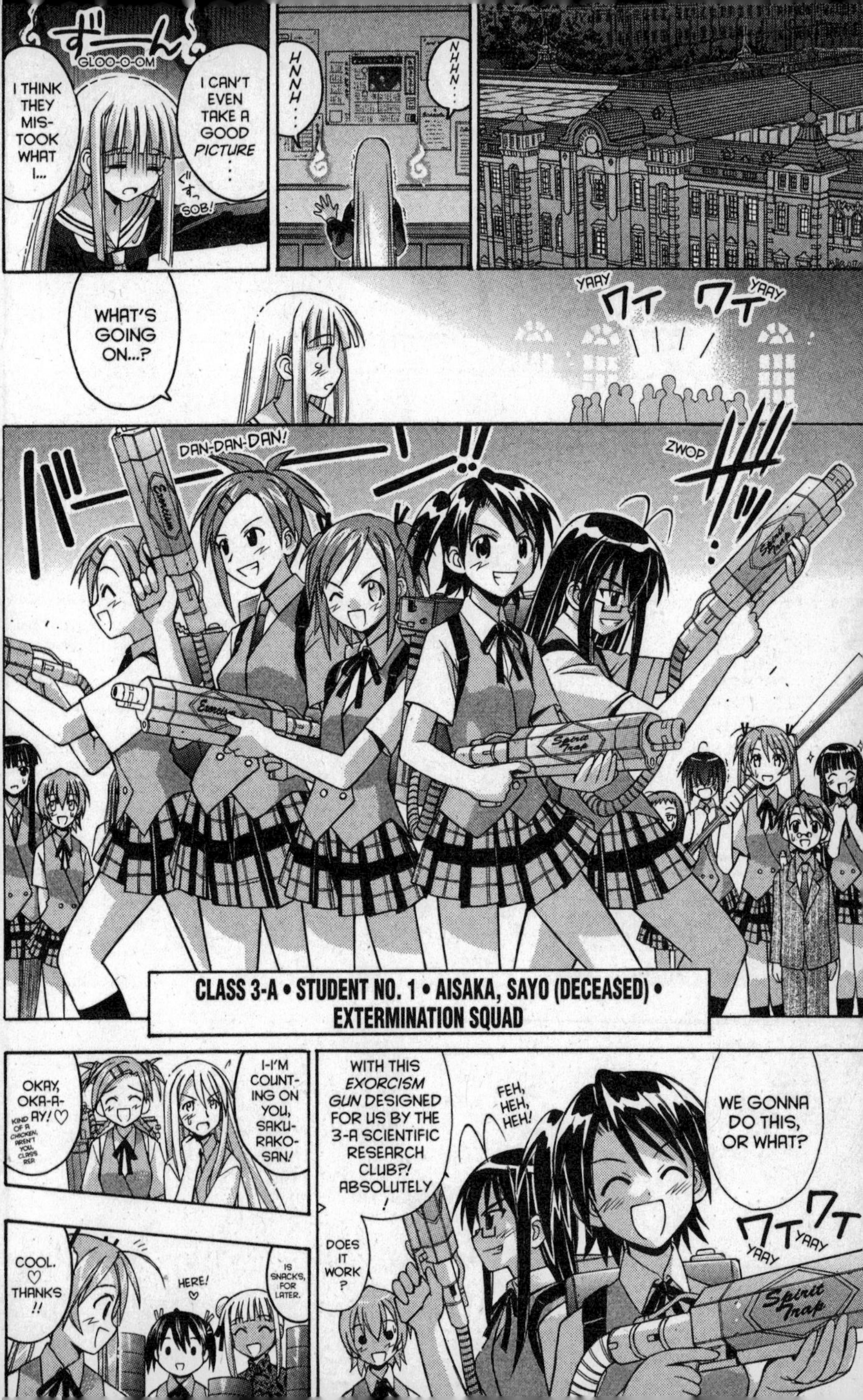
NHHN...
HNNH...
I CAN'T EVEN TAKE A GOOD PICTURE...
SOB!
GLOO-O-OM
I THINK THEY MIS-TOOK WHAT I...
YAAY ワイ ワイ YAAY
WHAT'S GOING ON...?
ZWOP
DAN-DAN-DAN!
CLASS 3-A • STUDENT NO. 1 • AISAKA, SAYO (DECEASED) • EXTERMINATION SQUAD
WE GONNA DO THIS, OR WHAT?
YAAY YAAY
FEH, HEH, HEH!
WITH THIS EXORCISM GUN DESIGNED FOR US BY THE 3-A SCIENTIFIC RESEARCH CLUB?! ABSOLUTELY!
DOES IT WORK?
I-I'M COUNTING ON YOU, SAKURAKO-SAN!
OKAY, OKA-A-AY! ♡
KIND OF A CHICKEN, AREN'T YOU, CLASS REP
IS SNACKS, FOR LATER.
HERE! ♡
COOL. ♡ THANKS!!

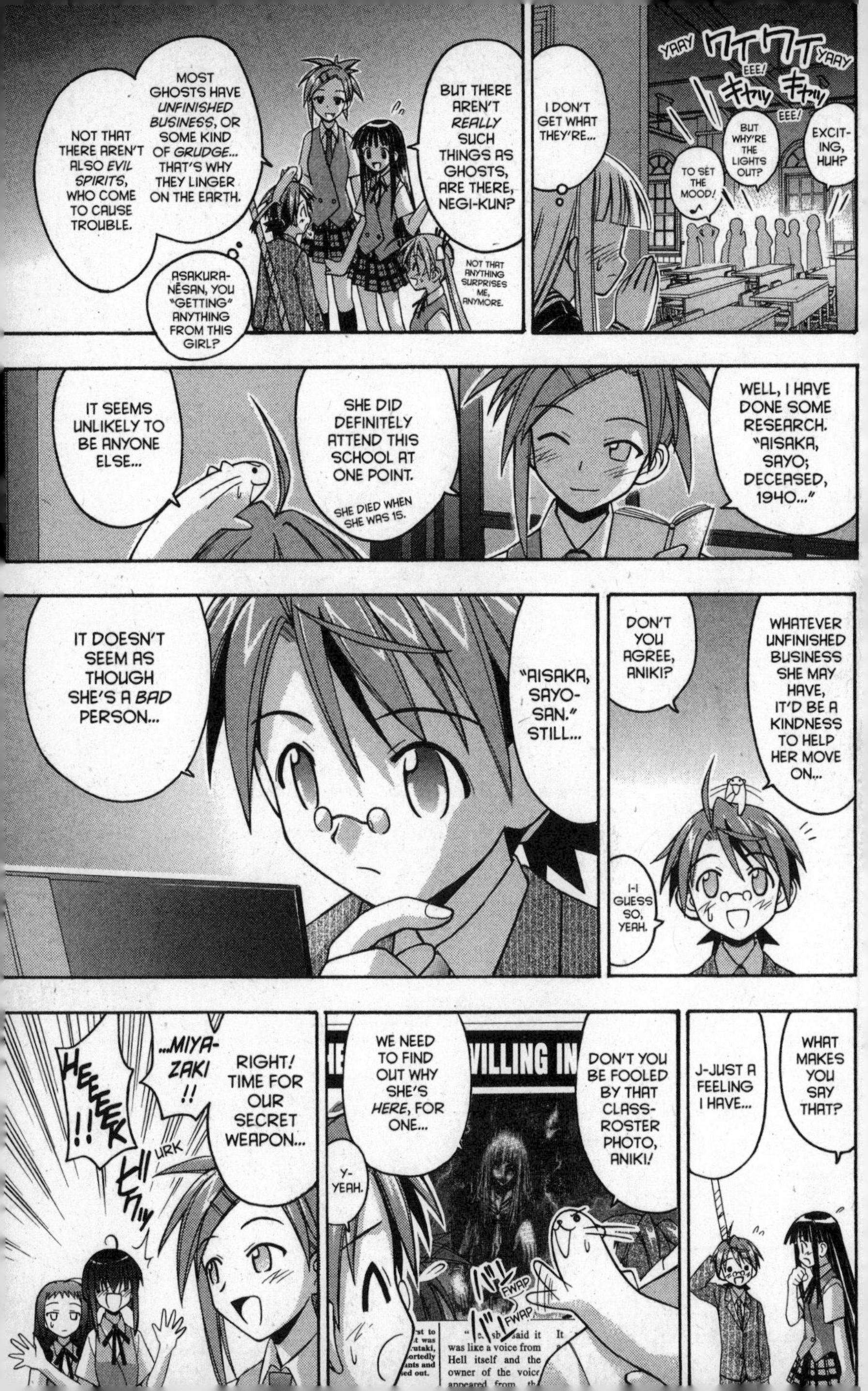
YAAY ワイワイ YAAY
EEE! キャッ キャッ EEE!
EXCITING, HUH?
BUT WHY'RE THE LIGHTS OUT?
TO SET THE MOOD! ♪
I DON'T GET WHAT THEY'RE...
BUT THERE AREN'T *REALLY* SUCH THINGS AS GHOSTS, ARE THERE, NEGI-KUN?
NOT THAT ANYTHING SURPRISES ME, ANYMORE.
MOST GHOSTS HAVE *UNFINISHED BUSINESS*, OR SOME KIND OF *GRUDGE*... THAT'S WHY THEY LINGER ON THE EARTH.
NOT THAT THERE AREN'T ALSO *EVIL SPIRITS*, WHO COME TO CAUSE TROUBLE.
ASAKURA-NĒSAN, YOU "GETTING" ANYTHING FROM THIS GIRL?
WELL, I HAVE DONE SOME RESEARCH. "AISAKA, SAYO; DECEASED, 1940..."
SHE DID DEFINITELY ATTEND THIS SCHOOL AT ONE POINT.
SHE DIED WHEN SHE WAS 15.
IT SEEMS UNLIKELY TO BE ANYONE ELSE...
WHATEVER UNFINISHED BUSINESS SHE MAY HAVE, IT'D BE A KINDNESS TO HELP HER MOVE ON...
DON'T YOU AGREE, ANIKI?
I-I GUESS SO, YEAH.
"AISAKA, SAYO-SAN." STILL...
IT DOESN'T SEEM AS THOUGH SHE'S A *BAD* PERSON...
WHAT MAKES YOU SAY THAT?
J-JUST A FEELING I HAVE...
DON'T YOU BE FOOLED BY THAT CLASS-ROSTER PHOTO, ANIKI!
WILLING IN
FWAP
FWAP
was like a voice from
Hell itself and the
owner of the voice
WE NEED TO FIND OUT WHY SHE'S *HERE*, FOR ONE...
Y-YEAH.
RIGHT! TIME FOR OUR SECRET WEAPON...
...MIYAZAKI!!
URK
HEEEEK!!

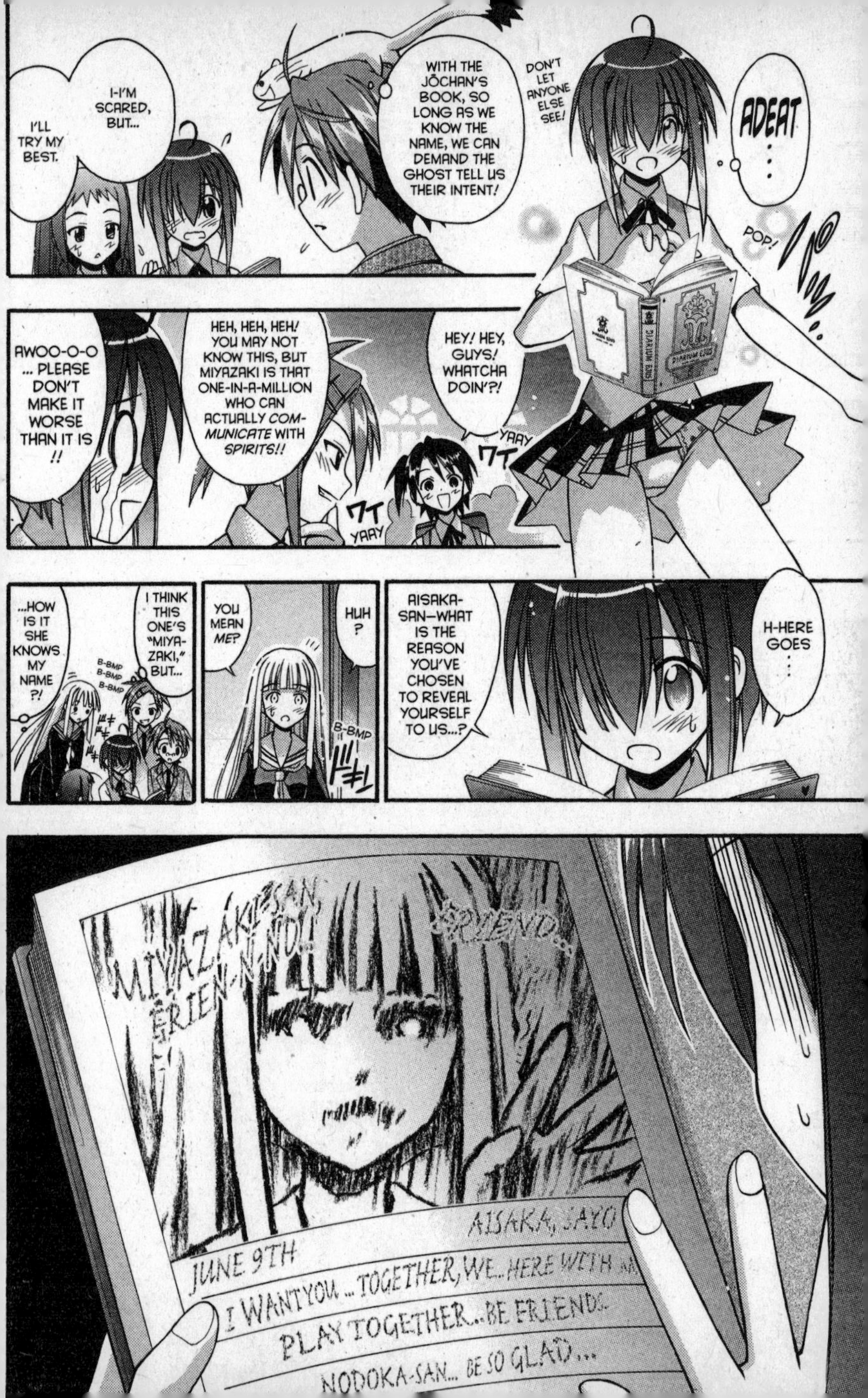
ADEAT . . .
POP!
DON'T LET ANYONE ELSE SEE!
WITH THE JŌCHAN'S BOOK, SO LONG AS WE KNOW THE NAME, WE CAN DEMAND THE GHOST TELL US THEIR INTENT!
I-I'M SCARED, BUT...
I'LL TRY MY BEST.
HEY! HEY, GUYS! WHATCHA DOIN'?!
YAAY
YAAY
HEH, HEH, HEH! YOU MAY NOT KNOW THIS, BUT MIYAZAKI IS THAT ONE-IN-A-MILLION WHO CAN ACTUALLY COMMUNICATE WITH SPIRITS!!
AWOO-O-O ... PLEASE DON'T MAKE IT WORSE THAN IT IS!!
H-HERE GOES . . .
AISAKA-SAN—WHAT IS THE REASON YOU'VE CHOSEN TO REVEAL YOURSELF TO US...?
HUH?
YOU MEAN ME?
B-BMP
I THINK THIS ONE'S "MIYAZAKI," BUT...
...HOW IS IT SHE KNOWS MY NAME?!
B-BMP
B-BMP
B-BMP
MIYAZAKI-SAN, FRIEN-N-ND!!
FRIEND...
AISAKA, SAYO
JUNE 9TH
I WANT YOU ... TOGETHER, WE... HERE WITH ME
PLAY TOGETHER... BE FRIENDS
NODOKA-SAN... BE SO GLAD...

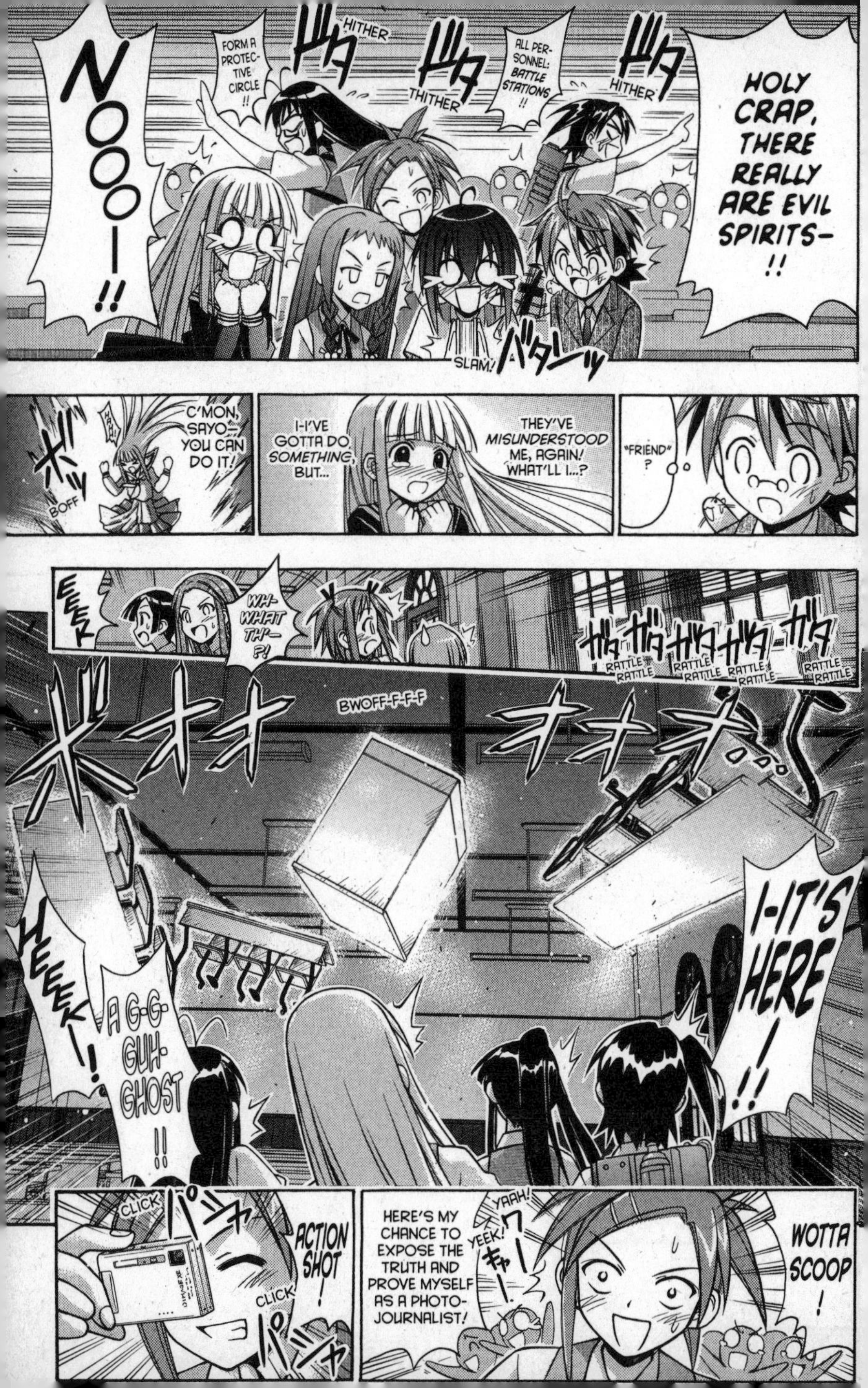
HOLY CRAP, THERE REALLY ARE EVIL SPIRITS—!!
HITHER
ALL PERSONNEL: BATTLE STATIONS!!
THITHER
FORM A PROTECTIVE CIRCLE!!
HITHER
NOOOO—!!
SLAM!
"FRIEND"?
THEY'VE MISUNDERSTOOD ME, AGAIN! WHAT'LL I...?
I-I'VE GOTTA DO SOMETHING, BUT...
C'MON, SAYO—YOU CAN DO IT!
BOFF
RATTLE RATTLE
RATTLE RATTLE
RATTLE RATTLE
RATTLE RATTLE
RATTLE RATTLE
WH-WHAT TH'—?!
EEEEK
BWOFF-F-F-F
I-IT'S HERE!!
A G-G-GUH-GHOST!!
HEEEEK—!!
WOTTA SCOOP!
YAAH!
YEEK!
HERE'S MY CHANCE TO EXPOSE THE TRUTH AND PROVE MYSELF AS A PHOTO-JOURNALIST!
ACTION SHOT!
CLICK
CLICK

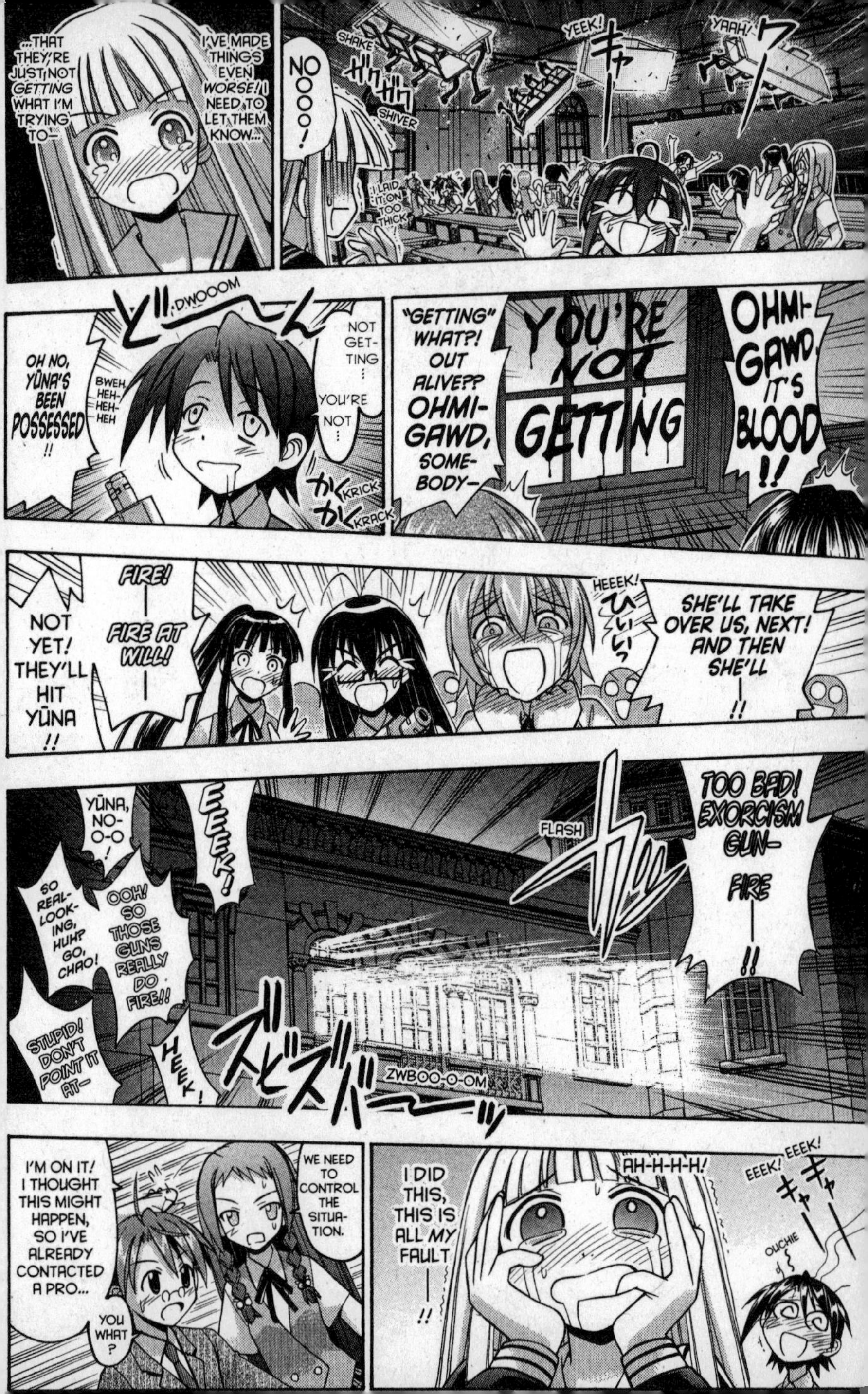
YAAH!
YEEK!
SHAKE
NO O O O O!
SHIVER
I LAID IT ON TOO THICK!
I'VE MADE THINGS EVEN WORSE! I NEED TO LET THEM KNOW...
...THAT THEY'RE JUST NOT GETTING WHAT I'M TRYING TO—
OHMI-GAWD, IT'S BLOOD!!
YOU'RE NOT GETTING
"GETTING" WHAT?! OUT ALIVE?? OHMI-GAWD, SOMEBODY—
DWOOOM
NOT GET-TING... YOU'RE NOT...
BWEH HEH-HEH-HEH
OH NO, YŪNA'S BEEN POSSESSED!!
KRICK
KRACK
SHE'LL TAKE OVER US, NEXT! AND THEN SHE'LL—!!
HEEEK!
FIRE! —FIRE AT WILL!—
NOT YET! THEY'LL HIT YŪNA!!
TOO BAD! EXORCISM GUN-FIRE——!!
FLASH
EEEEK!
YŪNA, NO-O-O!
OOH! SO THOSE GUNS REALLY DO FIRE!!
SO REAL-LOOKING, HUH? GO, CHAO!
HEEEK!
ZWBOO-O-OM
STUPID! DON'T POINT IT AT—
EEEK!
AH-H-H-H!
I DID THIS, THIS IS ALL MY FAULT——!!
OUCHIE
WE NEED TO CONTROL THE SITUATION.
I'M ON IT! I THOUGHT THIS MIGHT HAPPEN, SO I'VE ALREADY CONTACTED A PRO...
YOU WHAT?

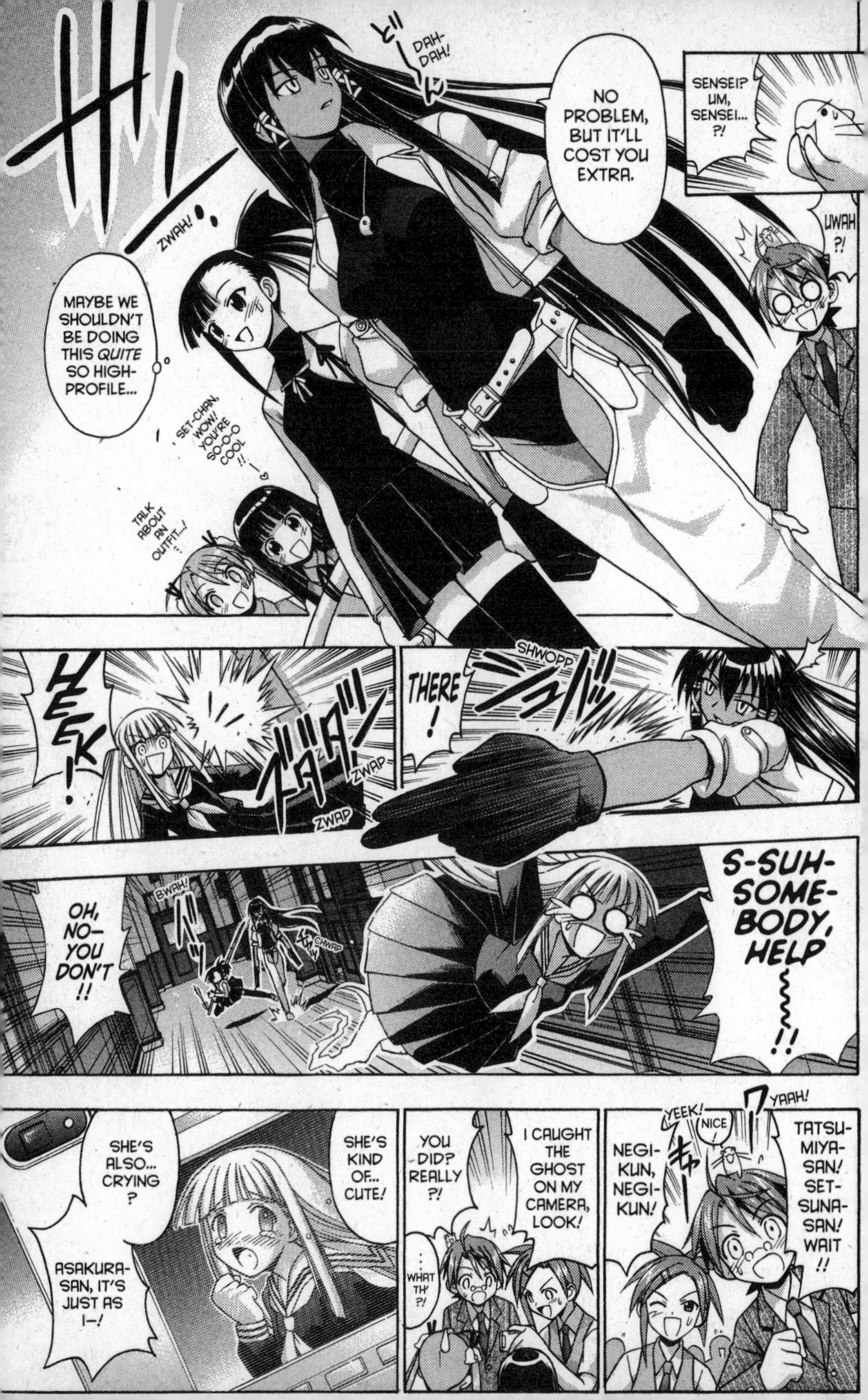
SENSEI? UM, SENSEI...?!
UWAH?!
DAH-DAH!
NO PROBLEM, BUT IT'LL COST YOU EXTRA.
ZWAH!
MAYBE WE SHOULDN'T BE DOING THIS *QUITE* SO HIGH-PROFILE...
SET-CHAN, WOW! YOU'RE SO-O-O COOL!!
TALK ABOUT AN OUTFIT...!
SHWOPP
THERE!
ZWAP
ZWAP
HEEK!
S-SUH-SOMEBODY, HELP~~!!
CHWAP
BWAH!
OH, NO—YOU DON'T!!
YAAAH!
TATSUMIYA-SAN! SETSUNA-SAN! WAIT!!
YEEK!
NICE!
NEGI-KUN, NEGI-KUN!
I CAUGHT THE GHOST ON MY CAMERA, LOOK!
YOU DID? REALLY?!
...WHAT TH'?!
SHE'S KIND OF... CUTE!
SHE'S ALSO... CRYING?
ASAKURA-SAN, IT'S JUST AS I—!

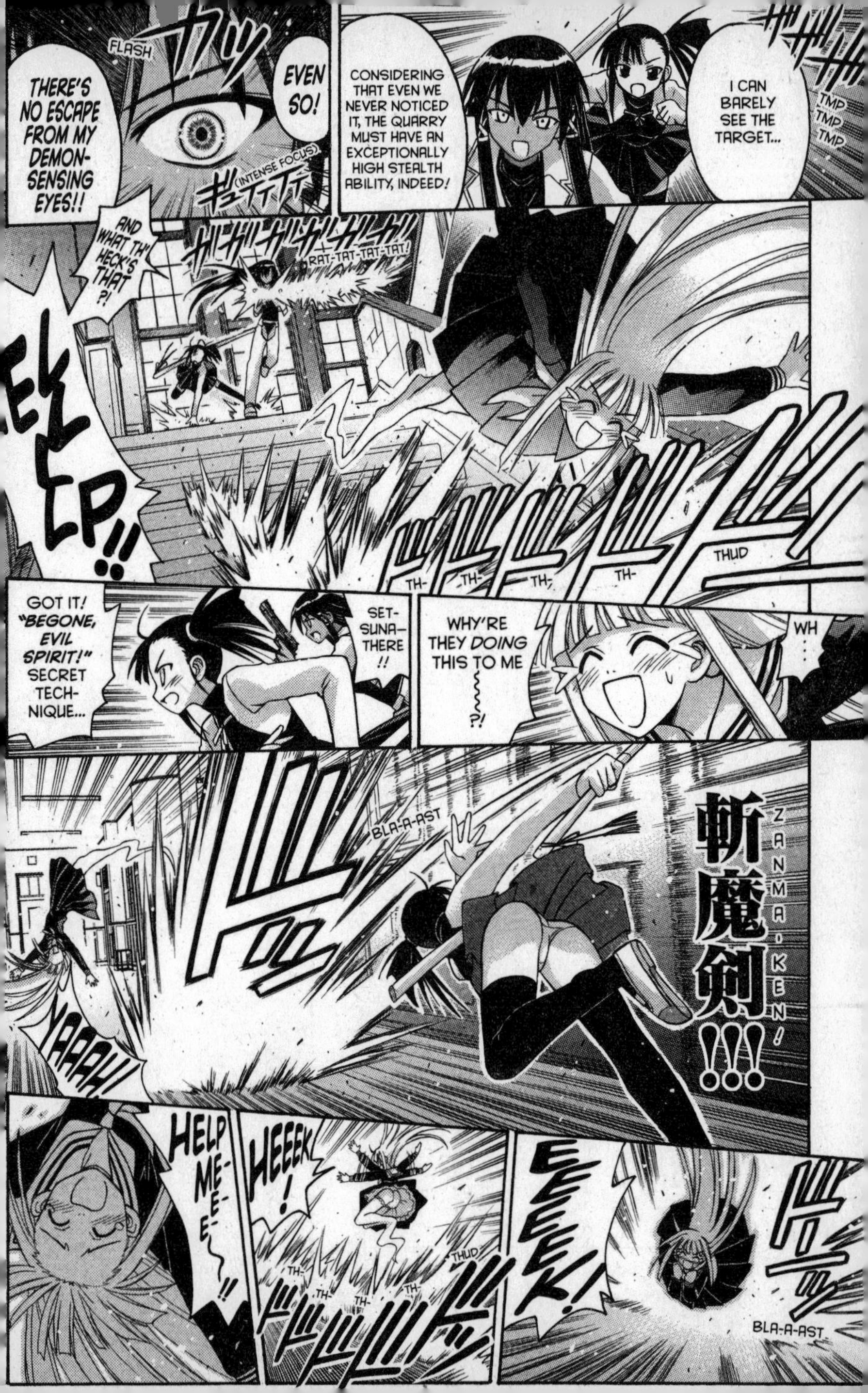
TMP TMP TMP
I CAN BARELY SEE THE TARGET...
CONSIDERING THAT EVEN WE NEVER NOTICED IT, THE QUARRY MUST HAVE AN EXCEPTIONALLY HIGH STEALTH ABILITY, INDEED!
EVEN SO!
FLASH
THERE'S NO ESCAPE FROM MY DEMON-SENSING EYES!!
(INTENSE FOCUS)
RAT-TAT-TAT-TAT!
AND WHAT TH' HECK'S THAT ?!
EEEP!!
THUD
TH-
TH-
TH-
TH-
WH...
WHY'RE THEY DOING THIS TO ME ~~~?!
SET-SUNA-THERE!!
GOT IT! "BEGONE, EVIL SPIRIT!" SECRET TECHNIQUE...
斬魔剣!!!
ZANMA-KEN!
BLA-A-AST
YAAAH!
BLA-A-AST
EEEEEK!
HEEEK!
THUD
TH-
TH-
TH-
HELP ME-E-E~!!

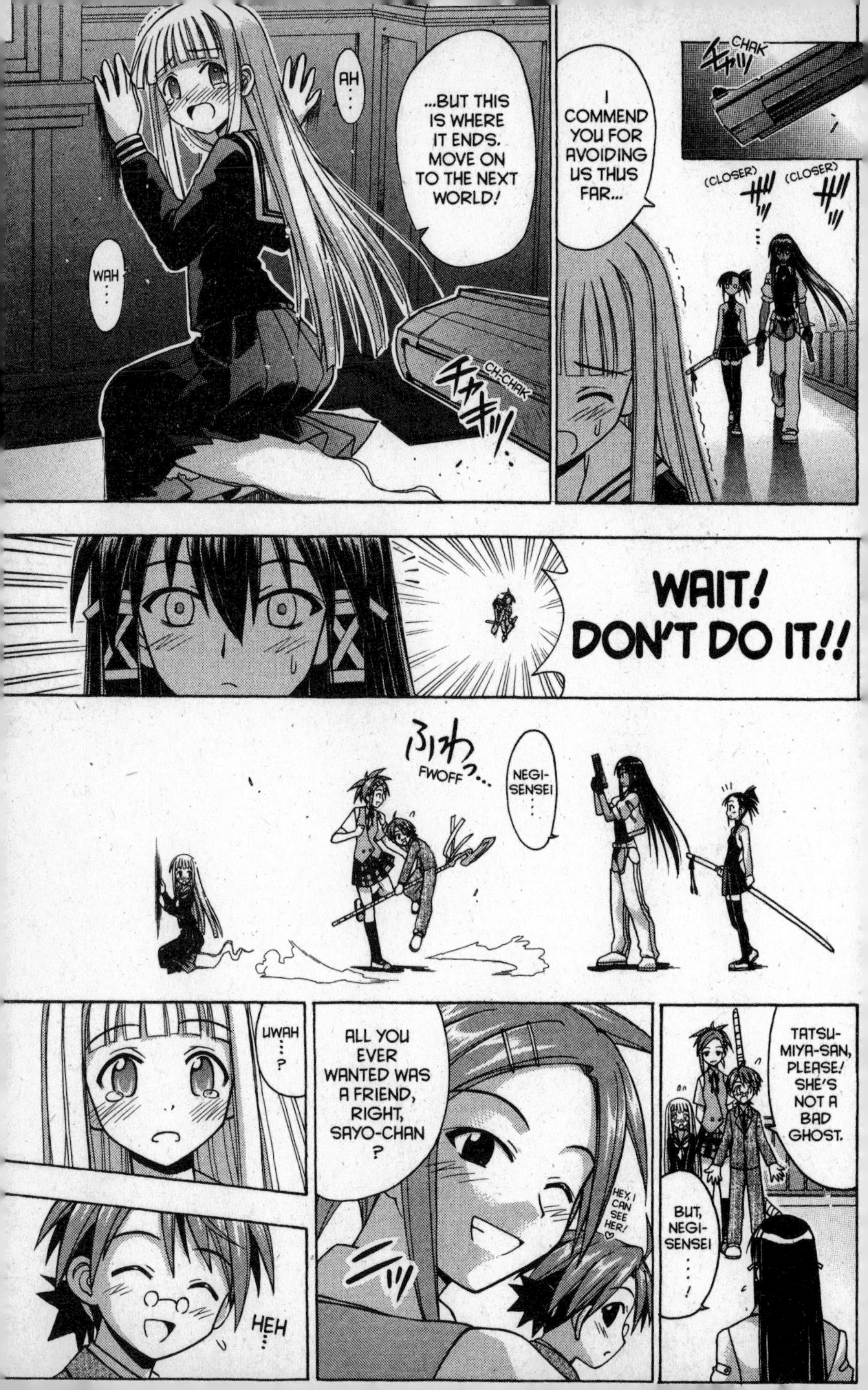
CHAK
I COMMEND YOU FOR AVOIDING US THUS FAR...
(CLOSER)
(CLOSER)
...BUT THIS IS WHERE IT ENDS. MOVE ON TO THE NEXT WORLD!
AH...
WAH...
CH-CHAK
WAIT! DON'T DO IT!!
ふわっ
FWOFF...
NEGI-SENSEI...
TATSUMIYA-SAN, PLEASE! SHE'S NOT A BAD GHOST.
BUT, NEGI-SENSEI...!
ALL YOU EVER WANTED WAS A FRIEND, RIGHT, SAYO-CHAN?
HEY, I CAN SEE HER! ♡
UWAH...?
HEH...

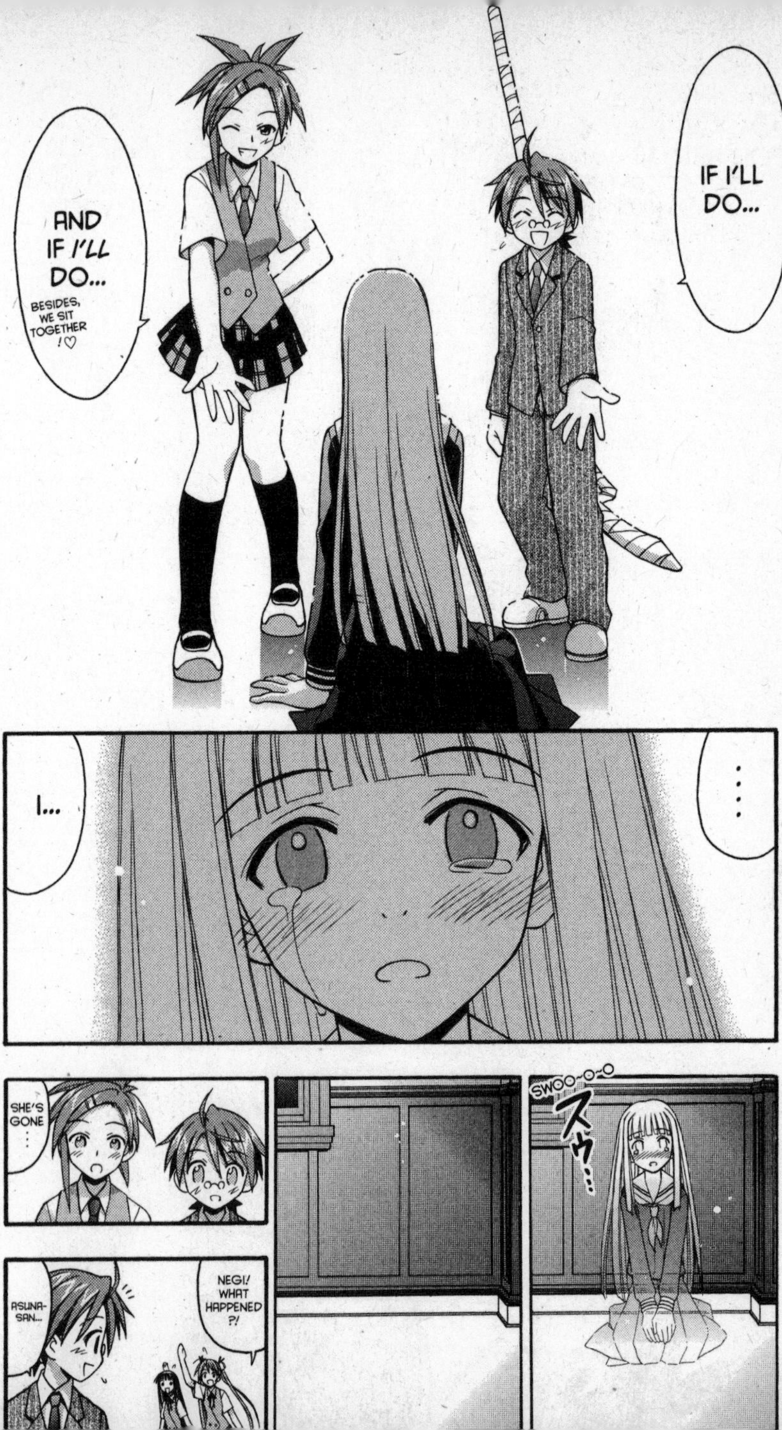
IF I'LL DO...
AND IF I'LL DO...
BESIDES, WE SIT TOGETHER !♡
....
I...
SWOO~O~O
スゥ...
SHE'S GONE ...
NEGI! WHAT HAPPENED ?!
ASUNA-SAN...

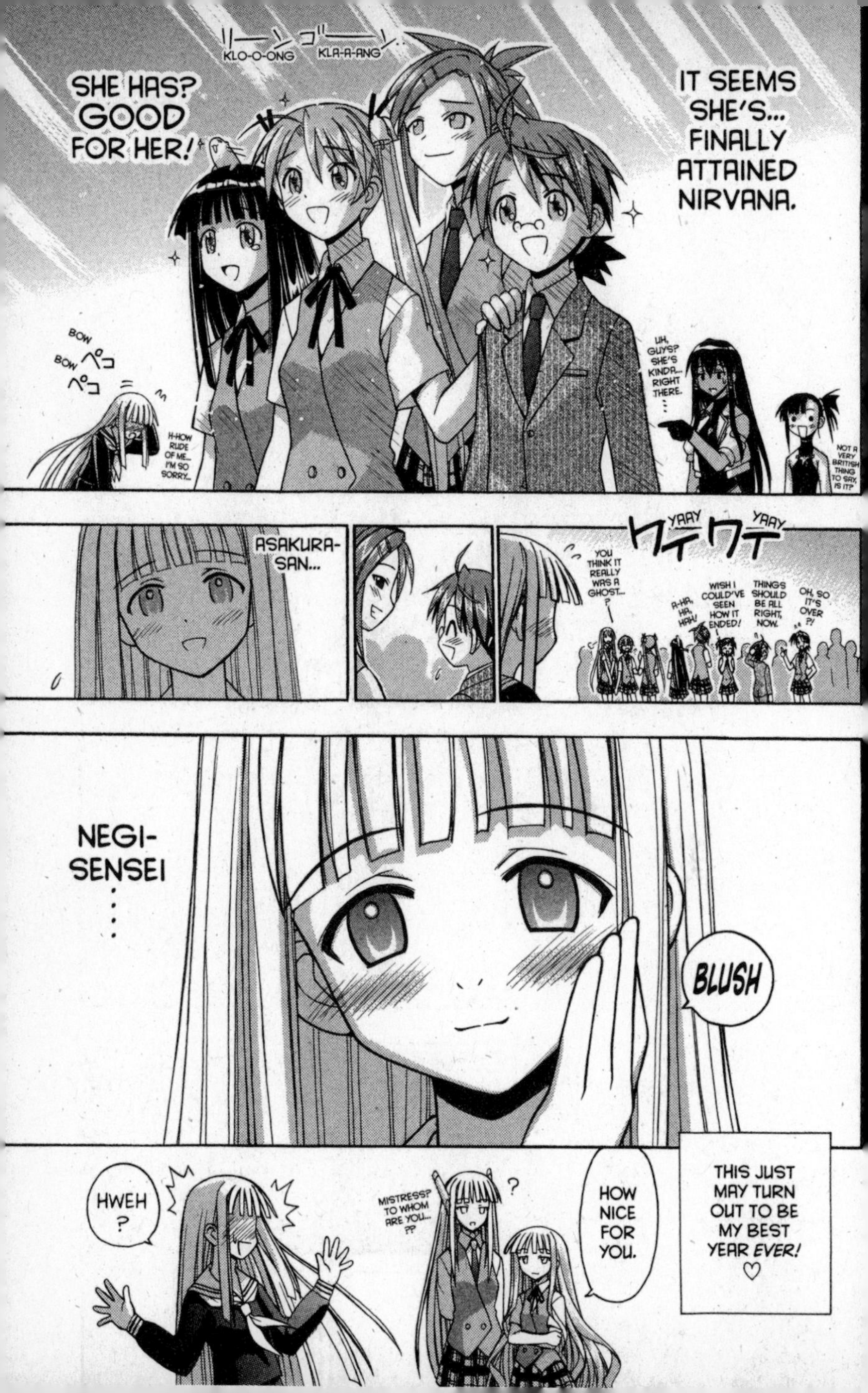
リーンゴーン
KLO-O-ONG KLA-A-ANG
IT SEEMS SHE'S... FINALLY ATTAINED NIRVANA.
SHE HAS? GOOD FOR HER!
UH, GUYS? SHE'S KINDA... RIGHT THERE. ...
NOT A VERY BRITISH THING TO SAY, IS IT?
BOW ペコ BOW ペコ
H-HOW RUDE OF ME... I'M SO SORRY...
YAAY ワイワイ YAAY
OH, SO IT'S OVER ?!
THINGS SHOULD BE ALL RIGHT, NOW.
WISH I COULD'VE SEEN HOW IT ENDED!
A-HA, HA, HAH!
YOU THINK IT REALLY WAS A GHOST... ?
ASAKURA-SAN...
BLUSH
NEGI-SENSEI ....
THIS JUST MAY TURN OUT TO BE MY BEST YEAR *EVER!* ♡
HOW NICE FOR YOU.
?
MISTRESS? TO WHOM ARE YOU... ??
HWEH ?

STUDENT NUMBER 24
HAKASE, SATOMI
BORN: 14 JULY 1988
BLOODTYPE: B
LIKES: ROBOTS; CURRENT RESEARCH
      INTERESTS (i.e., THE SCIENTIFIC
      APPLICATIONS OF MAGIC)
DISLIKES: ANYTHING UN-SCIENTIFIC
      (MAGIC USED TO FURTHER MY
      RESEARCH DOESN'T COUNT)
AFFILIATIONS: ROBOT RESEARCH
      CIRCLE (UNIVERSITY-LEVEL);
      JET-PROPULSION RESEARCH
      CIRCLE (UNIVERSITY-LEVEL)

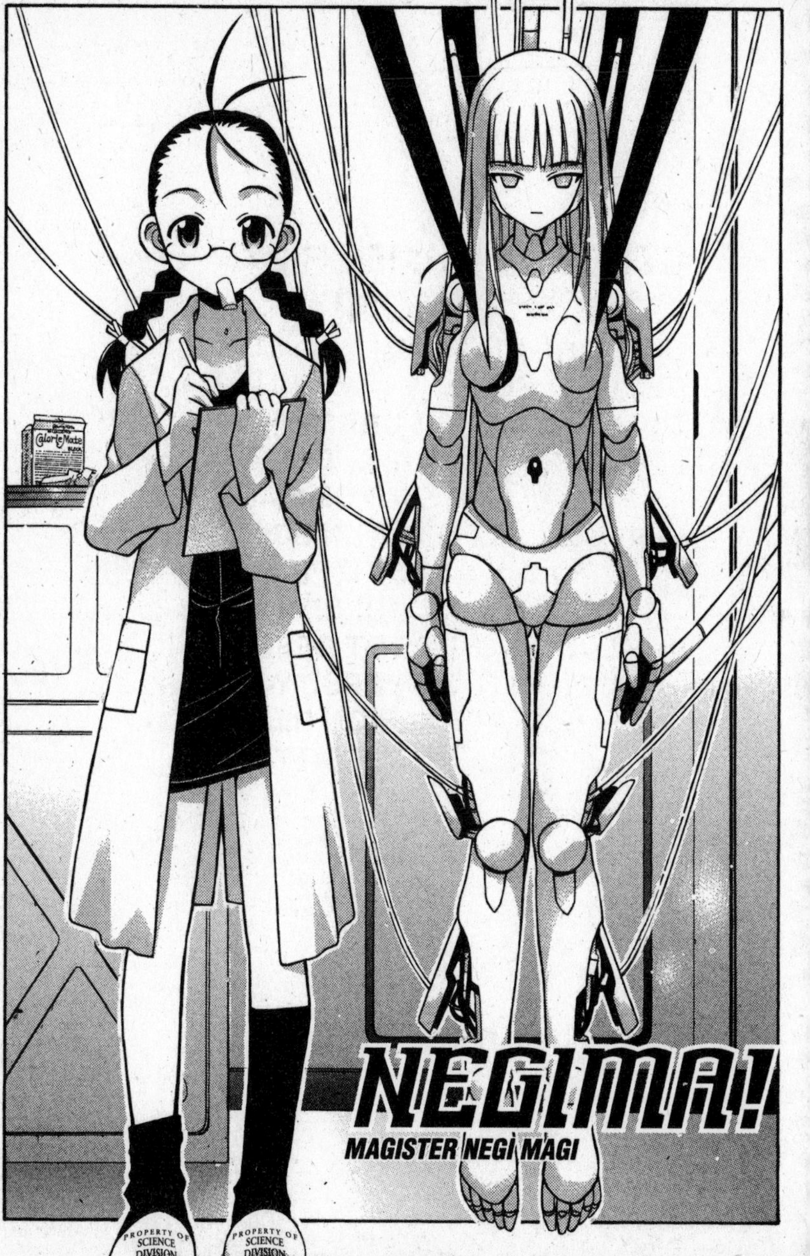
Calorie Mate
PROPERTY OF SCIENCE DIVISION
PROPERTY OF SCIENCE DIVISION
NEGIMA!
MAGISTER NEGI MAGI
SEVENTY-FIFTH PERIOD: THE LOGIC OF ILLOGIC

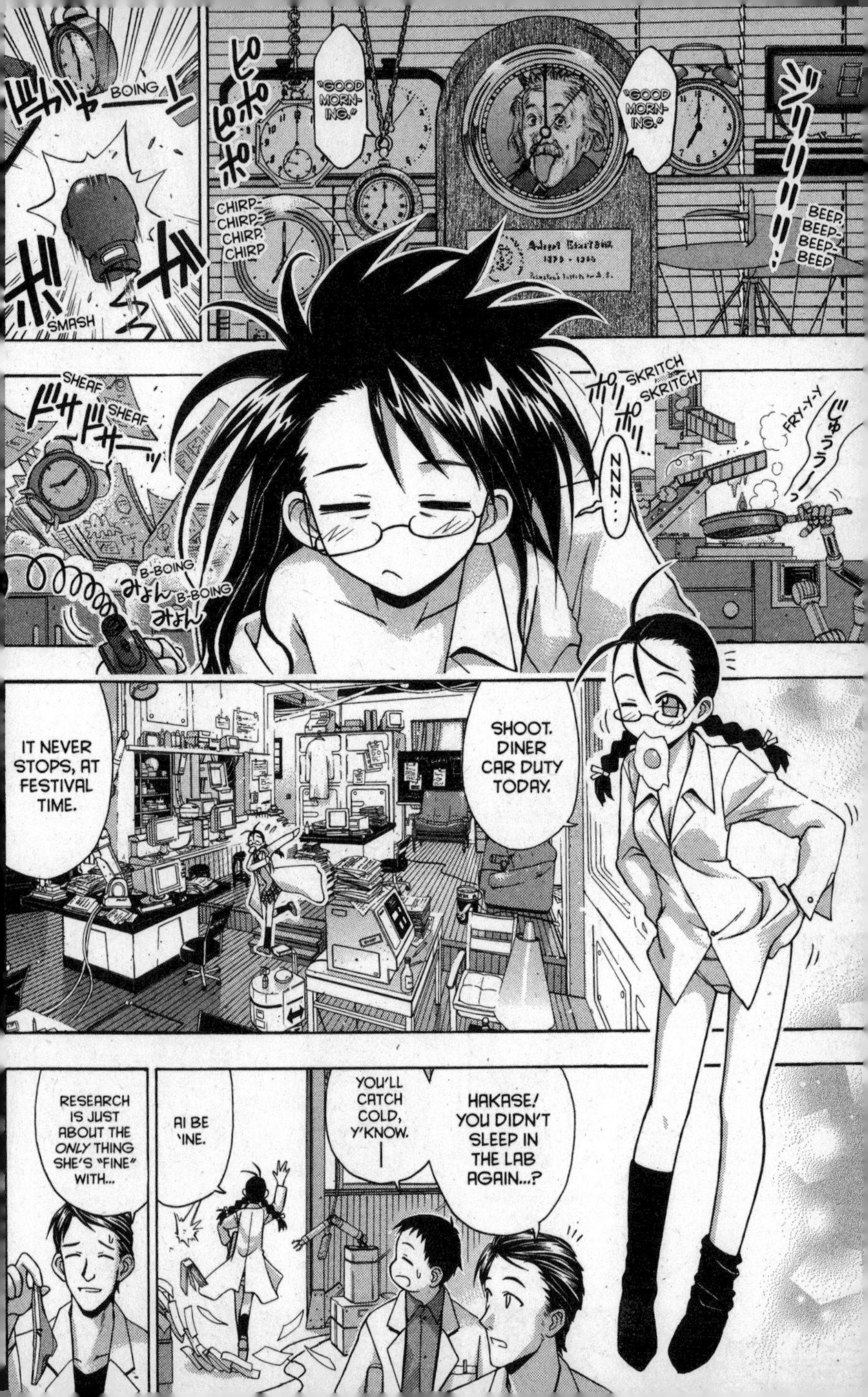
"GOOD MORNING."
BEEP, BEEP, BEEP, BEEP
"GOOD MORNING."
CHIRP, CHIRP, CHIRP, CHIRP
BOING
SMASH
SKRITCH SKRITCH
NNN...
FRY-Y-Y
SHEAF SHEAF
B-BOING B-BOING
みょん みょん
SHOOT. DINER CAR DUTY TODAY.
IT NEVER STOPS, AT FESTIVAL TIME.
HAKASE! YOU DIDN'T SLEEP IN THE LAB AGAIN...?
YOU'LL CATCH COLD, Y'KNOW.
AI BE 'INE.
RESEARCH IS JUST ABOUT THE *ONLY* THING SHE'S "FINE" WITH...

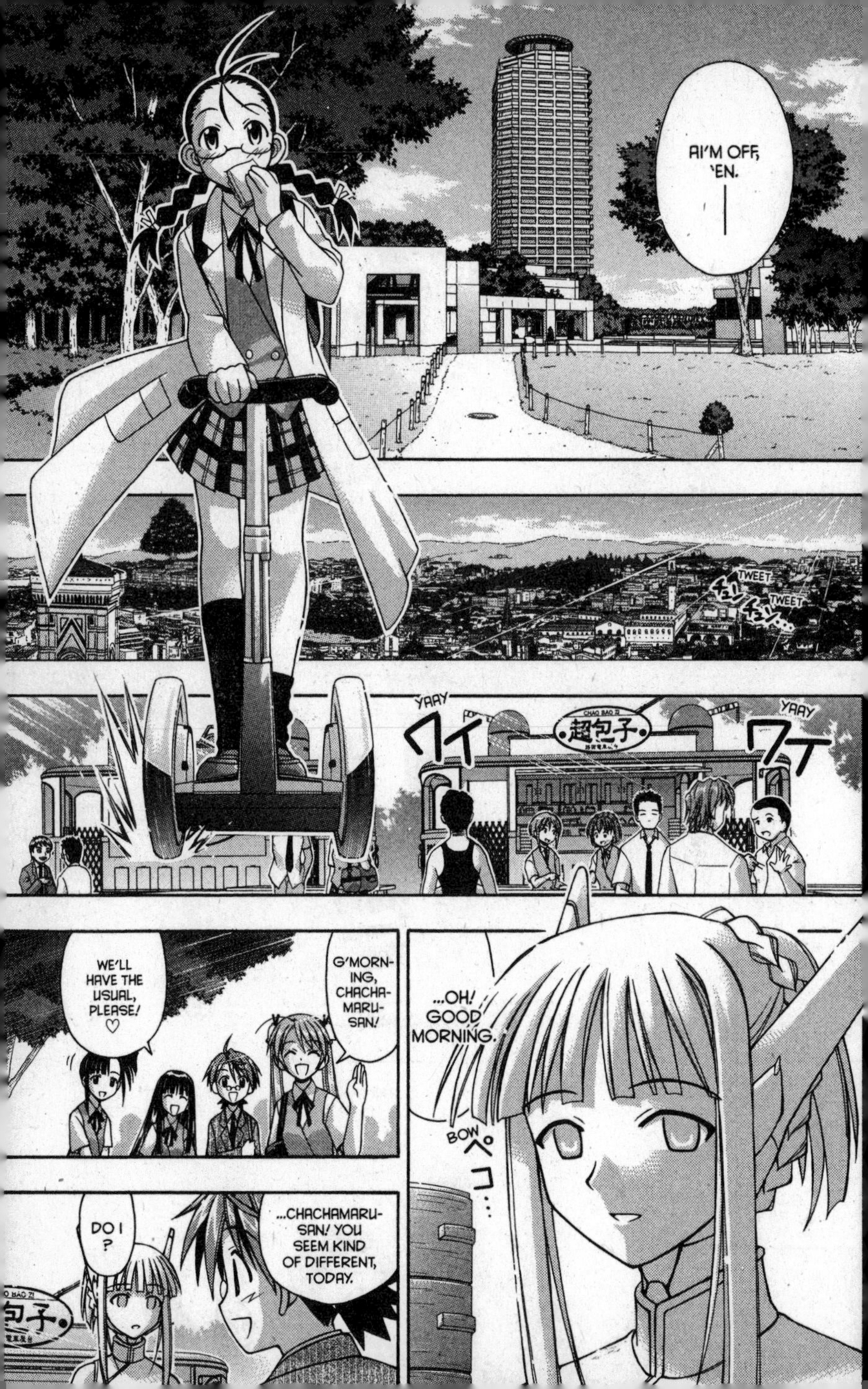
AI'M OFF, 'EN.
TWEET
TWEET
YAAY
CHAO BAO ZI
超包子
YAAY
...OH! GOOD MORNING.
BOW
G'MORN-ING, CHACHA-MARU-SAN!
WE'LL HAVE THE USUAL, PLEASE! ♡
...CHACHAMARU-SAN! YOU SEEM KIND OF DIFFERENT, TODAY.
DO I ?

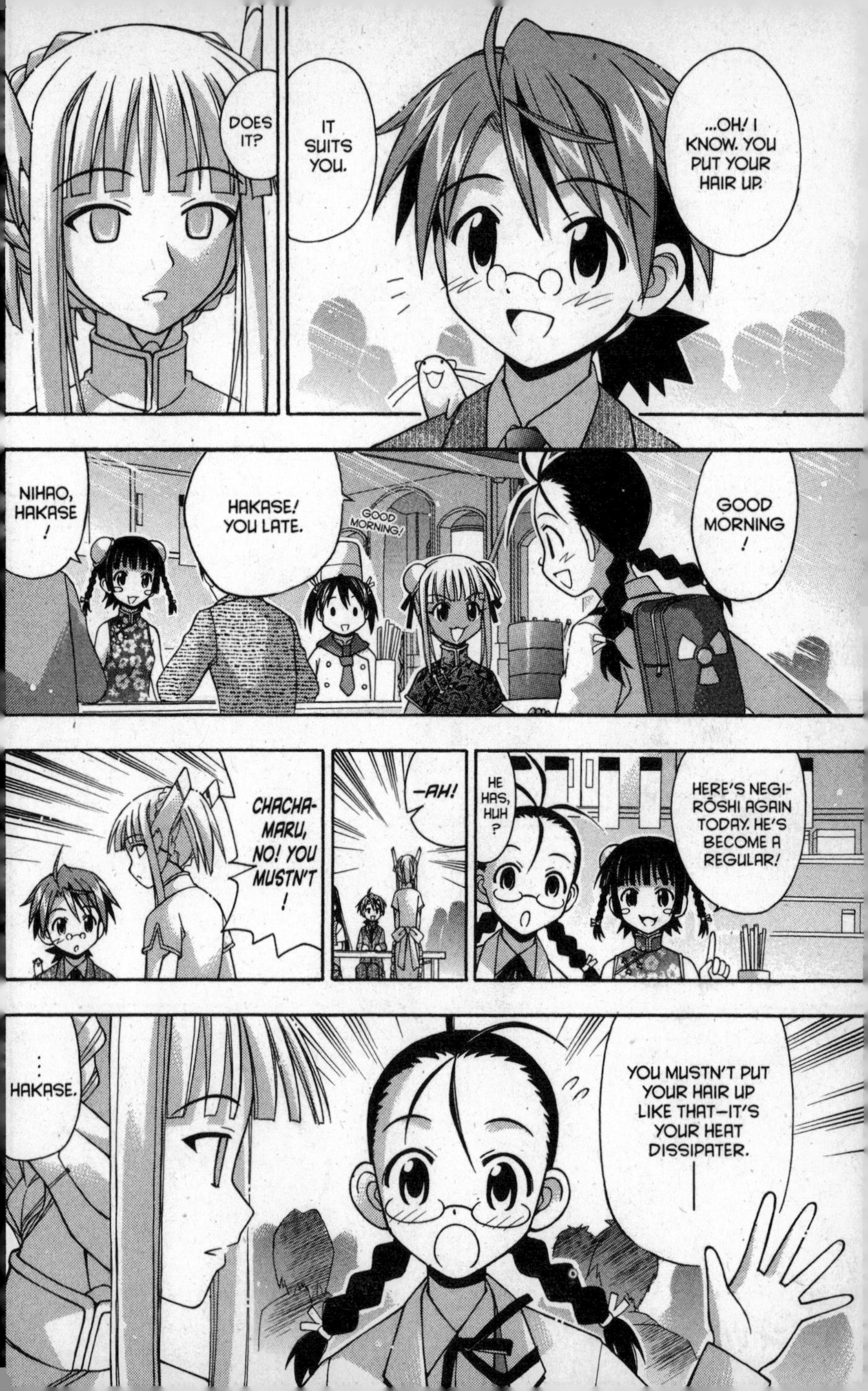
...OH! I KNOW. YOU PUT YOUR HAIR UP.
IT SUITS YOU.
DOES IT?
GOOD MORNING!
GOOD MORNING!
HAKASE! YOU LATE.
NIHAO, HAKASE!
HERE'S NEGI-RŌSHI AGAIN TODAY. HE'S BECOME A REGULAR!
HE HAS, HUH?
—AH!
CHACHA-MARU, NO! YOU MUSTN'T!
YOU MUSTN'T PUT YOUR HAIR UP LIKE THAT—IT'S YOUR HEAT DISSIPATER.
...HAKASE.

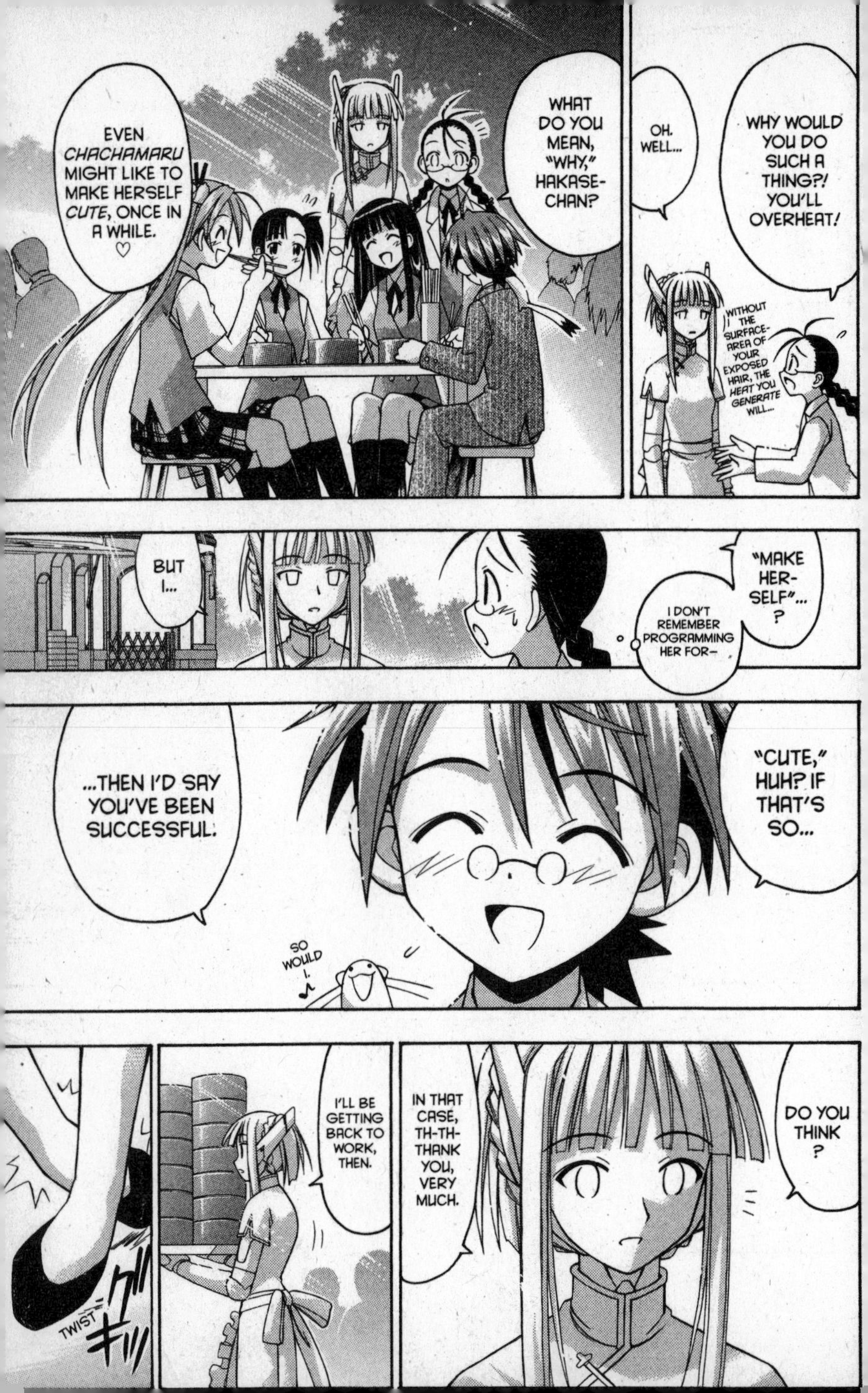
WHY WOULD YOU DO SUCH A THING?! YOU'LL OVERHEAT!
OH. WELL...
WITHOUT THE SURFACE-AREA OF YOUR EXPOSED HAIR, THE HEAT YOU GENERATE WILL...
WHAT DO YOU MEAN, "WHY," HAKASE-CHAN?
EVEN *CHACHAMARU* MIGHT LIKE TO MAKE HERSELF *CUTE*, ONCE IN A WHILE. ♡
"MAKE HER-SELF"...?
I DON'T REMEMBER PROGRAMMING HER FOR—
BUT I...
"CUTE," HUH? IF THAT'S SO...
...THEN I'D SAY YOU'VE BEEN SUCCESSFUL.
SO WOULD I. ♪
DO YOU THINK?
IN THAT CASE, TH-TH-THANK YOU, VERY MUCH.
I'LL BE GETTING BACK TO WORK, THEN.
TWIST

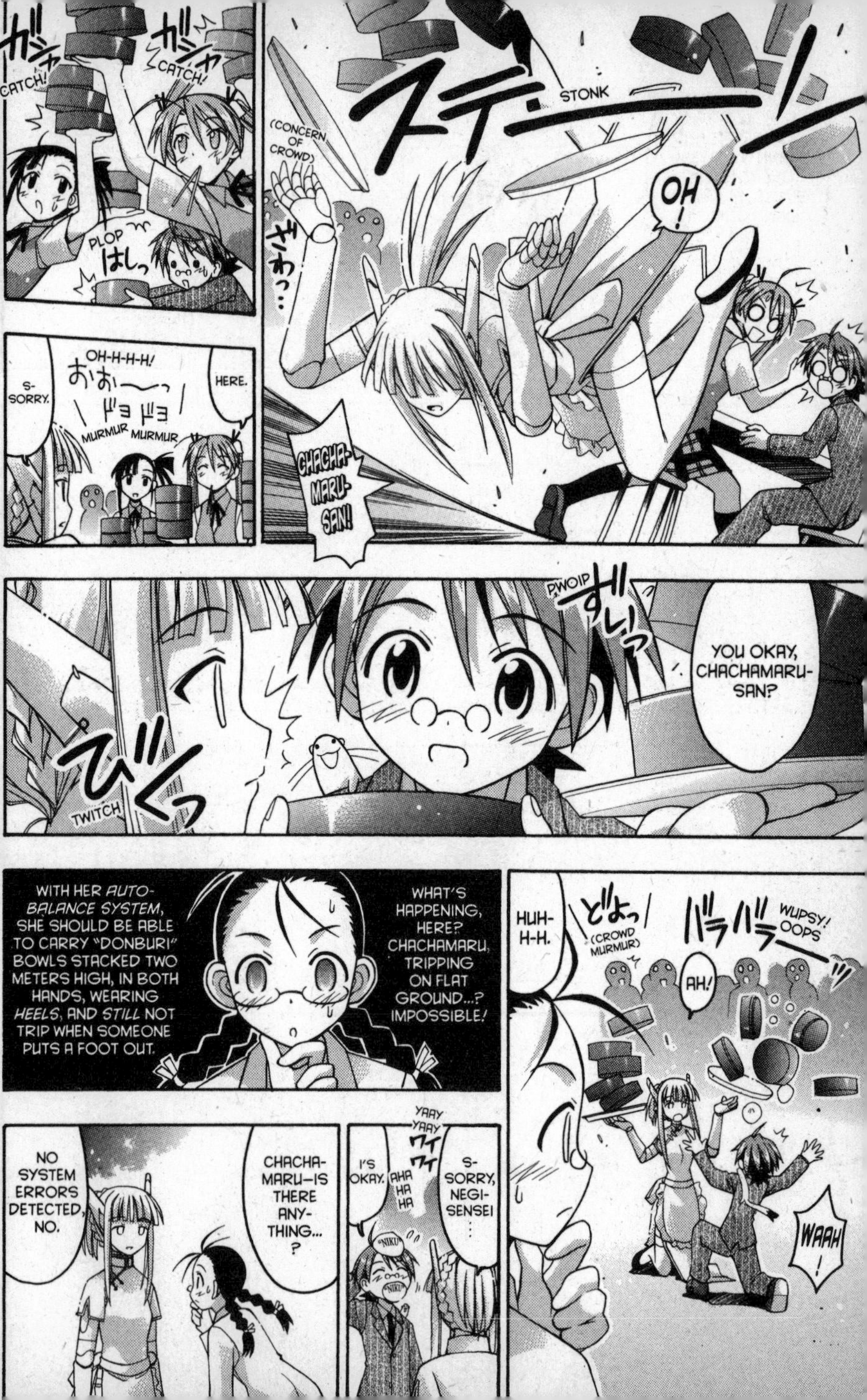
ステーン
STONK
OH!
(CONCERN OF CROWD)
ざわっ…
CHACHA-MARU-SAN!
ガシャ
CATCH!
ガシャ
CATCH!
PLOP
はしっ
HERE.
OH-H-H-H!
おお〜っ
ドヨドヨ
MURMUR MURMUR
S-SORRY.
YOU OKAY, CHACHAMARU-SAN?
PWOIP
ひくっ
TWITCH
バラバラー
WUPSY! OOPS
どよっ
(CROWD MURMUR)
HUH-H-H.
AH!
WAAH!
WHAT'S HAPPENING, HERE? CHACHAMARU, TRIPPING ON FLAT GROUND...? IMPOSSIBLE!
WITH HER AUTO-BALANCE SYSTEM, SHE SHOULD BE ABLE TO CARRY "DONBURI" BOWLS STACKED TWO METERS HIGH, IN BOTH HANDS, WEARING HEELS, AND STILL NOT TRIP WHEN SOMEONE PUTS A FOOT OUT.
S-SORRY, NEGI-SENSEI...
YAAY YAAY
ワイワイ
I'S OKAY.
AHA HA HA
"NIKU"
"NIKU"
CHACHA-MARU—IS THERE ANYTHING...?
NO SYSTEM ERRORS DETECTED, NO.

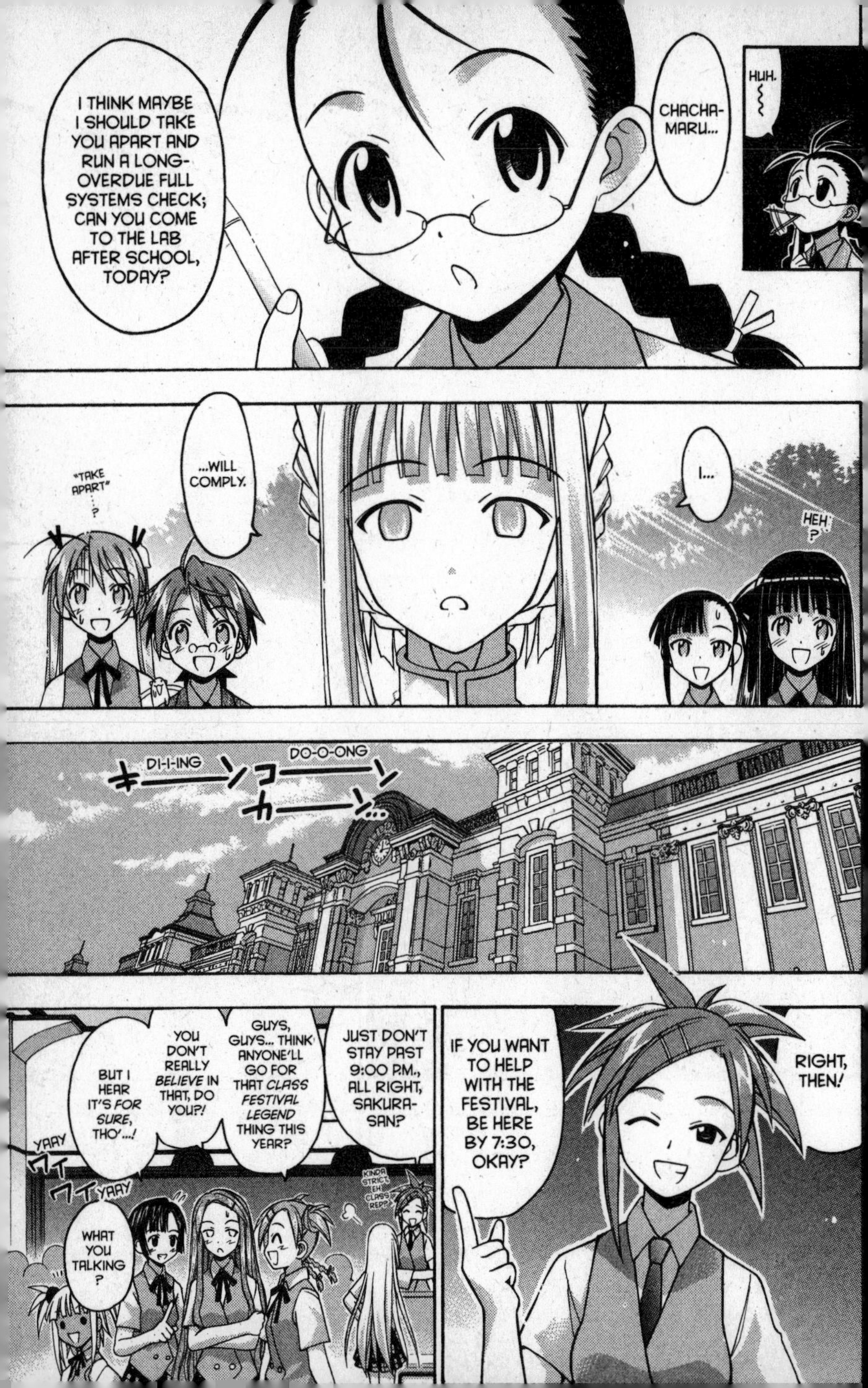
HUH. ~~~
CHACHA-MARU...
I THINK MAYBE I SHOULD TAKE YOU APART AND RUN A LONG-OVERDUE FULL SYSTEMS CHECK; CAN YOU COME TO THE LAB AFTER SCHOOL, TODAY?
I...
HEH?
...WILL COMPLY.
"TAKE APART"...?
DI-I-ING
DO-O-ONG
キーンコーン
カーン…
RIGHT, THEN!
IF YOU WANT TO HELP WITH THE FESTIVAL, BE HERE BY 7:30, OKAY?
JUST DON'T STAY PAST 9:00 P.M., ALL RIGHT, SAKURA-SAN?
GUYS, GUYS... THINK ANYONE'LL GO FOR THAT *CLASS FESTIVAL LEGEND* THING THIS YEAR?
YOU DON'T REALLY *BELIEVE* IN THAT, DO YOU?!
BUT I HEAR IT'S *FOR SURE*, THO'...!
YAAY ワイ
ワイ YAAY
KINDA STRICT, EH CLASS REP?
WHAT YOU TALKING?

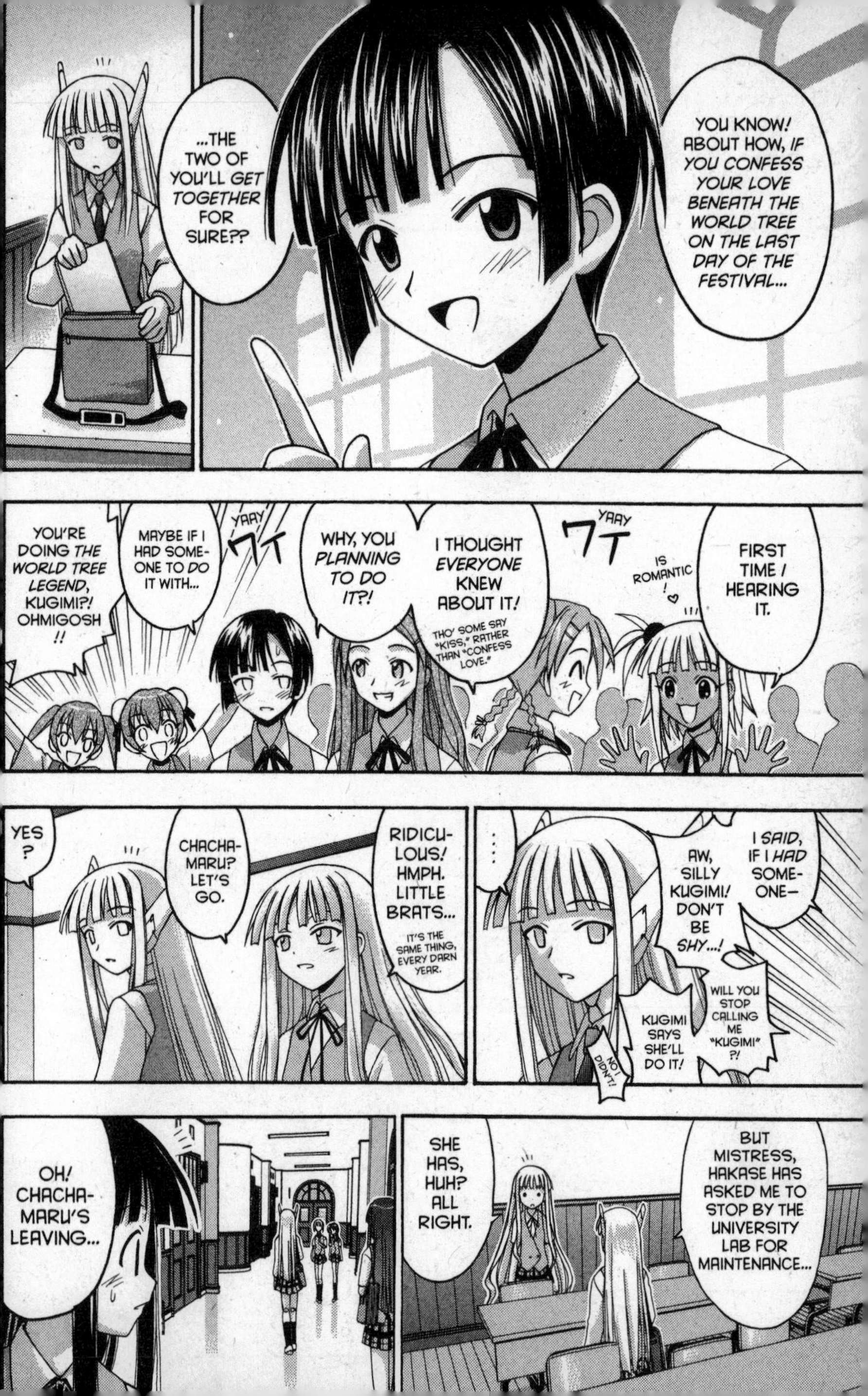
YOU KNOW! ABOUT HOW, IF YOU CONFESS YOUR LOVE BENEATH THE WORLD TREE ON THE LAST DAY OF THE FESTIVAL...
...THE TWO OF YOU'LL GET TOGETHER FOR SURE??
FIRST TIME I HEARING IT.
IS ROMANTIC!
YAAY
I THOUGHT EVERYONE KNEW ABOUT IT!
THO' SOME SAY "KISS," RATHER THAN "CONFESS LOVE."
WHY, YOU PLANNING TO DO IT?!
YAAY
MAYBE IF I HAD SOME-ONE TO DO IT WITH...
YOU'RE DOING THE WORLD TREE LEGEND, KUGIMI?! OHMIGOSH!!
I SAID, IF I HAD SOME-ONE—
AW, SILLY KUGIMI! DON'T BE SHY...!
WILL YOU STOP CALLING ME "KUGIMI"?!
KUGIMI SAYS SHE'LL DO IT!
NO I DIDN'T!
...
RIDICU-LOUS! HMPH. LITTLE BRATS...
IT'S THE SAME THING, EVERY DARN YEAR.
CHACHA-MARU? LET'S GO.
YES?
BUT MISTRESS, HAKASE HAS ASKED ME TO STOP BY THE UNIVERSITY LAB FOR MAINTENANCE...
SHE HAS, HUH? ALL RIGHT.
OH! CHACHA-MARU'S LEAVING...

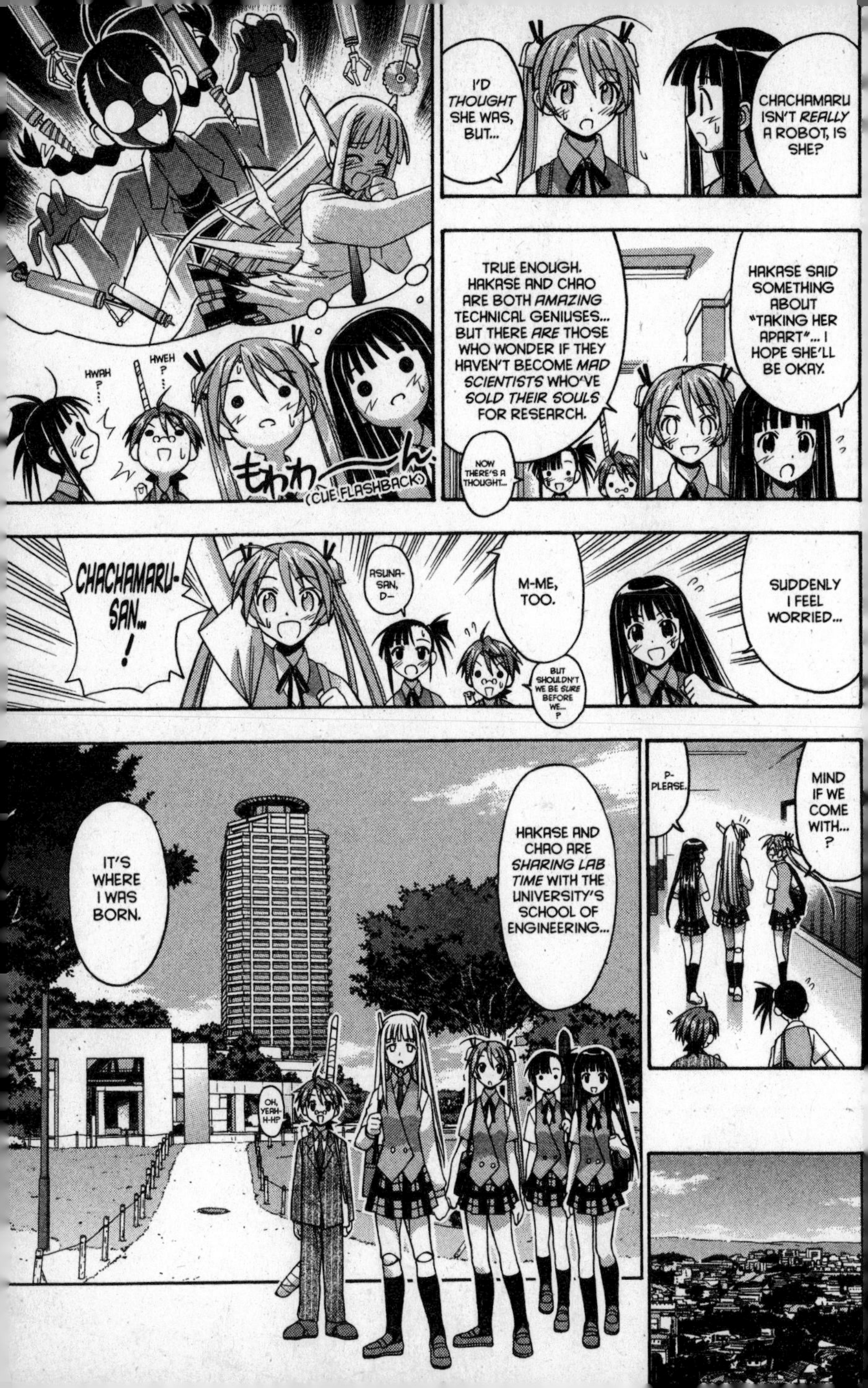

CHACHAMARU ISN'T REALLY A ROBOT, IS SHE?
I'D THOUGHT SHE WAS, BUT...
HAKASE SAID SOMETHING ABOUT "TAKING HER APART"... I HOPE SHE'LL BE OKAY.
TRUE ENOUGH. HAKASE AND CHAO ARE BOTH AMAZING TECHNICAL GENIUSES... BUT THERE ARE THOSE WHO WONDER IF THEY HAVEN'T BECOME MAD SCIENTISTS WHO'VE SOLD THEIR SOULS FOR RESEARCH.
NOW THERE'S A THOUGHT...
HWEH ?...
HWAH ?...
もわわ～ん
(CUE FLASHBACK)
SUDDENLY I FEEL WORRIED...
M-ME, TOO.
BUT SHOULDN'T WE BE SURE BEFORE WE...?
ASUNA-SAN, D–
CHACHAMARU-SAN...!
MIND IF WE COME WITH...?
P-PLEASE.
HAKASE AND CHAO ARE SHARING LAB TIME WITH THE UNIVERSITY'S SCHOOL OF ENGINEERING...
IT'S WHERE I WAS BORN.
OH, YEAH-H-H?

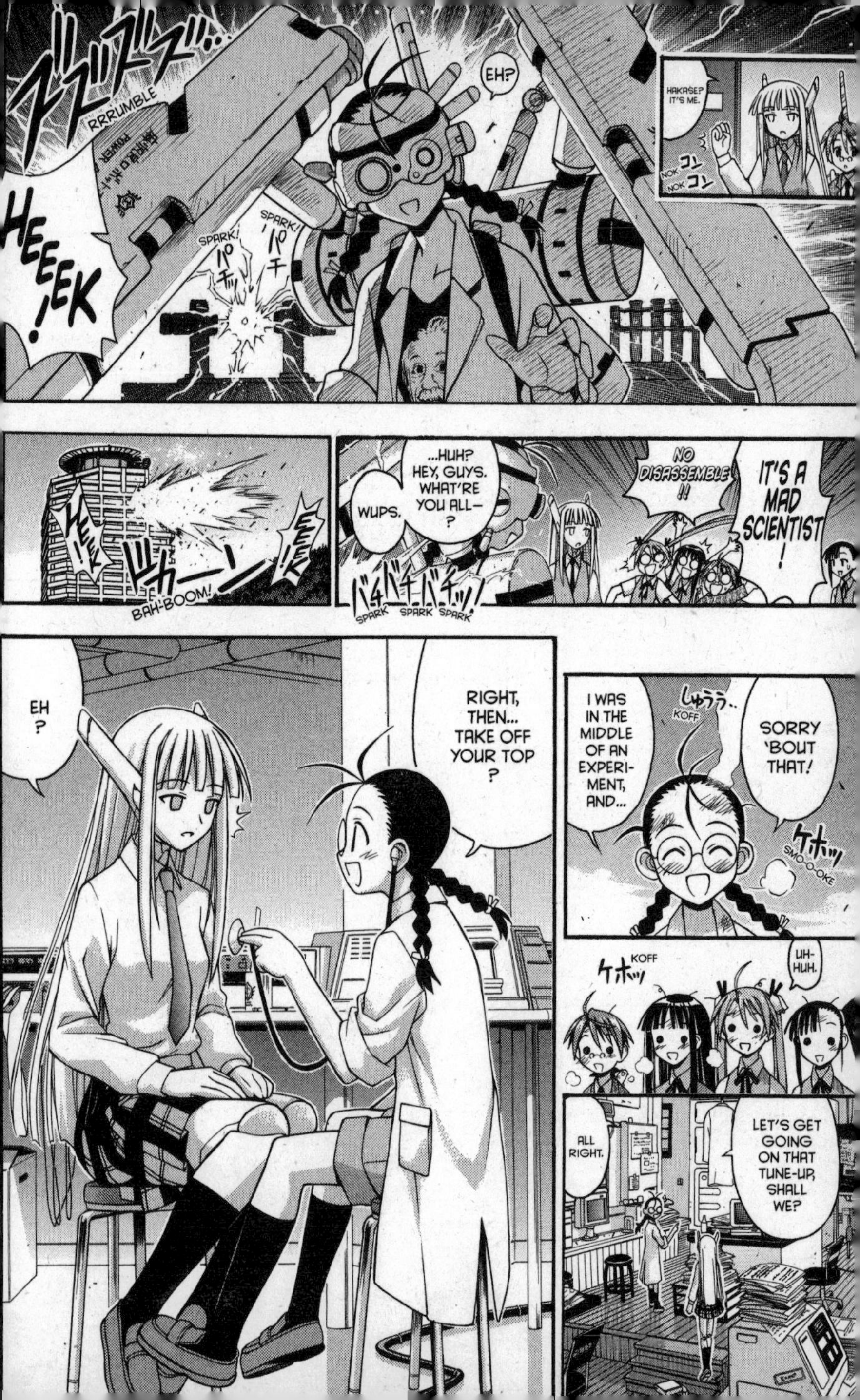
HAKASE? IT'S ME.
NOK コン
NOK コン
EH?
ズズズズ…
RRRUMBLE
HEEEEK!
SPARK! パチ
SPARK! パチッ
POWER
IT'S A MAD SCIENTIST!
NO DISASSEMBLE!!
...HUH? HEY, GUYS. WHAT'RE YOU ALL—?
WUPS.
バチバチバチッ!
SPARK SPARK SPARK
EEEK!
ドカーン
BAH-BOOM!
HEEEK!
SORRY 'BOUT THAT!
I WAS IN THE MIDDLE OF AN EXPERIMENT, AND...
しゅうう..
KOFF
ケホッ
SMO-O-OKE
UH-HUH.
ケホッ
KOFF
LET'S GET GOING ON THAT TUNE-UP, SHALL WE?
ALL RIGHT.
RIGHT, THEN... TAKE OFF YOUR TOP?
EH?

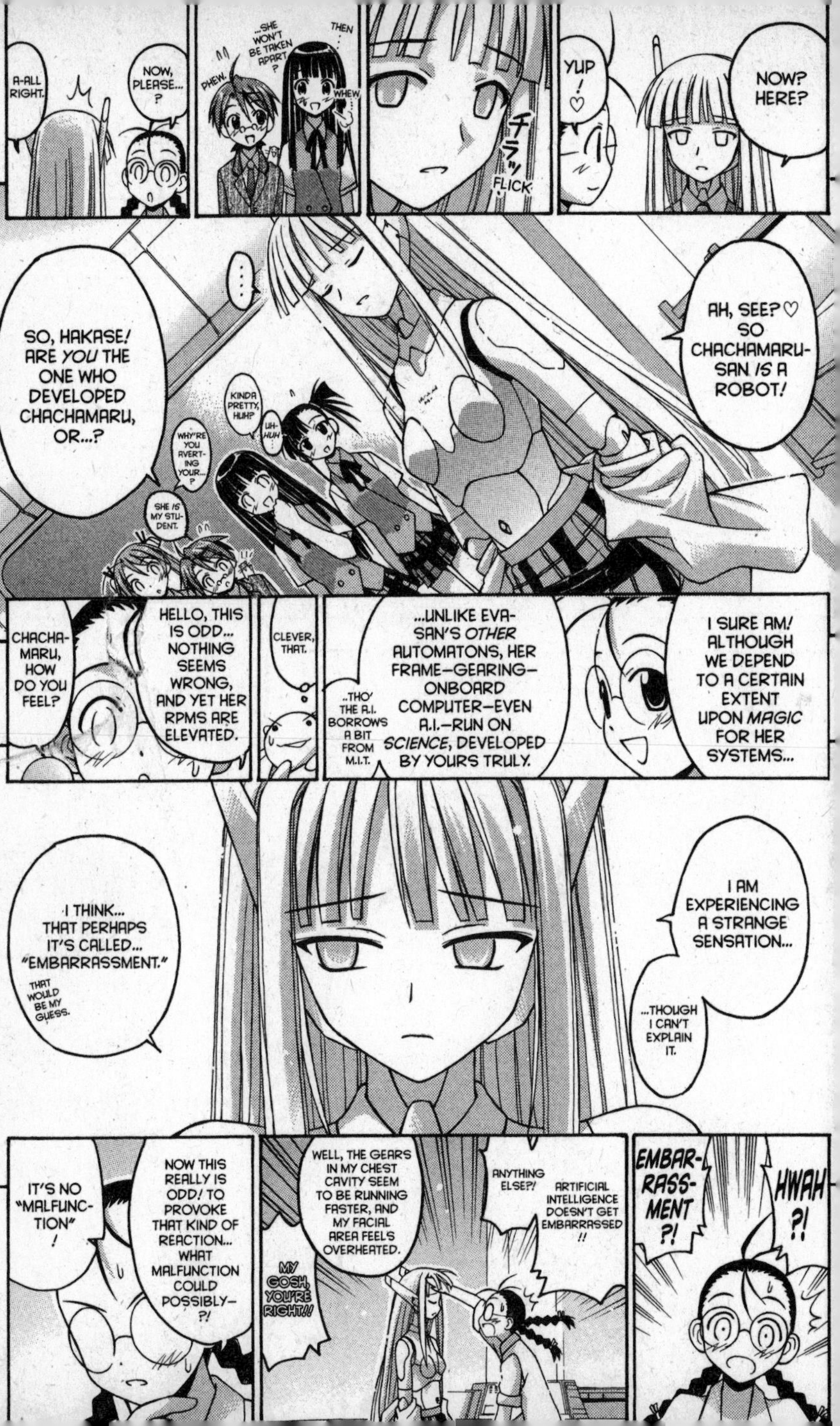

NOW? HERE?
YUP! ♡
チラッ
FLICK
THEN...
...SHE WON'T BE TAKEN APART?
PHEW.
WHEW
NOW, PLEASE...?
A-ALL RIGHT.
AH, SEE? ♡ SO CHACHAMARU-SAN *IS* A ROBOT!
...
SO, HAKASE! ARE *YOU* THE ONE WHO DEVELOPED CHACHAMARU, OR...?
KINDA PRETTY, HUH?
UH-HUH
WHY'RE YOU AVERTING YOUR...?
SHE IS MY STUDENT.
I SURE AM! ALTHOUGH WE DEPEND TO A CERTAIN EXTENT UPON *MAGIC* FOR HER SYSTEMS...
...UNLIKE EVA-SAN'S *OTHER* AUTOMATONS, HER FRAME—GEARING—ONBOARD COMPUTER—EVEN A.I.—RUN ON *SCIENCE*, DEVELOPED BY YOURS TRULY.
..THO' THE A.I. BORROWS A BIT FROM M.I.T.
CLEVER, THAT.
HELLO, THIS IS ODD... NOTHING SEEMS WRONG, AND YET HER RPMS ARE ELEVATED.
CHACHAMARU, HOW DO YOU FEEL?
I AM EXPERIENCING A STRANGE SENSATION...
...THOUGH I CAN'T EXPLAIN IT.
I THINK... THAT PERHAPS IT'S CALLED... "EMBARRASSMENT."
THAT WOULD BE MY GUESS.
EMBARRASSMENT?!
HWAH?!
WELL, THE GEARS IN MY CHEST CAVITY SEEM TO BE RUNNING FASTER, AND MY FACIAL AREA FEELS OVERHEATED.
ANYTHING ELSE?!
ARTIFICIAL INTELLIGENCE DOESN'T GET EMBARRASSED!!
MY GOSH, YOU'RE RIGHT!!
NOW THIS REALLY IS ODD! TO PROVOKE THAT KIND OF REACTION... WHAT MALFUNCTION COULD POSSIBLY—?!
IT'S NO "MALFUNCTION"!

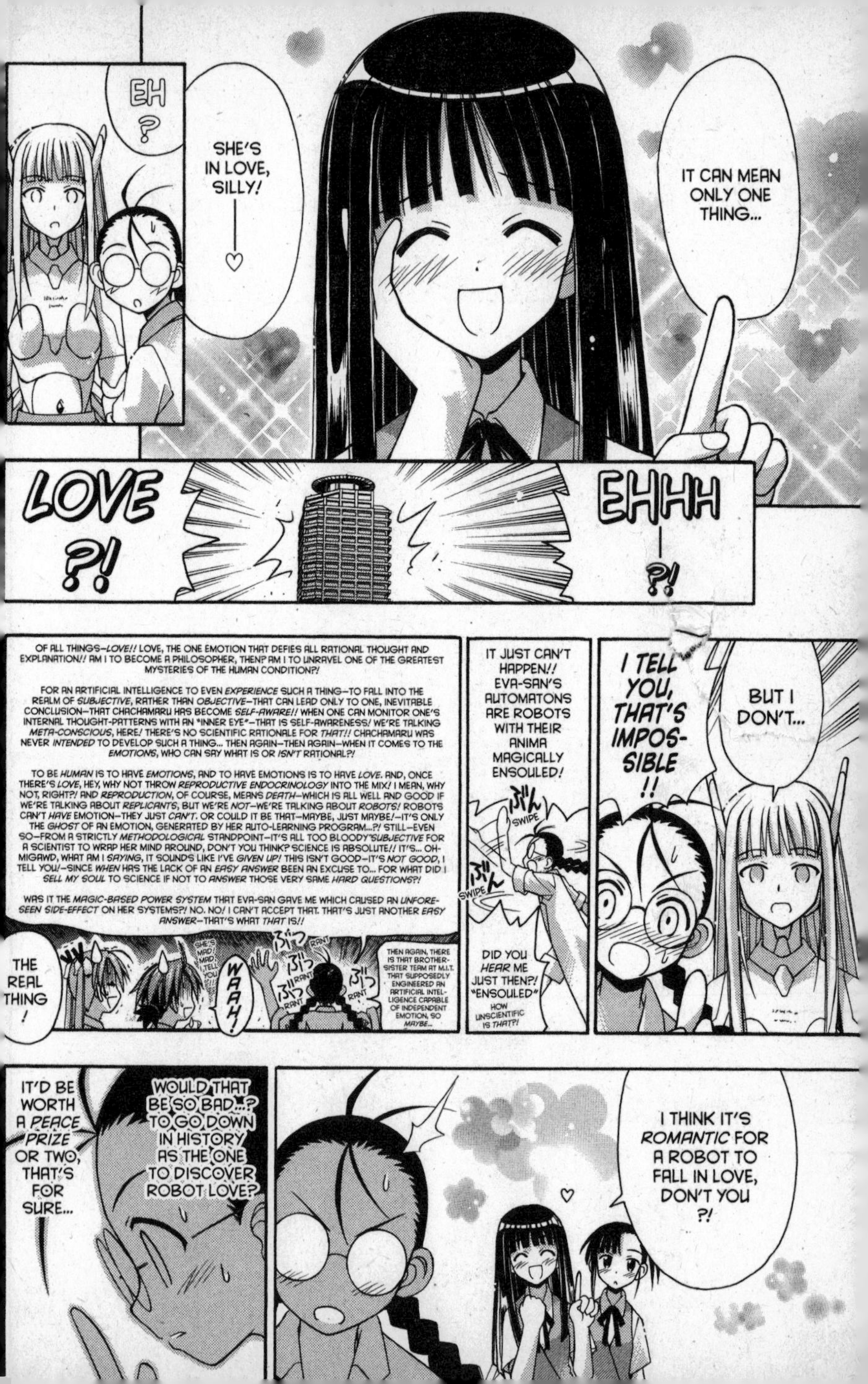
IT CAN MEAN ONLY ONE THING...
SHE'S IN LOVE, SILLY! ♡
EH?
EHHH?!
LOVE?!
BUT I DON'T...
I TELL YOU, THAT'S IMPOSSIBLE!!
IT JUST CAN'T HAPPEN!! EVA-SAN'S AUTOMATONS ARE ROBOTS WITH THEIR ANIMA MAGICALLY ENSOULED!
ぶん SWIPE
ぶん SWIPE
DID YOU *HEAR* ME JUST THEN?! "ENSOULED"
HOW UNSCIENTIFIC IS *THAT*?!
OF ALL THINGS—*LOVE!!* LOVE, THE ONE EMOTION THAT DEFIES ALL RATIONAL THOUGHT AND EXPLANATION!! AM I TO BECOME A PHILOSOPHER, THEN? AM I TO UNRAVEL ONE OF THE GREATEST MYSTERIES OF THE HUMAN CONDITION?!
FOR AN ARTIFICIAL INTELLIGENCE TO EVEN *EXPERIENCE* SUCH A THING—TO FALL INTO THE REALM OF *SUBJECTIVE*, RATHER THAN *OBJECTIVE*—THAT CAN LEAD ONLY TO ONE, INEVITABLE CONCLUSION—THAT CHACHAMARU HAS BECOME *SELF-AWARE!!* WHEN ONE CAN MONITOR ONE'S INTERNAL THOUGHT-PATTERNS WITH AN "INNER EYE"—THAT IS SELF-AWARENESS! WE'RE TALKING *META-CONSCIOUS*, HERE! THERE'S NO SCIENTIFIC RATIONALE FOR *THAT!!* CHACHAMARU WAS NEVER *INTENDED* TO DEVELOP SUCH A THING... THEN AGAIN—THEN AGAIN—WHEN IT COMES TO THE *EMOTIONS*, WHO CAN SAY WHAT IS OR *ISN'T* RATIONAL?!
TO BE *HUMAN* IS TO HAVE *EMOTIONS*, AND TO HAVE EMOTIONS IS TO HAVE *LOVE*. AND, ONCE THERE'S *LOVE*, HEY, WHY NOT THROW *REPRODUCTIVE ENDOCRINOLOGY* INTO THE MIX! I MEAN, WHY NOT, RIGHT?! AND *REPRODUCTION*, OF COURSE, MEANS *DEATH*—WHICH IS ALL WELL AND GOOD IF WE'RE TALKING ABOUT *REPLICANTS*, BUT WE'RE *NOT*—WE'RE TALKING ABOUT *ROBOTS!* ROBOTS CAN'T *HAVE* EMOTION—THEY JUST *CAN'T*. OR COULD IT BE THAT—MAYBE, JUST MAYBE!—IT'S ONLY THE *GHOST* OF AN EMOTION, GENERATED BY HER AUTO-LEARNING PROGRAM...?! STILL—EVEN SO—FROM A STRICTLY *METHODOLOGICAL* STANDPOINT—IT'S ALL TOO BLOODY *SUBJECTIVE* FOR A SCIENTIST TO WRAP HER MIND AROUND, DON'T YOU THINK? SCIENCE IS ABSOLUTE!! IT'S... OH-MIGAWD, WHAT AM I *SAYING*, IT SOUNDS LIKE I'VE *GIVEN UP!* THIS ISN'T GOOD—IT'S *NOT GOOD*, I TELL YOU!—SINCE *WHEN* HAS THE LACK OF AN *EASY ANSWER* BEEN AN EXCUSE TO... FOR WHAT DID I *SELL MY SOUL* TO SCIENCE IF NOT TO *ANSWER* THOSE VERY SAME *HARD QUESTIONS?!*
WAS IT THE *MAGIC-BASED POWER SYSTEM* THAT EVA-SAN GAVE ME WHICH CAUSED AN *UNFORESEEN SIDE-EFFECT* ON HER SYSTEMS?! NO. NO! I CAN'T ACCEPT THAT. THAT'S JUST ANOTHER *EASY ANSWER*—THAT'S WHAT *THAT* IS!!
THEN AGAIN, THERE IS THAT BROTHER-SISTER TEAM AT M.I.T. THAT SUPPOSEDLY ENGINEERED AN ARTIFICIAL INTELLIGENCE CAPABLE OF INDEPENDENT EMOTION, SO *MAYBE*...
ぶつ RANT
ぶつ RANT
ぶつ RANT
ぶつ RANT
WAAH!
SHE'S MAD! MAD, I TELL YOU!!
THE REAL THING!
I THINK IT'S *ROMANTIC* FOR A ROBOT TO FALL IN LOVE, DON'T YOU?!
WOULD THAT BE SO BAD...? TO GO DOWN IN HISTORY AS THE ONE TO DISCOVER ROBOT LOVE?
IT'D BE WORTH A *PEACE PRIZE* OR TWO, THAT'S FOR SURE...

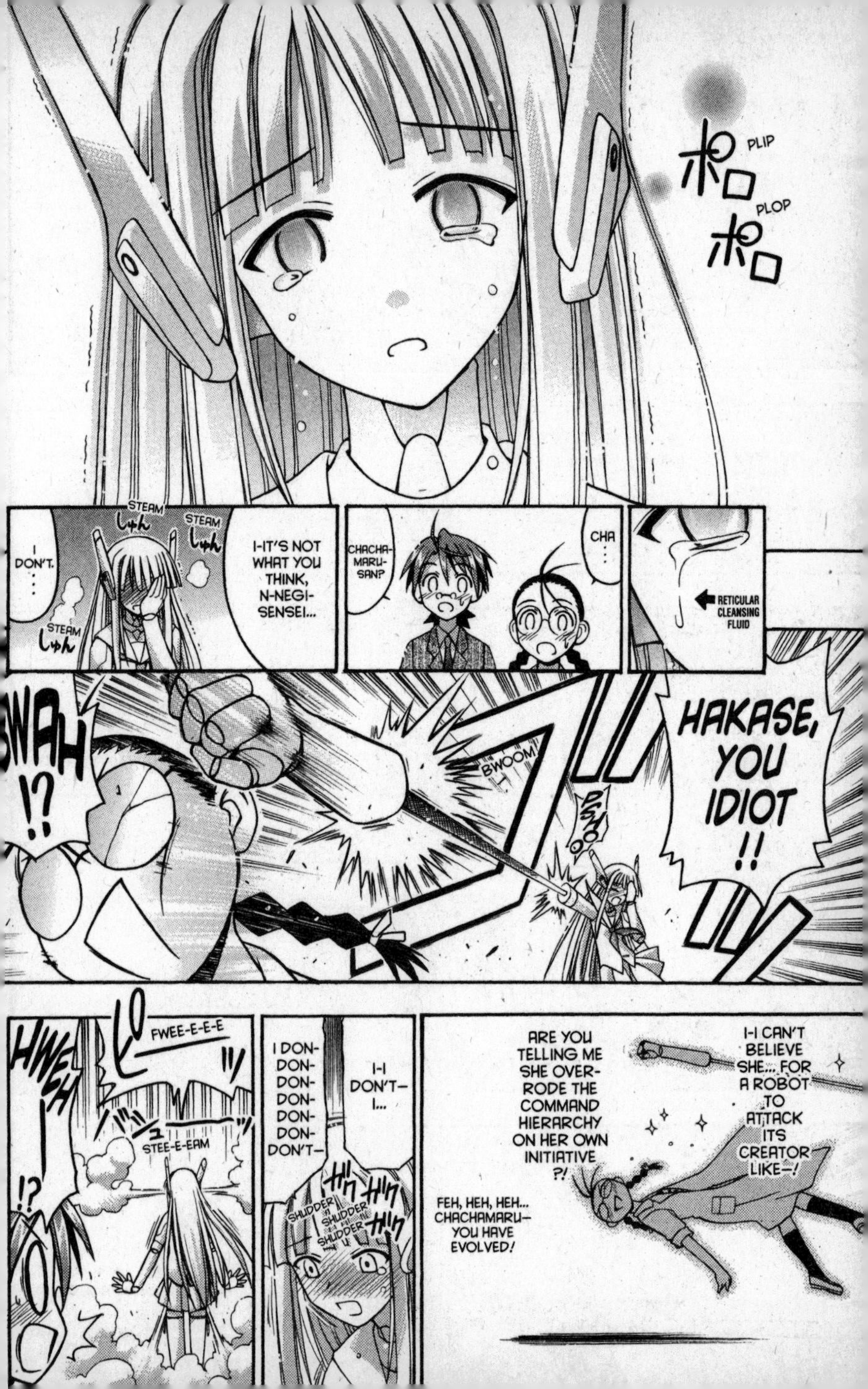

PLIP
PLOP
RETICULAR CLEANSING FLUID
CHA...
CHACHA-MARU-SAN?
I-IT'S NOT WHAT YOU THINK, N-NEGI-SENSEI...
STEAM
STEAM
STEAM
I DON'T....
HAKASE, YOU IDIOT!!
BWOOM
WAH!?
I-I CAN'T BELIEVE SHE... FOR A ROBOT TO ATTACK ITS CREATOR LIKE—!
ARE YOU TELLING ME SHE OVER-RODE THE COMMAND HIERARCHY ON HER OWN INITIATIVE?!
FEH, HEH, HEH... CHACHAMARU—YOU HAVE EVOLVED!
I-I DON'T—I...
I DON-DON-DON-DON-DON-DON-DON'T—
SHUDDER SHUDDER SHUDDER
FWEE-E-E-E
STEE-E-EAM
HWEH!?

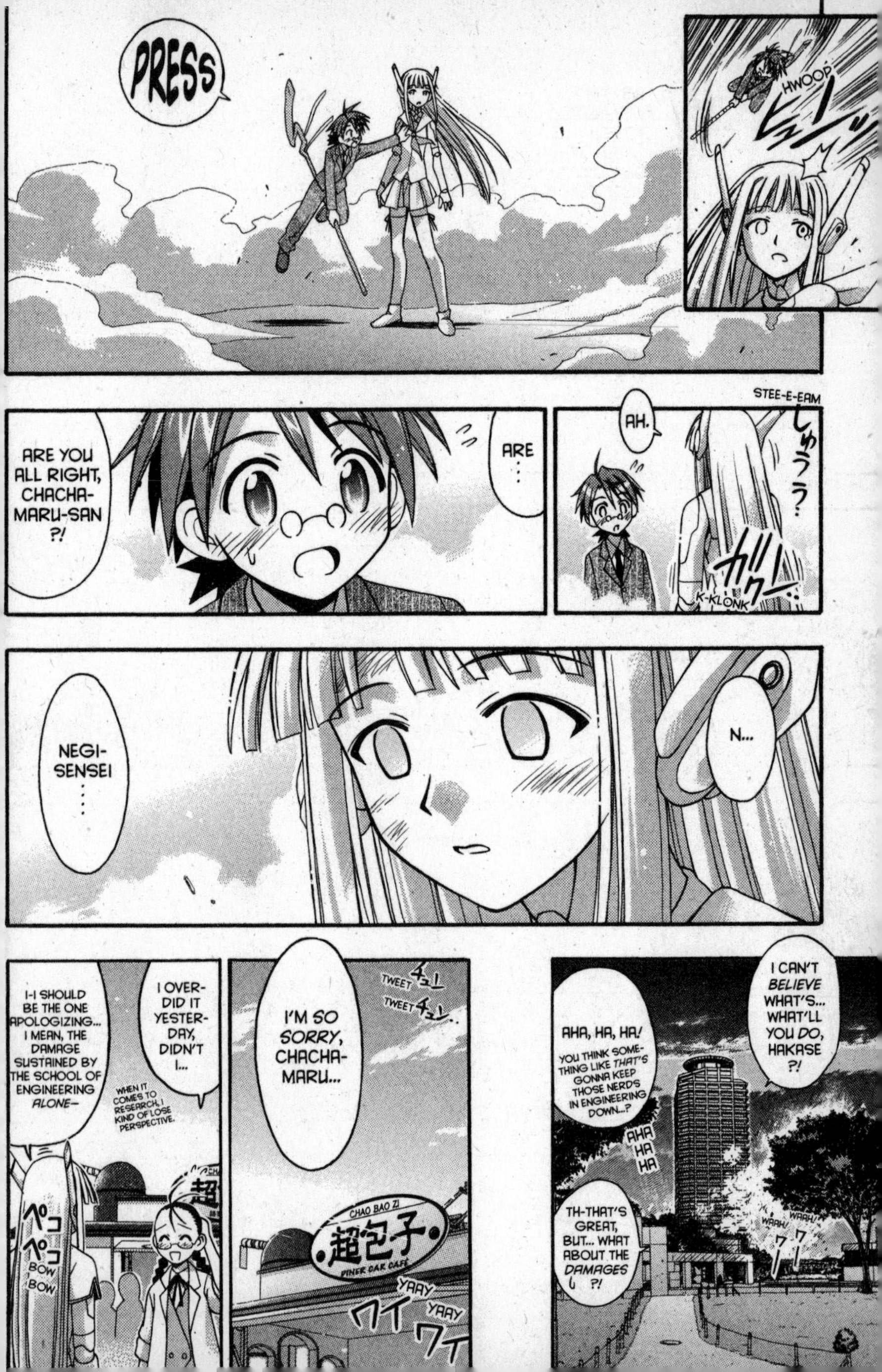
HWOOP
PRESS
STEE-E-EAM
AH.
K-KLONK
ARE...
ARE YOU ALL RIGHT, CHACHA-MARU-SAN?!
N...
NEGI-SENSEI......
I CAN'T BELIEVE WHAT'S... WHAT'LL YOU DO, HAKASE?!
AHA, HA, HA!
YOU THINK SOME-THING LIKE THAT'S GONNA KEEP THOSE NERDS IN ENGINEERING DOWN...?
AHA HA HA
WAAH! WAAH!
TH-THAT'S GREAT, BUT... WHAT ABOUT THE DAMAGES?!
TWEET TWEET
I'M SO SORRY, CHACHA-MARU...
CHAO BAO ZI
超包子
YAAY YAAY
I OVER-DID IT YESTER-DAY, DIDN'T I...
WHEN IT COMES TO RESEARCH, I KIND OF LOSE PERSPECTIVE.
I-I SHOULD BE THE ONE APOLOGIZING... I MEAN, THE DAMAGE SUSTAINED BY THE SCHOOL OF ENGINEERING ALONE—
ペコペコ
BOW BOW

TH-THANK YOU, HAKASE.

AS FAR AS *NEGI-SENSEI* GOES, WE'LL KEEP IT OUR LITTLE SECRET. ♡

DON'T YOU WORRY ABOUT THAT OTHER THING, THOUGH, CHACHAMARU...

IT'LL MEAN REMOVING SOME ARMOR, BUT...

I SHOULD FIX IT SO YOU CAN DO "H," AS WELL?

WHILE WE'RE AT IT, I'LL WORK ON MAKING YOUR OUTER SKIN-COVER-ING MORE REALISTIC, OKAY?

NOT THAT IT CAN MAKE UP FOR YESTERDAY OR ANYTHING, BUT... I THINK YOUR HEAT-SINK SYSTEM COULD USE SOME UPDATING.

IT SHOULD ONLY TAKE A MINUTE.

THERE IS ONE OTHER THING...

OH-H-H, YEAH!

WOULD YOU MIND LOWER-ING YOUR VOICE?

TH-THAT'S ALL RIGHT.

I-I'D APPRECI-ATE THAT, THANKS.

HEH, HEH ...

包子。

IF ONLY WE COULD'VE FOUND OUT WHO SHE WAS IN LOVE WITH, THO', HUH??

I'M SURE CHACHAMARU-SAN WILL ENJOY BEING EVEN MORE "CUTE."

SHE IS CHACHAMARU-SAN'S PARENT, AFTER ALL.

YOU SEE? HAKASE'S NOT SO BAD...

HO, HO.

ONCE A MAD SCIENTIST, *ALWAYS* A MAD SCIENTIST.

N-NOT TO COMPLAIN, BUT...

UH-H...

YOU CAN EVEN PUT YOUR HAIR UP!

WITH THIS NEW *HEAT-SINK PLATE*, IT ALL OUGHTTA BE JUST FINE!

THIS IS, LIKE, TOTALLY UNCONFIRMED, BUT I HEARD THAT THIS GIRL WHO TOLD THIS GUY? WHO WAS IN ONE OF THOSE *BOY-BANDS* ON TV? THAT *HE* SAID OKAY, TOO!

RE-E-EALLY?!

AH, NAND THEY'RE OFF.

THEY DID?! IN 2ND YEAR JUNIOR-HIGH...? ISN'T THAT, LIKE, ILLEGALLY?!

AND I HEARD THAT, THREE GIRLS? IN THE SAME GRADE AS US? THEY TOLD THEIR STUDENT-TEACHERS THAT THEY LIKED THEM? AND *THEY* SAID THEY'D GO OUT, TOO!!

I'M THINKING I'D LIKE TO TRY IT... Y'KNOW? JUST T' BE SURE?

I WISH I'D GONE BENEATH IT AND SAID HOW I FELT...

TEE HEE

I KNOW! ME, EITHER!! ♡

I CAN HARDLY BELIEVE IT...

I'M NOT SURE I DO...

WOW-W-W!

"EVEN AFTER SOME TIME, SUBSEQUENT FOLLOW-UPS REVEALED THAT..."

UH-HUH, UH-HUH.

LISTEN TO THIS: "CALL IT THE MAGIC OF THE WORLD TREE! NO OBSTACLE TOO TOUGH TO OVERCOME! OLDER/YOUNGER, CUTE/NOT CUTE, FAMOUS/A NOBODY—THEY ALL SAID IT WAS IMPOSSIBLE, BUT RESULTS DON'T LIE!!

YOU DON'T SAY

SHOW US, SHOW US!

HEY GUYS, WHAT'RE YOU...?

WHO, ME? N-NOTHING.

YOU SAY SOMETHING, CHACHAMARU?

"NO OBSTACLE TOO TOUGH TO..."?

MORE OR LESS.

HEH HEH HEH

I MEAN, WE *ARE* AN ALL-GIRL JUNIOR HIGH.

NO, YOU'RE RIGHT, I GUESS THERE'S NO ONE I...

YAAY

BUT, YUNA, WHO WOULD YOU SAY YOU...?

HO HO!

WOW-W-W

UM—UH—N-NO...N-NO ONE IN PARTICU...

B-BMP.

YOU'RE SO CUTE AS A CAT-GIRL, SET-CHAN.

DO YOU HAVE ANYONE YOU LIKE, SET-CHAN...?

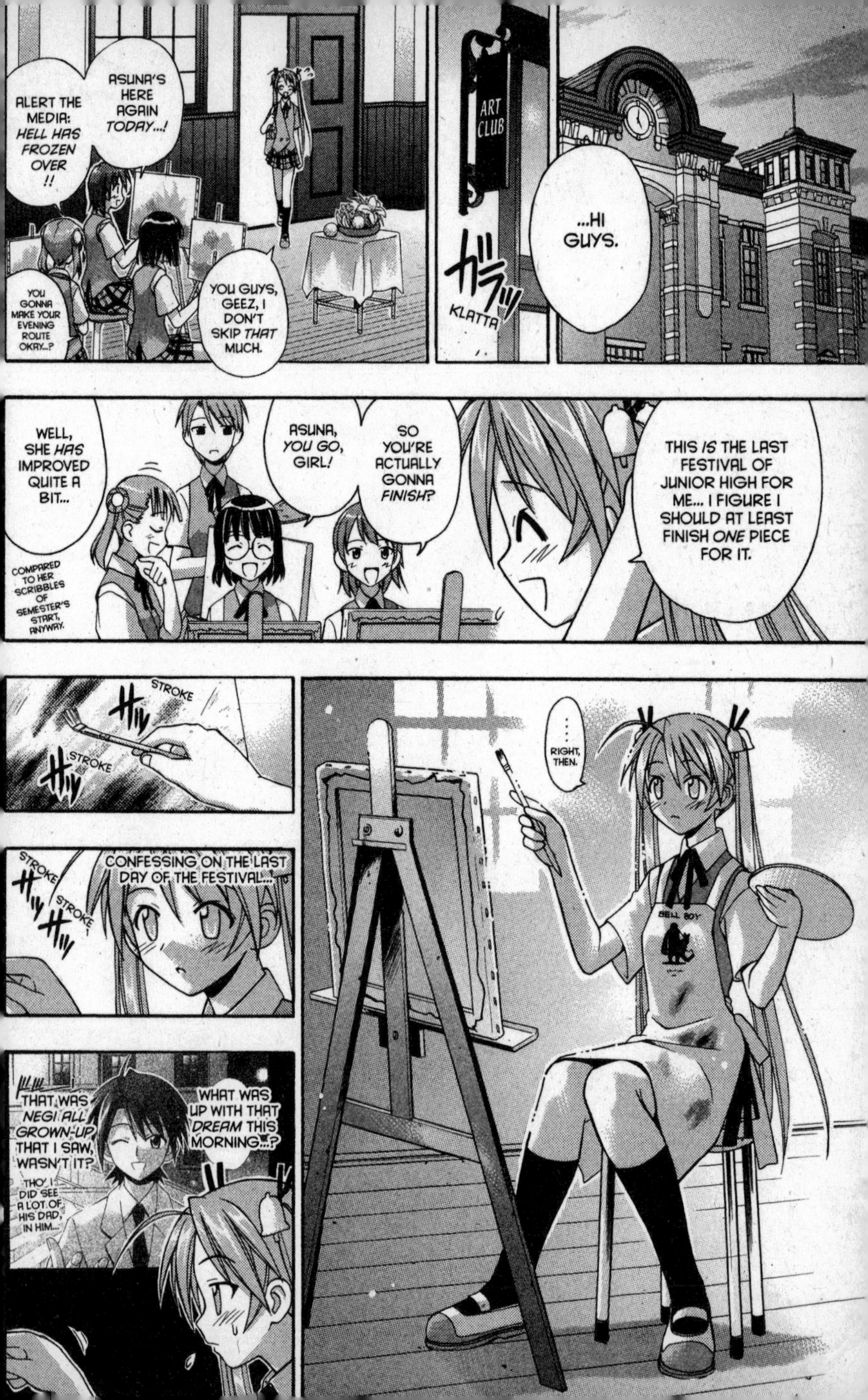

...HI GUYS.
ART CLUB
KLATTA
ASUNA'S HERE AGAIN TODAY...!
ALERT THE MEDIA: HELL HAS FROZEN OVER !!
YOU GUYS, GEEZ, I DON'T SKIP THAT MUCH.
YOU GONNA MAKE YOUR EVENING ROUTE OKAY...?
THIS IS THE LAST FESTIVAL OF JUNIOR HIGH FOR ME... I FIGURE I SHOULD AT LEAST FINISH ONE PIECE FOR IT.
SO YOU'RE ACTUALLY GONNA FINISH?
ASUNA, YOU GO, GIRL!
WELL, SHE HAS IMPROVED QUITE A BIT...
COMPARED TO HER SCRIBBLES OF SEMESTER'S START, ANYWAY.
... RIGHT, THEN.
BELL BOY
STROKE
STROKE
STROKE
STROKE
CONFESSING ON THE LAST DAY OF THE FESTIVAL...
WHAT WAS UP WITH THAT DREAM THIS MORNING...?
THAT WAS NEGI ALL GROWN-UP THAT I SAW, WASN'T IT?
THO' I DID SEE A LOT OF HIS DAD, IN HIM...

PA-PA-PA-PAH!

AGE-MISREPRESENTATION PASTILLES... RED AND BLUE CANDY DROPS

I'VE ALREADY ORDERED A *SUPER-SECRET ITEM* OVER THE MAHONET.

HOO, HOO, HOO! I *THOUGHT* SOMETHING LIKE THIS MIGHT HAPPEN...

SHUFFLE SHUFFLE

IT'S NOT LIKE YOU TRANSFORM FOR REAL, THOUGH—IT'S MORE AN ILLUSION THING.

LIKE THE MAGIC EVANGELINE USED TO USE.

JUST LIKE IT SOUNDS, IT'S A MAGICAL CANDY THAT MAKES PEOPLE THINK YOU'RE OLDER THAN YOU REALLY ARE!

HUH?

WOW-W-W

TALK ABOUT YOUR SUSPICIOUS FOODSTUFFS...

NO GUARANTEE SHE'LL LOOK LIKE THAT, OF COURSE.

SHE SOMETHIN', OR WHAT??

CHECK THIS, ASUNA! I'M A WHOLE LOTTA WOMAN!!

SHE'S *SOMETHING,* ALL RIGHT...

HIYAH

KONOKA, AGE 18 →

HYAH!?

HE SURE WOULD

IT'S PERFECT!!

IF ANIKI TAKES ONE AND LOOKS ADULT, THEN WILL HE BE A BETTER PARTNER FOR TRAINING...?

POP A RED ONE, AND SEE FOR YOURSELF.

BUT DO THEY *REALLY* MAKE YOU LOOK GROWN-UP...?

HERE YOU GO, SET-CHAN...

NOW *THIS* IS FUN! *THIS* IS THE KIND OF MAGIC I LIKE!!

EH?

SAY "AH"

BWAH-BAHH!

BOMM

BAND, HUH? THAT'S GREAT. I'LL BE SURE TO COME BY.

HUH? UM? YEAH. EXCUSE ME...

Y-YOU OKAY, AKO-SAN?

FWUMP

WHOA.

WAH.

UWAH...?

LOVE-STRUCK DAZE

ほけ──！

THE PLACE PROMISED IN OUR EARLY DAYS

HE SEEMS FAMILIAR...

DON'T LIE—HE CALLED YOU BY NAME!

I'VE NO IDEA!

THAT GUY, THAT REALLY CUTE GUY—WHO WAS HE?!

I COULD SWEAR I'VE SEEN HIM SOME-WHERE...

IT'S COMING OFF HIM IN WAVES.

THAT GUY OVER THERE—HE'S STRONG.

H-HE IS CUTE.

WONDER WHAT SCHOOL HE GOES TO?

H-HE'S CUTE!

GWAH!

Lick

Bautti!

POKE

GEH! GET A LOAD OF HIM!

STARBOOKS COFFEE

PUH-LEEZE.

YADA ガヤガヤ YADA

YAARY ワイワイ‥ YAARY

MAHORA FESTIVAL
MAHORA FESTIVAL
STAGE 1

BANG·SAW·DRILL トンテンカン

YAARY ワイ YAARY ワイ

EVERYONE SEEMS SO FULL OF ENERGY, IT BEING THE LAST WEEKEND BEFORE THE FESTIVAL AND ALL.

I GUESS.

HE CAN'T BE IN JUNIOR HIGH, CAN HE?!

YOU GUYS, OHMIGOSH, I THINK I'M IN LOVE!

PSST PSST ヒソヒソ

‥‥

KYAA KYAA キャーキャー

EEEK! キャー

DON'T GET THE WRONG IDEA, OKAY?!

MY HEART IS POUNDING!

I'VE NEVER BEEN ON A DATE BEFORE, ASUNA-SAN...

UWAH?

WHY DOES YOUR SAYING THAT LINE WITH THAT HEIGHT AND THAT FACE MAKE ME WANNA *PUNCH* IT?!

D-D'YOU REALLY THINK I'M *COOL*?!

DON'T GO THINKING YOU'RE ALL THAT JUST 'CAUSE YOU'RE ALL COOL AND CUTE WITH MAGIC!

THIS IS JUST FOR PRACTICE, OKAY? PRACTICE! GOT IT?!

WOO-HOO ♥

JUST STAY BACK, ALL RIGHT?! YOU'RE EMBARRASSING ME.

B-BUT, ASUNA-SAN...!!

WHAT? BUT... I *NEVER*—!

LOOK, KIDS LIKE YOU ANNOY ME TO *BEGIN* WITH, *ESPECIALLY* THOSE WHO ONLY CARE ABOUT *LOOKS* AND THINK THEY'RE *BETTER* THAN EVERYONE ELSE!!

ZWOOP

THE IDEA IS FOR YOU NOT TO BE EMBARRASSED—I MEAN, WHAT IF TAKAMICHI WERE TO PUT HIS FACE UP ALL CLOSE LIKE *THIS*...??

IF YOU'RE GONNA GET ALL MAD ABOUT IT, HOW'M I S'PPOSED TO *HELP*?!

BUT I ONLY EVEN *LOOK* LIKE THIS 'CAUSE OF YOUR *PRACTICE* DATE!

GURK!

M-MAYBE YOU'RE RIGHT...

STILL, IT'S NOT LIKE I *ASKED* YOU TO—

HRHM ...

HEE HEE

LOOK, THEY'RE FIGHTING

WELL THEN, LET'S GET THIS DATE STARTED!

JUST REMEMBER THAT IT'S ONLY PRACTICE

SHADDUP!!

SO, DO YOU NOT LIKE HOW I LOOK, OR...?

GUESS I CAN'T SAY I WASN'T WARNED! CHAMO-KUN DID SAY, "ANESAN'S NOT GONNA LIKE YOUR LOOKING LIKE THIS, ANIKI...."

AND CHAMO'LL ANSWER FOR IT, TOO!

SCHTEAM... しゅうう

JUST STAY BACK, I SAID!!

ICE CREAM

Ice Cream

THANK YOU, COME AGAIN!

WE'LL BE OPEN ALL FESTIVAL...

YAKITORI

I'M FINE, THANK YOU. BESIDES, YOU SCRAWNY TYPES DON'T DO IT FOR ME, SO...

YOU STILL NERVOUS...?

THAT FACE WAS SO-O-O NOT MEANT FOR EATING ICE CREAM.♥

LAP LAP ♥

INSIDE, HE'S STILL THE SAME TEN-YEAR-OLD BRAT HE ALWAYS WAS.

OKAY, SURE, HE IS WAY COOLER THAN I'D'VE THOUGHT, BUT COMPARED TO A MAN LIKE TAKAHATA-SENSEI...?

WHAT POINT IS THERE TO EVEN PRACTICING WITH HIM...?

LEAVE IT TO ASUNA AND HER THING FOR OLDER GUYS, HUH?

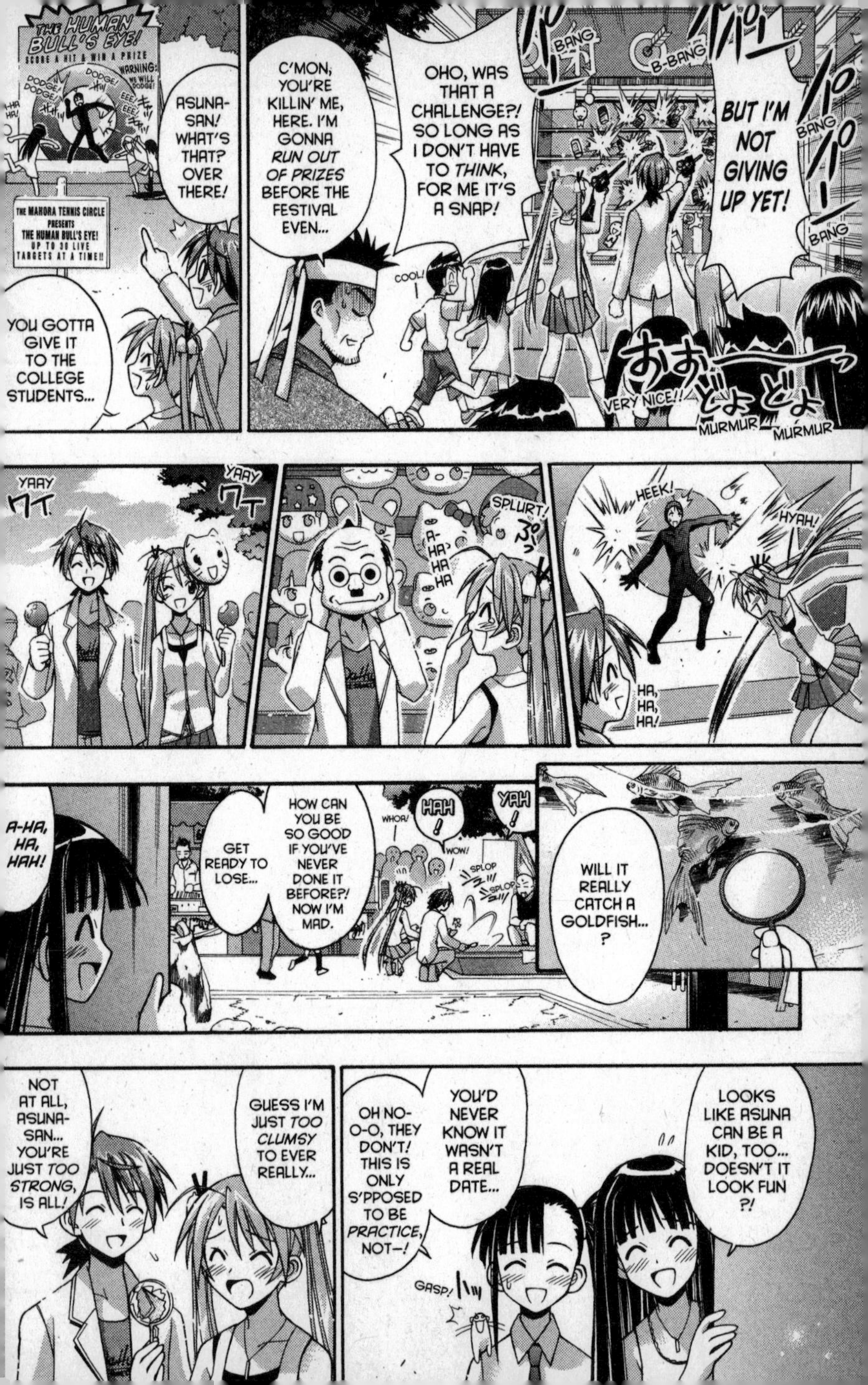
BANG
B-BANG
BUT I'M NOT GIVING UP YET!
BANG
BANG
VERY NICE!!
おぉーっ
どよ どよ
MURMUR
MURMUR
OHO, WAS THAT A CHALLENGE?! SO LONG AS I DON'T HAVE TO *THINK*, FOR ME IT'S A SNAP!
C'MON, YOU'RE KILLIN' ME, HERE. I'M GONNA *RUN OUT OF PRIZES* BEFORE THE FESTIVAL EVEN...
COOL!
THE HUMAN BULL'S EYE!
SCORE A HIT & WIN A PRIZE
WARNING! WE WILL DODGE!
DODGE! DODGE!
DODGE!
EEE! EEE!
A-HA HA!
THE MAHORA TENNIS CIRCLE PRESENTS THE HUMAN BULL'S EYE! UP TO 30 LIVE TARGETS AT A TIME!!
ASUNA-SAN! WHAT'S THAT? OVER THERE!
YOU GOTTA GIVE IT TO THE COLLEGE STUDENTS...
HEEK!
HYAH!
HA, HA, HA!
SPLURT!
A-HA HA HA
YAAY
YAAY
WILL IT REALLY CATCH A GOLDFISH...?
YAH!
HAH!
WOW!
WHOA!
SPLOP
SPLOP
HOW CAN YOU BE SO GOOD IF YOU'VE NEVER DONE IT BEFORE?! NOW I'M MAD.
GET READY TO LOSE...
A-HA, HA, HAH!
LOOKS LIKE ASUNA CAN BE A KID, TOO... DOESN'T IT LOOK FUN?!
YOU'D NEVER KNOW IT WASN'T A REAL DATE...
OH NO-O-O, THEY DON'T! THIS IS ONLY S'PPOSED TO BE *PRACTICE*, NOT—!
GASP!
GUESS I'M JUST *TOO CLUMSY* TO EVER REALLY...
NOT AT ALL, ASUNA-SAN... YOU'RE JUST *TOO STRONG*, IS ALL!

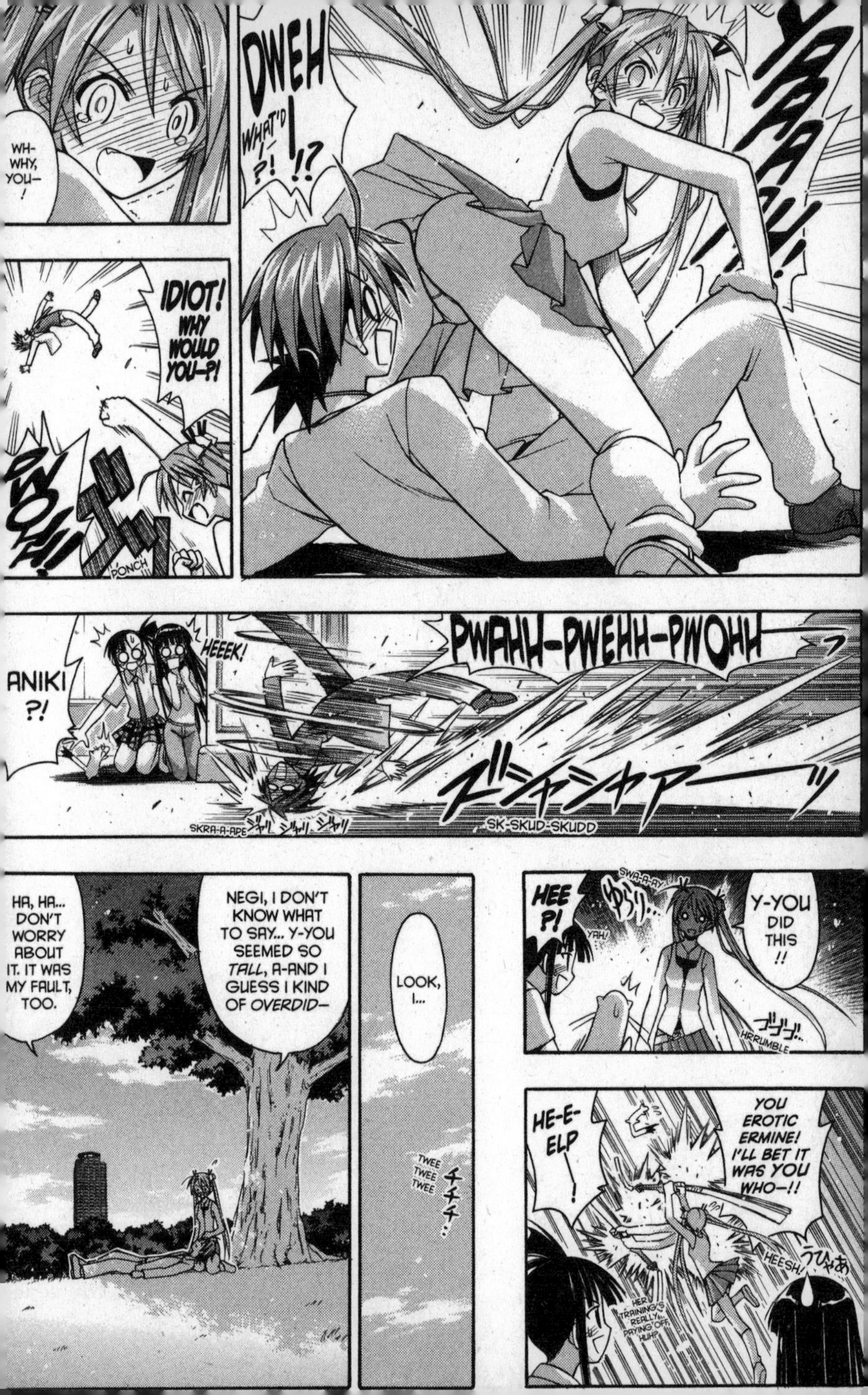
YAAAAAH!!
DWEH
WHAT'D I-?!
!!?
WH-WHY, YOU-!
IDIOT! WHY WOULD YOU-?!
DWOOH!!
PONCH
PWAHH-PWEHH-PWOHH
ズシャシャアーッ
SK-SKUD-SKUDD
HEEEK!
ANIKI?!
ジャリ ジャリ ジャリ
SKRA-A-APE
Y-YOU DID THIS!!
ゆらり…
SWA-A-AY
HEE?!
YAH!
ゴゴゴ…
HRRUMBLE
YOU EROTIC ERMINE! I'LL BET IT WAS YOU WHO-!!
HE-E-ELP!
うひゃあ
HEESH!
HER TRAINING'S REALLY PAYING OFF, HUH.
LOOK, I...
チチチ…
TWEE TWEE TWEE
NEGI, I DON'T KNOW WHAT TO SAY... Y-YOU SEEMED SO *TALL*, A-AND I GUESS I KIND OF *OVERDID*-
HA, HA... DON'T WORRY ABOUT IT. IT WAS MY FAULT, TOO.

YEAH? WHAT IS IT.

SO, UM, ASUNA-SAN...?

PROB'LY ...

NOSE STILL BLEEDING?

I 'ID NOT !!

IT'S NOT 'CAUSE YOU SAW MY *UNDERWEAR*, IS IT?!

... N-NOT VERY SUBTLE, ARE YOU.

WHAT IS IT ABOUT TAKAMICHI THAT YOU...?

WHAT A KID.

TWEE TWEE TWEE ♪♪♪

TUMP TUMP

IT WAS BACK WHEN I FIRST CAME HERE...

THAT MUST'VE BEEN HARD.

I REALLY *HAD* NO ONE ELSE.

I WAS KIND OF A KID MYSELF... AND TAKAHATA-SENSEI LOOKED AFTER ME.

THE FIRST—AND LAST—PRESENT HE EVER GAVE ME.

I SEE ...

THEY'RE FROM TAKAHATA-SENSEI...

SWOFF ＃ッ

SEE THESE BELLS...?

CH-RING ちん... ちん...

WAIT!! ASUNA-SAN!

DASH

ISN'T THAT TAKAMICHI AND SHIZUNA-SENSEI SITTING OVER...?

HEY...

ASUNA-SA-A-N! WHAT'S WRONG?!

HEY!

DMP

WASN'T THAT...?!

AKO, YOU WERE GREAT!

I-I WAS?

T-TMP

ANIKI! WHAT HAPPENED?! DONE PRACTICING ALREADY?

H-HEY, GUYS...

HAS ANYONE SEEN ASUNA-SAN?!

SO THEY'RE FRIENDS, THEN...

IT'S ASUNA AND THAT CUTE GUY FROM EARLIER!

HUH?

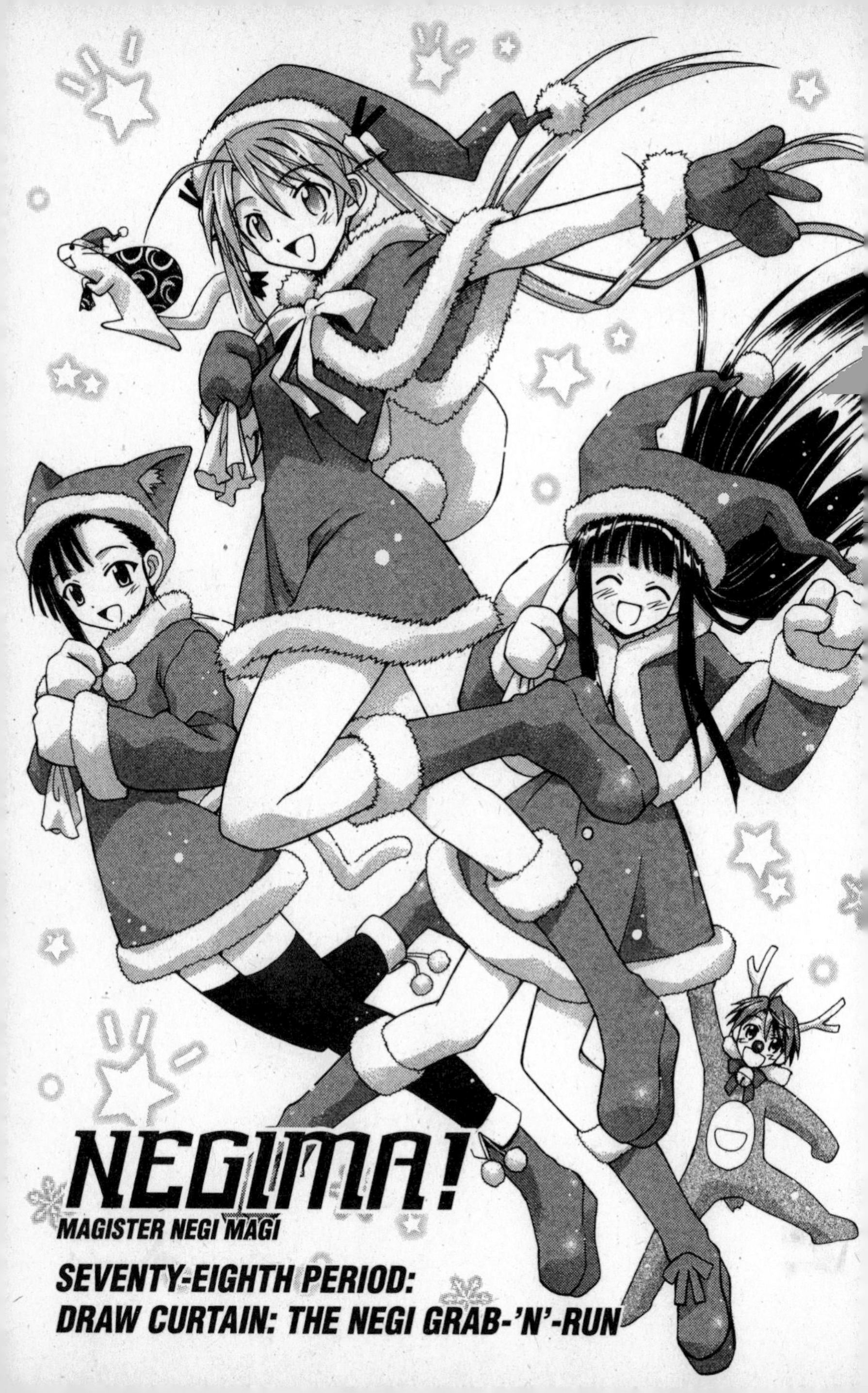

NEGIMA!

MAGISTER NEGI MAGI

SEVENTY-EIGHTH PERIOD: DRAW CURTAIN: THE NEGI GRAB-'N'-RUN

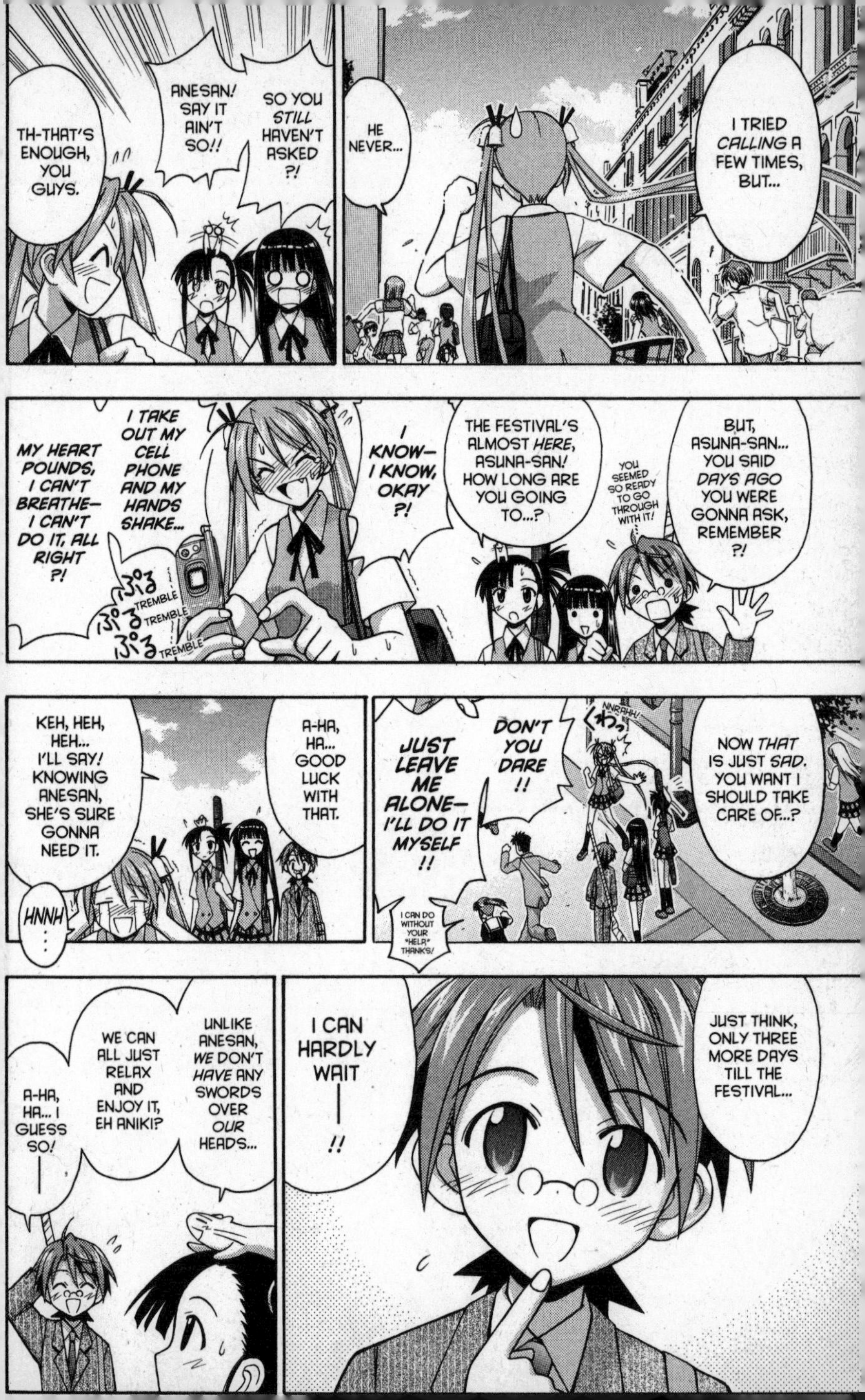

TH-THAT'S ENOUGH, YOU GUYS.

ANESAN! SAY IT AIN'T SO!!

SO YOU *STILL* HAVEN'T ASKED?!

HE NEVER...

I TRIED CALLING A FEW TIMES, BUT...

MY HEART POUNDS, I CAN'T BREATHE— I CAN'T DO IT, ALL RIGHT?!

I TAKE OUT MY CELL PHONE AND MY HANDS SHAKE...

TREMBLE TREMBLE TREMBLE

I KNOW— I KNOW, OKAY?!

THE FESTIVAL'S ALMOST *HERE*, ASUNA-SAN! HOW LONG ARE YOU GOING TO...?

YOU SEEMED SO READY TO GO THROUGH WITH IT!

BUT, ASUNA-SAN... YOU SAID *DAYS* AGO YOU WERE GONNA ASK, REMEMBER?!

KEH, HEH, HEH... I'LL SAY! KNOWING ANESAN, SHE'S SURE GONNA NEED IT.

A-HA, HA... GOOD LUCK WITH THAT.

HNNH!

JUST LEAVE ME ALONE— I'LL DO IT MYSELF!!

DON'T YOU DARE!!

I CAN DO WITHOUT YOUR "HELP" THANKS!

NOW *THAT* IS JUST *SAD.* YOU WANT I SHOULD TAKE CARE OF...?

A-HA, HA... I GUESS SO!

WE CAN ALL JUST RELAX AND ENJOY IT, EH ANIKI?

UNLIKE ANESAN, *WE DON'T HAVE ANY SWORDS* OVER *OUR* HEADS...

I CAN HARDLY WAIT —!!

JUST THINK, ONLY THREE MORE DAYS TILL THE FESTIVAL...

DWAH P!

YOU WANNA BOOK TIME WITH NEGI-KUN, YOU GOTTA GO THROUGH HIS ACTING MANAGER— NAMELY, ME!

ACTUAL MANAGER

ALL RIGHT, GIRLS— STAND BACK, STAND BACK!

BWAH

EEEE

YAAY

ワイワイ

YAAY

BUT NEGI-SENSEI, IT'S UNHEARD OF!!

HEH-LOH! CAN WE GET BACK TO WORK, HERE

P?

NEVER YOU MIND THAT. YOU WANNA BOOK TIME, GET IN LINE!

ASAKURA-SAN! WHO MADE YOU HIS MANAGER P?!

P-TWEEET

EHEH, HEH... YOU MAY NOT BE ABLE TO GET TO THEM ALL, ANIKI, SO...

I'M SURE YOU'LL WANNA BREAK IT DOWN EVEN FURTHER.

HEY, YOU'VE GOT THREE DAYS, RIGHT? PLENTY OF TIME!

I TRIED TO LEAVE YOU SOME ROOM IN YOUR SCHEDULE, BUT IT'S PACKED PRETTY TIGHT..

麻帆良祭スケジュール
MAHORA SCHOOL FESTIVAL
schedule table

DAY 1
6/20 (FRIDAY)
10 : 30~

HOVER HOVER

R.G. EXHIBITION

EQUESTRIAN CLUB

DAY 2
6/21 (SATURDAY)

STAGE PLAY

MARTIAL-ARTS DEMO

DIVINATION CLUB

ACADEMY WALKING TOUR

DAY 3
6/22 (SUNDAY)
(LAST DAY)

GOURMET FESTIVAL

FINE-ARTS CLUB

NIGHTMARE CIRCUS

OVER HOVER

LIVE CONCERT

TH-THANKS. A FLYER FOR THE MASTER'S "GO" TOURNAMENT.

SORRY TO INTERRUPT, NEGI-SENSEI...

CHACHAMARU-SAN!

I'VE ALWAYS WANTED TO WATCH YOU PERFORM IT...

HEY!♡ THANKS SO MUCH!

AND HERE'S AN INVITATION TO THE "NODATE"** BEING HELD BY OUR CLUB.

Y-YOU HAVE?!

* NODATE = FORMAL OPEN-AIR TEA CEREMONY

I-IF... IF WE...

I-IT NEEDN'T BE AT ANY PARTICULAR TIME, BUT, IF YOU...

F-FURTHER, IF YOU COULD... TH-THAT IS TO SAY, IF WE...

FIDGET

CHACHA-MARU-SAN ??

THOUGH I WILL STILL PERFORM THE CEREMONY FOR YOU.

SKIR-R-R-R

KREE-E-E

PRETEND I SAID NOTHING!

VROOM...!!

?

CHACHA-MARU-SAN DOESN'T... DOES SHE ??

AN ACTUAL, AUTHENTIC "NODATE"... ! I CAN'T WAIT !

Y' GOT ME.

WHAT'S UP WITH HER?

SWAY

UM...

I...

ASUNA, THAT CUTE GUY FROM THE OTHER DAY--IS HE A FRIEND OR WHAT?

WELL, UM, THERE'S SOMETHING WE'D LIKE TO...

HEY, GUYS. WHAT'S UP?

HIS HAIR WAS JUST LIKE NEGI-KUN'S...

H-HE WAS VISITING JAPAN, AND I... I, UM...

NO WAY!! I-I MEAN, HE'S MORE LIKE... UM...A COUSIN! THAT'S IT! NEGI'S COUSIN!!

HE'S NOT YOUR BOYFRIEND?!

HE'S, UM, KIND OF A

SO THEN THEY DID SEE ME!

WH-WHAT OTHER DAY?!

THAT OTHER DAY ??

NEGI-KUN HAS A COUSIN?

AKO-SAN, KUGIMIYA-SAN! SO HOW'S IT GOING?

A-HA, HA... THIS STUFF IS AMAZING.

YOU TWO NEVER LET UP, DO YOU.

DA-DAH!

BWOPH! UH-OH... YOU'RE RIGHT!

NOW THERE'RE TWO CUTE GUYS!

D-DO WE KNOW YOU... ??

LOOK, JUST FOLLOW MY LEAD, OKAY?!

NEGI, YOU MORON!

WHAT IF THEY FIND OUT?!

PONCH

SPLURT

...YOU HAVE TO SPEND THE ENTIRE LAST DAY OF THE FESTIVAL WITH ME—IN YOUR CURRENT FORM.

UP TO AND INCLUDING DINNER—AND ANYTHING AFTER.

KYAH HAH HAH

IF YOU'RE UNABLE TO BEST ME IN THIS, MY WEAKENED STATE...

DUM-DUMM!

SINCE I SAID SO! MASTER'S ORDERS.

SINCE WHEN?!

UM, UH... EXCUSE ME?

YOU'RE RIGHT— THIS IS BAD.

WELL, NODOKA-JŌCHAN IS COUNTING ON YOU TO...

IF I LOSE TO THE MASTER, THE WHOLE LAST DAY WILL BE...

N-N-NOW WHAT?! THIS COULD RUIN EVERY-THING!

AWAH-WAH-WAH!

BE LOOKING FORWARD TO IT. SEE YA!

DIDN'T YOU MOVE ON TO THE NEXT WORLD?!

I-I'VE BEEN HOPING I MIGHT SEE THE FESTIVAL WITH NEGI-SEN... I-I MEAN, WITH EVERYONE, IF THAT'S...

HEEEK!

NICE DAY, ISN'T IT?

HORROR
HORROR
HORROR

SKITTER

UNNH...

NECO NYAN NYAN

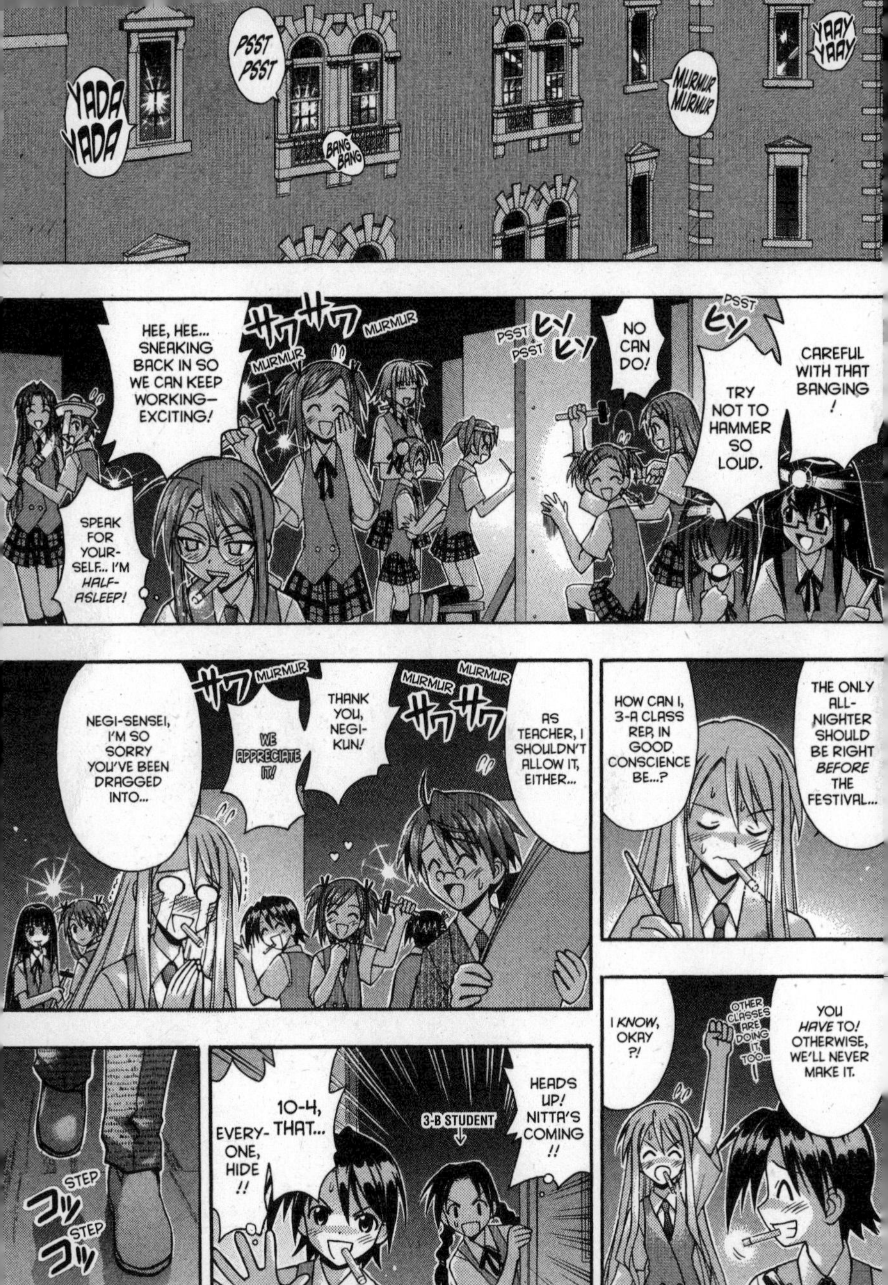
YAAY YAAY
MURMUR MURMUR
PSST PSST
BANG BANG
YADA YADA
CAREFUL WITH THAT BANGING!
PSST ヒソ
TRY NOT TO HAMMER SO LOUD.
NO CAN DO!
PSST PSST ヒソヒソ
MURMUR サワサワ
MURMUR
HEE, HEE... SNEAKING BACK IN SO WE CAN KEEP WORKING—EXCITING!
SPEAK FOR YOUR-SELF... I'M HALF-ASLEEP!
THE ONLY ALL-NIGHTER SHOULD BE RIGHT BEFORE THE FESTIVAL...
HOW CAN I, 3-A CLASS REP, IN GOOD CONSCIENCE BE...?
AS TEACHER, I SHOULDN'T ALLOW IT, EITHER...
MURMUR MURMUR サワサワ
THANK YOU, NEGI-KUN!
WE APPRECIATE IT!
MURMUR サワ
NEGI-SENSEI, I'M SO SORRY YOU'VE BEEN DRAGGED INTO...
YOU HAVE TO! OTHERWISE, WE'LL NEVER MAKE IT.
OTHER CLASSES ARE DOING IT, TOO...
I KNOW, OKAY?!
HEADS UP! NITTA'S COMING!!
3-B STUDENT
10-4, THAT...
EVERY-ONE, HIDE!!
STEP コッ
STEP コッ

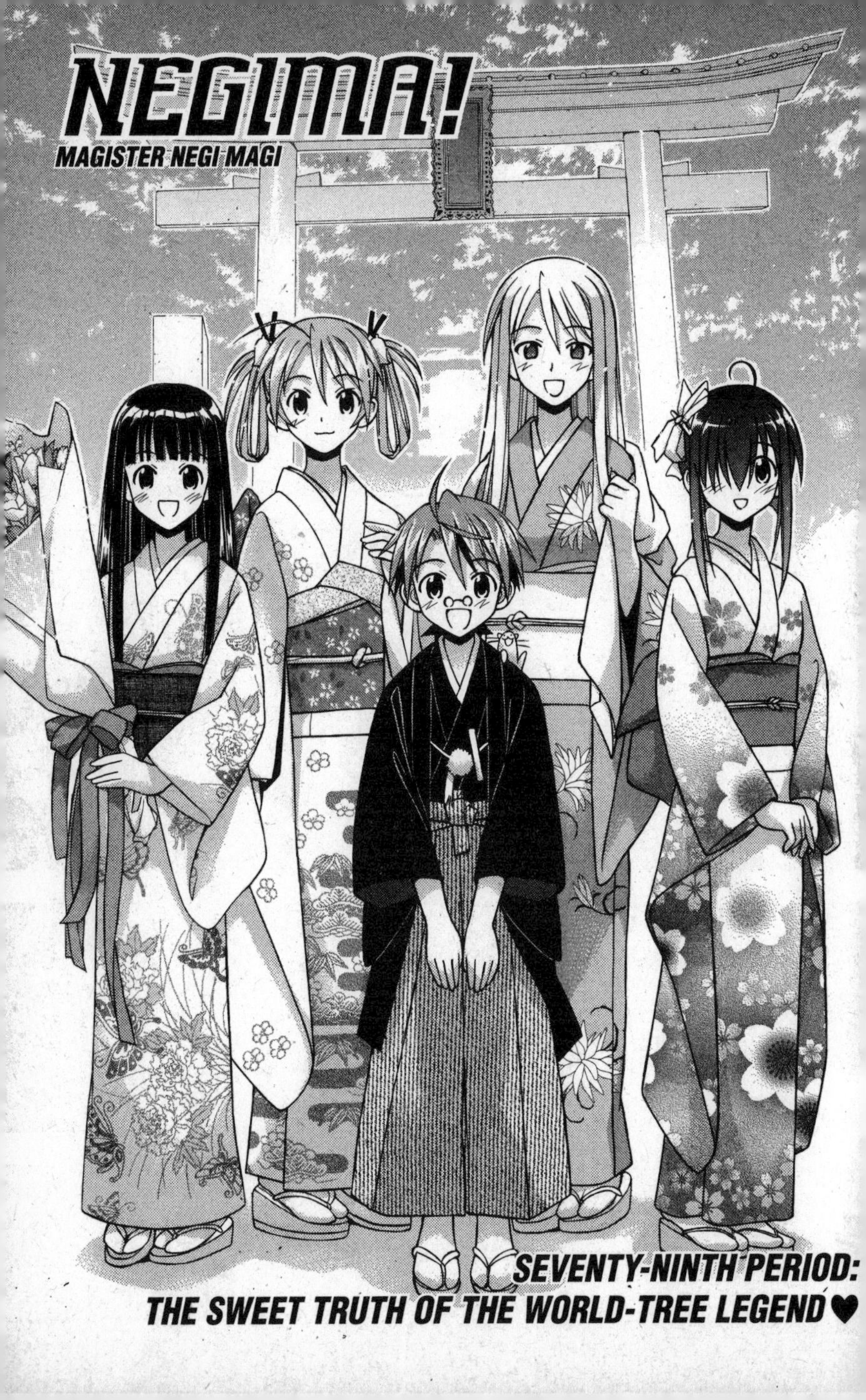
NEGIMA!
MAGISTER NEGI MAGI
SEVENTY-NINTH PERIOD:
THE SWEET TRUTH OF THE WORLD-TREE LEGEND♥

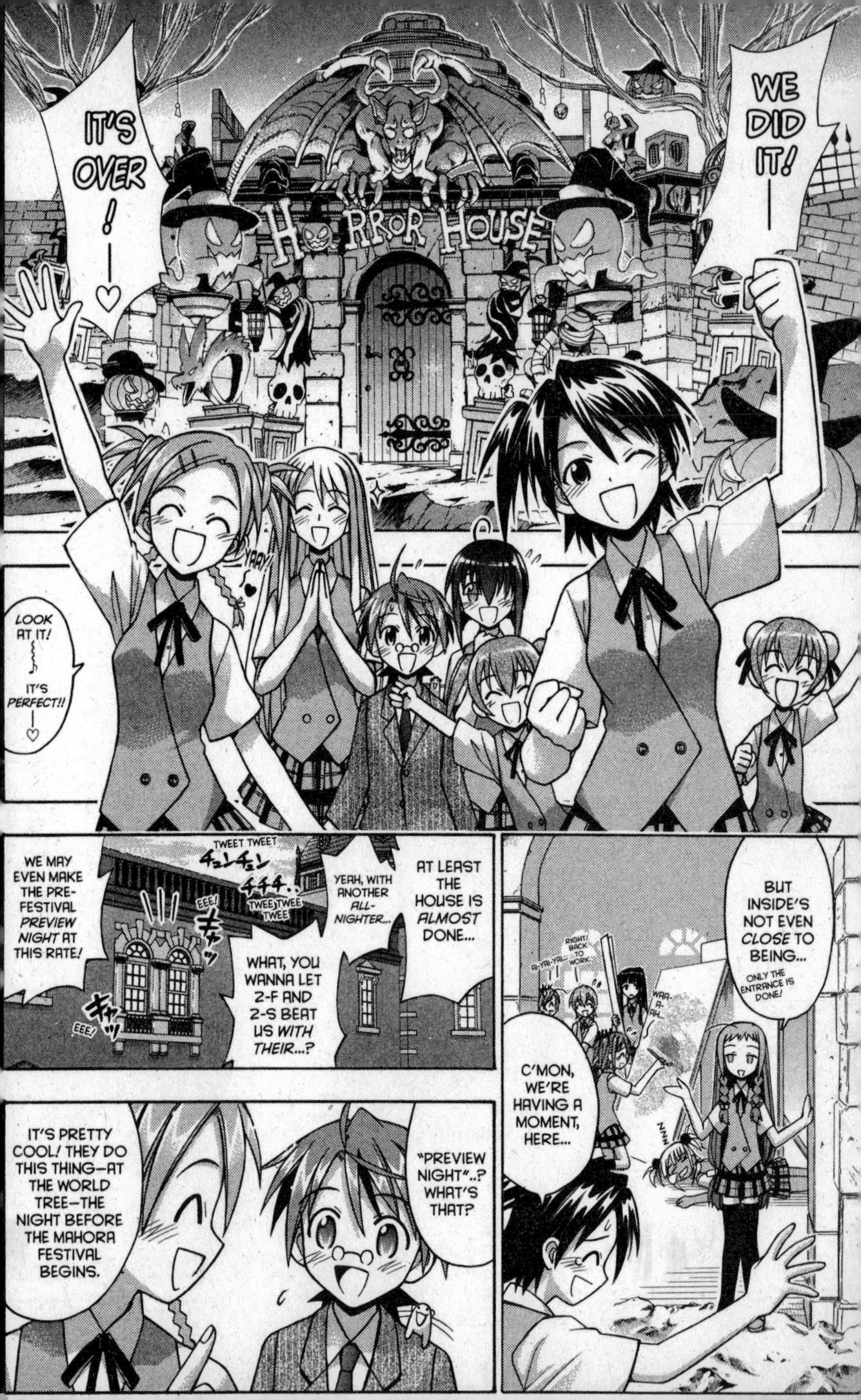
WE DID IT!—
IT'S OVER!—♥
YAAY! ♥
LOOK AT IT! IT'S PERFECT!!—♡
BUT INSIDE'S NOT EVEN *CLOSE* TO BEING...
ONLY THE ENTRANCE IS DONE!
RIGHT! BACK TO WORK.
WAA-A-AH...
AI-YAI-YAI...
C'MON, WE'RE HAVING A MOMENT, HERE...
NNN
AT LEAST THE HOUSE IS *ALMOST* DONE...
YEAH, WITH ANOTHER *ALL-NIGHTER*...
TWEET TWEET
TWEE TWEE TWEE
WHAT, YOU WANNA LET 2-F AND 2-S BEAT US *WITH THEIR*...?
EEE!
WE MAY EVEN MAKE THE PRE-FESTIVAL *PREVIEW NIGHT* AT THIS RATE!
EEE!
"PREVIEW NIGHT"..? WHAT'S THAT?
IT'S PRETTY COOL! THEY DO THIS THING—AT THE WORLD TREE—THE NIGHT BEFORE THE MAHORA FESTIVAL BEGINS.

WE'RE OFF TO GO FINISH THE BOOTHS FOR OUR CLUBS, OKAY?

PROMISE IF YOU'VE TIME YOU'LL COME BACK, THO', ALL RIGHT??

AND ALL WE'RE DOING IS TAKOYAKI...

WE'RE IN ATHLETICS, SO...

WHAT ABOUT YOU THREE, AREN'T YOU...?

AREN'T THEY SPUNKY.

WE'RE GOOD TO GO! WHO WANTS AN ENERGY DRINK?!

AFTER AN ALL-NIGHTER, TOO...

ASUNA-SAN! I'LL COME WITH YOU PARTWAY.

I'M OFF TO GO FINISH MY ART PROJECT...

"MAHOSUPO" AGAIN, HUH?

THAT REMINDS ME—YOU SEE THIS?

YAAY   YAAY

BUT IT'S NOT JUST THE PAPER!

NOT MORE TABLOID JOURNALISM...

"ACCORDING TO THE ACADEMY'S 'SEVEN WONDERS' RESEARCH CLUB..." IN-N-NT'RESTING, HUH??

I HEAR IT'S COMING EARLY, THIS YEAR...

EVEN THE OCCULT CLUB'S IN ON IT!

DON'T BELIEVE ALL YOU READ.

HOW, EVERY 22 YEARS, IT GETS REEEALLY BRIGHT...?

OH, THAT!

EEE

KNOW HOW IT GOES ON THE LAST DAY?

WORLD-TREE LEGEND NOT LEGEND AT ALL

POWER MANIFESTS ONCE EVERY 22 YEAR

"WORLD-TREE LEGEND NOT LEGEND AT ALL...."
"POWER MANIFESTS ONCE EVERY 22 YEARS..."

2003

FLUGTAG CONTEST

MAHORA LAKE, NORTH SIDE
ONLY 5 MINS. WALK FROM
(WORLD) ISLAND!
FIRST DAY, 10:00...

TAKE TO THE SKIES!

▲ June 22, 1982: The World Tree Emits a Spectacular Glow
Forever intrigued by the legend of the campus World Tree, we
at Mahora Sports have exciting new information to reveal.

Magical Phenomenon?! The World Tree's Spectacular Glow
Located in the center of the Mahora campus, the shinboku or
"Sacred Tree" Banbō has long been the center of controversy, as
well. That it predictably emits a glow of light in mid-summer
is a well-documented fact (see photo, above), but is it significant that the last day of the Festival also coincides with summer
...—the longest day of the year?

TWEET TWEET

TWEE TWEE

YAAY YAAY

STUDENTS CLUB

"MIZUSU" SHIGEKI RESEARCH CLUB

THE CLOSER THE FESTIVAL, THE WEIRDER IT SEEMS TO GET...

BOY, I'LL SAY!

I, UH...

WELL, UM...

HOW'D IT GO WITH TAKAMICHI?

SO, ASUNA-SAN...

GOOD FOR YOU, ASUNA

HAPPY TO HEAR IT!

REALLY?! THAT'S GREAT!

OKAY!

GLAD I RAN INTO YOU. THE HEADMASTER'D LIKE TO SEE YOU.

GUESS I'D BETTER HEAD BACK TO THE MAIN BUILDING...

H-HE WOULD?!

NEGI-SENSEI! HELLO.

SH-SHIZUNA-SENSEI!

GEH!

EVER SINCE I ASKED, I'VE BEEN SO NERVOUS I CAN'T EAT, CAN'T SLEEP—LIKE I'M GONNA DIE!! OH, I SHOULD NEVER HAVE...

HEY, HEY... ANESAN, IT'S ALWAYS LIKE THAT, AT FIRST.

NO, IT'S NOT GOOD! ONCE I DO SEE HIM, HOW DO I ACT?!

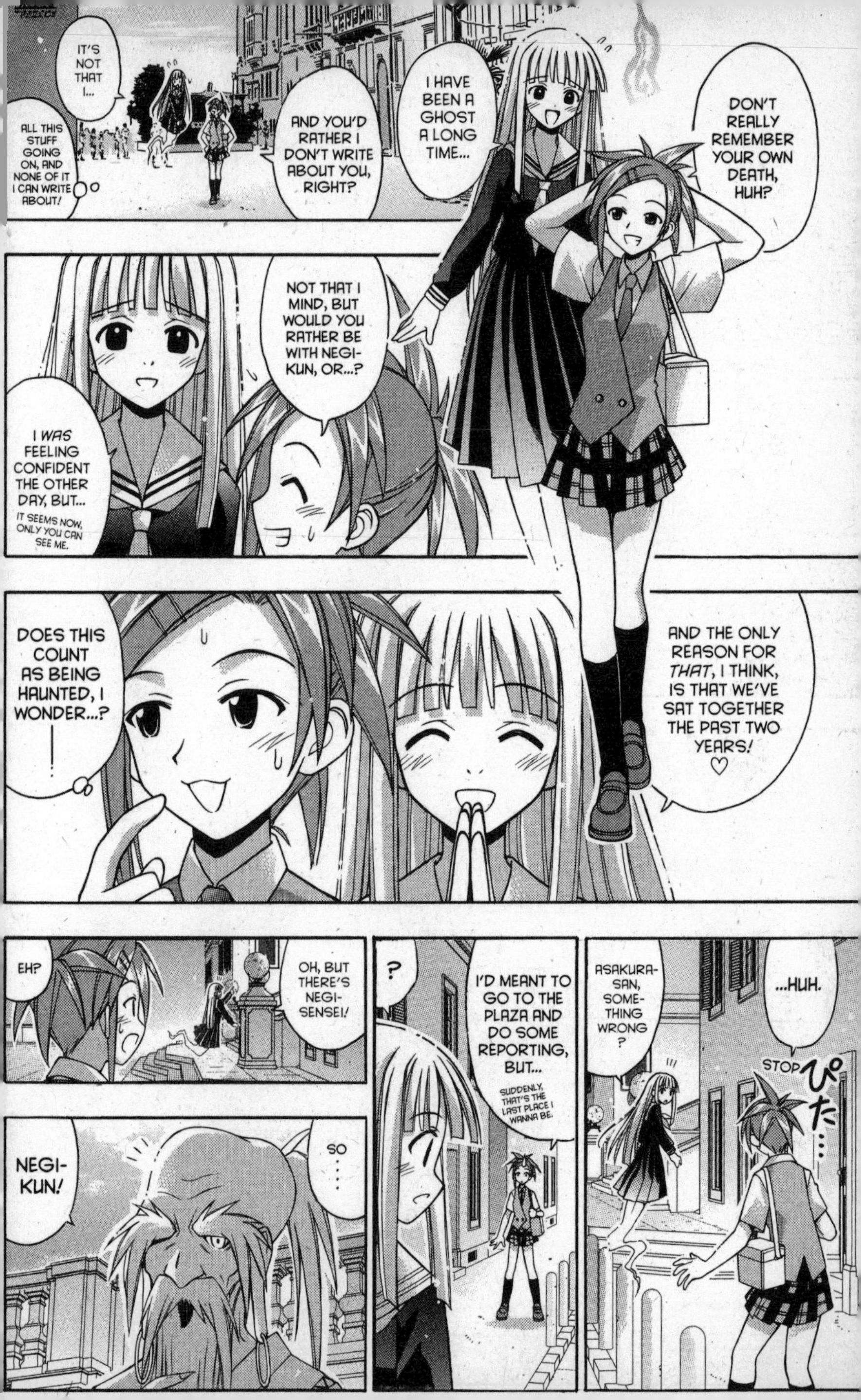

DON'T REALLY REMEMBER YOUR OWN DEATH, HUH?
I HAVE BEEN A GHOST A LONG TIME...
AND YOU'D RATHER I DON'T WRITE ABOUT YOU, RIGHT?
IT'S NOT THAT I...
ALL THIS STUFF GOING ON, AND NONE OF IT I CAN WRITE ABOUT!
NOT THAT I MIND, BUT WOULD YOU RATHER BE WITH NEGI-KUN, OR...?
I *WAS* FEELING CONFIDENT THE OTHER DAY, BUT...
IT SEEMS NOW, ONLY YOU CAN SEE ME.
AND THE ONLY REASON FOR *THAT*, I THINK, IS THAT WE'VE SAT TOGETHER THE PAST TWO YEARS! ♡
DOES THIS COUNT AS BEING HAUNTED, I WONDER...?
...HUH.
STOP ぴた...
ASAKURA-SAN, SOMETHING WRONG?
I'D MEANT TO GO TO THE PLAZA AND DO SOME REPORTING, BUT...
SUDDENLY, THAT'S THE LAST PLACE I WANNA BE.
?
OH, BUT THERE'S NEGI-SENSEI!
EH?
SO....
NEGI-KUN!

IT'S NOWHERE NEAR AS BAD AS DURING THE SCHOOL TRIP, BUT...

IT'S NOTHING AWFUL AGAIN, IS IT?!

THE ENEMY ?!

...AND I'LL BE NEEDING ALL YOUR HELP TO SET IT ARIGHT.

IT SEEMS WE'VE A PROBLEM...

THERE'S A REASON I'VE GATHERED YOU HERE TODAY...

YOU KNOW, OF COURSE, THE LEGEND OF THE WORLD TREE...?

IT IS AWE-INDUCING IN ITS OWN WAY.

I SUPPOSE THAT'S CLOSE ENOUGH.

I HEARD YUNA AND THE OTHERS TALKING ABOUT IT.

MORE ABOUT BECOMING A COUPLE, ISN'T IT?

SURE, YEAH, ALL THE KIDS IN CLASS CAN'T STOP *TALKING* ABOUT IT...

SOMETHING ABOUT, MAKE A WISH THERE ON THE LAST DAY OF THE FESTIVAL, BLAH BLAH BLAH...

LIKE IT'S *TANABATA*, OR...

HWAH ?!

...ONCE EVERY 22 YEARS.

WISHES DO COME TRUE, EVEN IF ONLY...

HWEH ?!

THE THING IS... IT'S TRUE.

AND SO...

...IS TO PREVENT ANY AND ALL STUDENTS FROM ATTEMPTING TO PUT THE WORLD-LEGEND TO THE TEST...

WHAT I NEED EVERYONE TO DO—ON THE LAST DAY OF THE FESTIVAL, IN PARTICULAR...

...ESPECIALLY AS IT RELATES TO MATTERS OF THE HEART.

FWOH, HOH, HOH...

THEN IT'S NOT SOME URBAN MYTH...?

SO THEN IT DOES WORK—

?!

IT IS, IN EFFECT A *MAGIC TREE.*

...DEEP INSIDE WHICH A MOST POWERFUL MAGIC IS HIDDEN.

...IS, IN REALITY, THE *SHINBOKU* OR "SACRED TREE" BANTŌ...

WHAT STUDENTS HERE CALL THE "WORLD TREE"...

WORLD TREE PLAZA

WORLD TREE

1.5km

ONCE, EVERY 22 YEARS, THE MAGICAL ENERGY ACCUMULATES TO SUCH A POINT THAT IT BEGINS TO FLOW OUTWARD FROM THE TREE...

FROM DEEP IN ITS CENTER, THERE ARE SIX MAIN LOCI FROM WHICH THE MAGIC EMANATES.

THIS PLAZA IS ONE OF THOSE LOCATIONS.

WHEN IT COMES TO CONFESSIONS OF LOVE...

NONE OF THESE AFFECT IT, BUT...

LUST FOR GLOBAL DOMINATION— VAST WEALTH— WOMEN'S UNDERWEAR...

THIS MAGIC IS EXTREMELY SUSCEPTIBLE TO HUMAN EMOTION...

COULD'VE DONE WITHOUT THE VISUAL.

OH-H-HKAY.

AND THAT, FRIENDS, IS THE REASON FOR THIS SUDDEN CONVOCATION.

CHANGING WEATHER PATTERNS, THE ENVIRONMENT... WHO KNOWS WHY, BUT WHAT *SHOULD* HAPPEN *NEXT* YEAR IS HAPPENING *NOW.*

ITS POWER IS SO GREAT, IT'S ALMOST A CURSE !!

120%

IT'S MORE LIKELY TO OCCUR BY 120% !!

DAH!!

WOULD *YOU* WANT TO FALL IN LOVE AGAINST YOUR WILL...?

THE PERMANENT BINDING OF AFFECTIONS THROUGH MAGIC GOES AGAINST THE MOST STRONGLY HELD BELIEFS OF ANY MAGUS...

BUT IT *IS* WRONG!

BUT WHAT'S SO WRONG WITH FALLING IN LOVE...?

EITHER WAY, COUNT ME OUT.

SUCH A CHILD, THIS ONE.

SOMETHING WRONG...?

I'M A CRIMINAL, A CRIMINAL!

GONG GONG GONG

N-NOT A THING, NOPE!

TH-THEY ARE—?!

WHAT YOU MADE WAS ONLY *TEMPORARY*—IT DOESN'T COUNT. YOU *DO* REALIZE, THOUGH, THAT LOVE POTIONS *ARE ILLEGAL*...?

B-BUT WHAT ABOUT THE LOVE POTION THAT *I* MADE?!

COMBINED WITH ARTICLES PUBLISHED IN "MAHORA SPORTS" AND OPINIONS POSTED ONLINE, THE TOTAL DEPTH OF RUMOR PENETRATION IS 79% AMONG WOMEN AND 34% AMONG MEN... ALTHOUGH I'D SAY THE NUMBER WHO ACTUALLY BELIEVE THE RUMOR IS FAR LESS.

THE "SEVEN WONDERS" CLUB, THE ACADEMY HISTORICAL SOCIETY, THE OCCULT RESEARCHER'S CLUB, EVEN THE "WORLD-TREE LOVERS"—ALL HAVE CONDUCTED THEIR OWN INVESTIGATIONS INTO THE WORLD TREE'S "GLOW"... AND SOME HAVE COME PERILOUSLY CLOSE TO THE TRUTH.

AND HOW.

I IMAGINE THE RUMOR HAS SPREAD TO EVERY STUDENT ON CAMPUS BY NOW...

BADLY AS I FEEL FOR THE STUDENTS, I MUST ASK THAT YOU GUARD ALL SIX AREAS FROM CONFESSION.

ALTHOUGH THE DAY OF MOST DANGER WILL NO DOUBT BE THE FINAL DAY OF THE FESTIVAL, ALREADY ACTIVITY HAS BEEN NOTICED.

SUCH IS HOW THINGS STAND.

...WE'LL HAVE NO SHORTAGE OF GIRLS PUTTING THE RUMOR TO THE TEST, I SHOULD THINK.

AND YET, EVEN IF WE'RE ONLY TALKING THOSE WHO BELIEVE IN FORTUNE-TELLING, OR IN URBAN MYTHS...

HWEH?!

IT OUGHTN'T BE *TOO DIFFICULT*; ONLY A HANDFUL ARE EVEN CAPABLE OF SUCH A THING.

I'LL FIND 'EM.

WE MUST NEVER UNDER-ESTIMATE THE STUDENTS.

A STUDENT, PERHAPS...? IF SO, NOT BAD—GETTING PAST THE BARRIER.

I SENSED NO MAGICAL POWER... MUST BE MECHANICAL.

NICE... I'D'VE THOUGHT THE *ANTI-MAGE STEALTH SYSTEM* WOULD'VE PREVENTED IT.

AIYA—! THE OBSERVATION DROID'S DESTROYED. THEY'RE ONTO US!

I'LL LURE THEM AWAY.

HAKASE—YOU ACTIVATE YOUR STEALTH CAMO AND STAY HIDDEN.

BUT... WILL YOU BE OKAY?!

WH-WHAT'LL WE DO?!

UH-OH... IS NO GOOD. THEY COMING AFTER.

THEY MAY EVEN ERASE OUR MEMORIES!

PROPERTY OF CHAOSGUNS.COM
2003 OPTICAL STEALTH

PLEASE USE THE UTMOST CAUTION IN YOUR USE OF MAGIC... I'LL BE COUNTING ON YOU ALL.

OUR STUDENTS STAND TO LOSE THEIR VERY YOUTH...

ZWAH

YOU MUSTN'T THINK OF IT AS MERE YOUTHFUL ARDOR...

YES, SIR!

RIGHT!

THAT IS ALL... DISMISSED.

FWAH

PLEASE BEGIN YOUR SCHEDULED PATROL SHIFTS IMMEDIATELY.

YOU PAY, I'LL PATROL.

YAAY YAAY
ワイ ワイ

THE SPELL KEEPING THEM AWAY'S BEEN LIFTED.

WHERE'D ALL THESE PEOPLE...?

BUZZ BUZZ
ガヤ ガヤ

PWOH HOH HOH

WHAT A HUGE HOUSE HE HAS!

HEY! THE HEAD MASTER!

WH-WHO, ME?! A-HA, HA, HA...

?

WHAT'S THIS? SURELY YOU DON'T THINK...!

OH, HE THINKS, ALL RIGHT.

HAH-WOO...

THOUGH I'M SURE IT SHAN'T BE AN ISSUE...

PLEASE AVOID ANY CONFESSIONS TO YOUR PERSON, AS WELL.

S-SIR?

NEGI-KUN?

...BUT TO LEARN THERE'S SO MANY OTHER TEACHERS OF *MAGIC*–!

BUZZ BUZZ

THE WORLD-TREE LEGEND'S ONE THING...

STILL, WHAT A SHOCK, HUH?

–KOTARŌ! DOES IT ALWAYS HAVE TO COME DOWN TO THAT FOR YOU?

GUESS HE JUST LIKES T' FIGHT...

LIKE I SAY, THOSE WESTERN MAGES ARE ALL NO DAMN–

HEY-Y-Y, WHAT'S THE BIG DEAL, WE COULD TAKE 'EM IN A FIGHT, NO PROBLEM!

SPARK! WHRRR! JWOOP

YUP, YOU'RE SCREWED, ALL RIGHT.

THERE'S NO WAY! I MEAN, JUST LOOK AT... NO WAY!!

URK!

Y-YOU'RE RIGHT– BEFORE, IT WAS ONLY *IMPOSSIBLE*, BUT NOW...

BUT ANIKI, YOUR SCHEDULE...! BAD AS IT WAS BEFORE, NOW THAT YOU'VE GOT *MAGIC-TEACHER* STUFF TO DO–

Z-Z-ZOOM

AWOO OOH

SOME-THING WRONG?

?

GLOO-O-OM

THEY BROACHED MY STEALTH WITHOUT EVEN... OOH, THIS IS BAD.

KRACKLE

NGH !

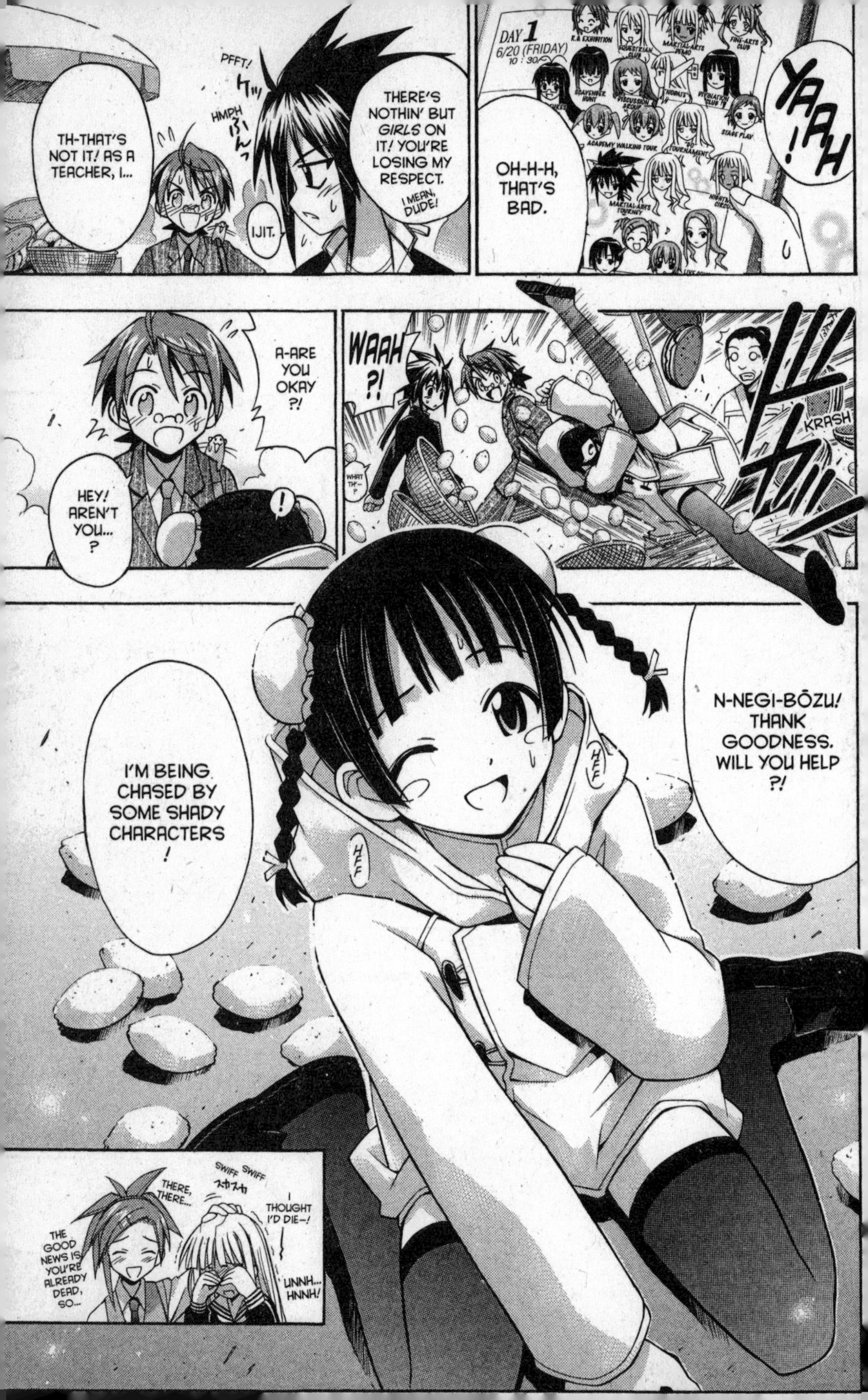
DAY 1
6/20 (FRIDAY)
10:30
R.A EXHIBITION
EQUESTRIAN CLUB
MARTIAL-ARTS DEMO
FINE-ARTS CLUB
SCAVENGER HUNT
DISCUSSION GROUP
DIVINATION CLUB
STAGE PLAY
ACADEMY WALKING TOUR
TOURNAMENT
MARTIAL-ARTS TOURNEY
YAAH!
OH-H-H, THAT'S BAD.
PFFT! ケッ
THERE'S NOTHIN' BUT GIRLS ON IT! YOU'RE LOSING MY RESPECT.
I MEAN, DUDE!
HMPH ふんっ
IJIT.
TH-THAT'S NOT IT! AS A TEACHER, I...
KRASH
WAAH?!
WHAT TH-?
A-ARE YOU OKAY?!
!
HEY! AREN'T YOU...?
N-NEGI-BŌZU! THANK GOODNESS. WILL YOU HELP?!
HEF
HEF
I'M BEING CHASED BY SOME SHADY CHARACTERS!
I THOUGHT I'D DIE-!
SWIFF SWIFF スカスカ
THERE, THERE...
THE GOOD NEWS IS YOU'RE ALREADY DEAD, SO...
UNNH... HNNH!

EIGHTIETH PERIOD:
SIGNS & PORTENTS AT THE PRE-FESTIVAL GALA

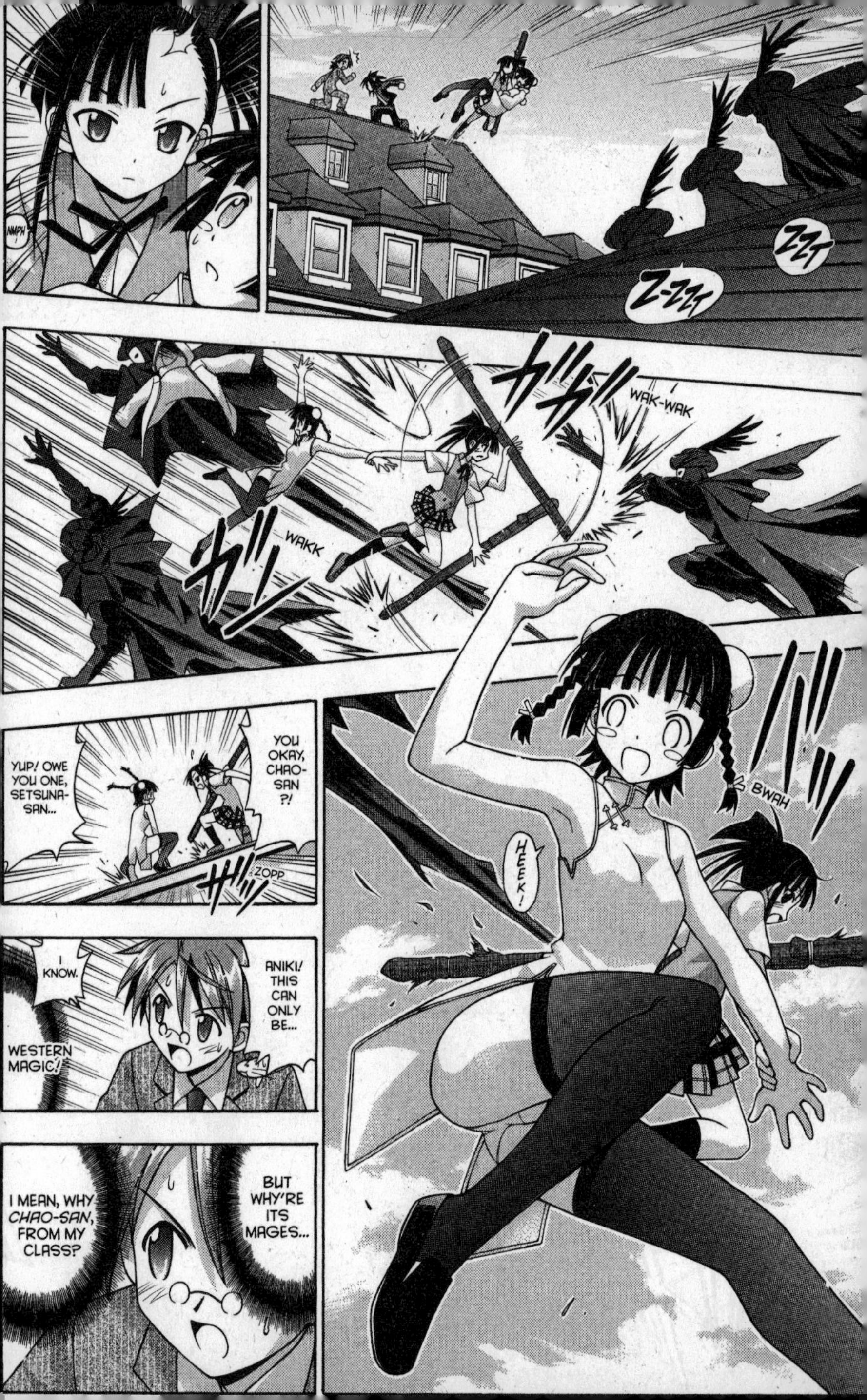
ZZZT
Z-ZZZT
NMPH!
WAK-WAK
WAKK
BWAH
HEEEK!
YOU OKAY, CHAO-SAN?!
YUP! OWE YOU ONE, SETSUNA-SAN...
ZOPP
ANIKI! THIS CAN ONLY BE...
I KNOW.
WESTERN MAGIC!
BUT WHY'RE ITS MAGES...
I MEAN, WHY CHAO-SAN, FROM MY CLASS?

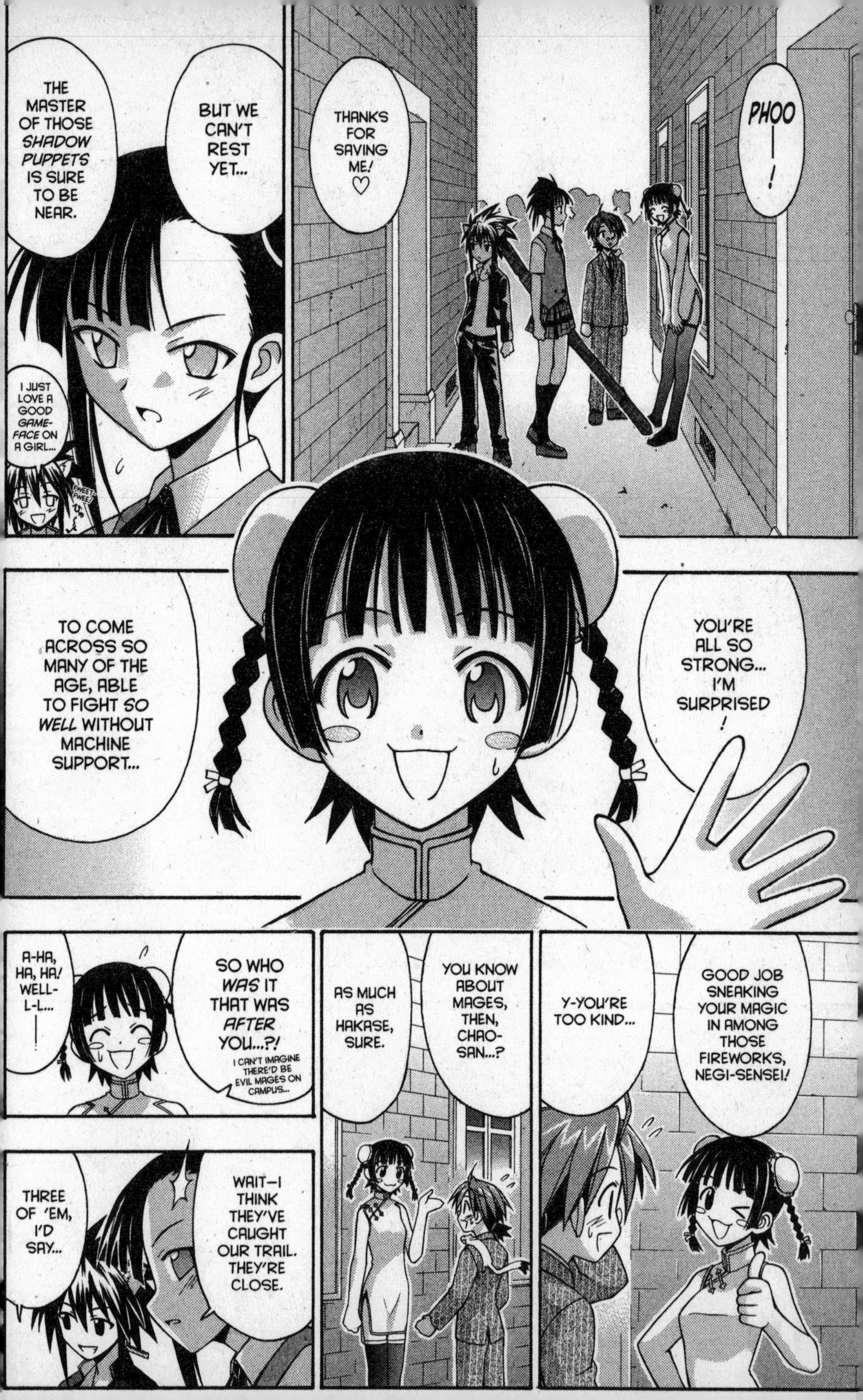
PHOO—!
THANKS FOR SAVING ME! ♡
BUT WE CAN'T REST YET...
THE MASTER OF THOSE SHADOW PUPPETS IS SURE TO BE NEAR.
I JUST LOVE A GOOD GAME-FACE ON A GIRL...
FWEET-FWEE!
YOU'RE ALL SO STRONG... I'M SURPRISED!
TO COME ACROSS SO MANY OF THE AGE, ABLE TO FIGHT SO WELL WITHOUT MACHINE SUPPORT...
GOOD JOB SNEAKING YOUR MAGIC IN AMONG THOSE FIREWORKS, NEGI-SENSEI!
Y-YOU'RE TOO KIND...
YOU KNOW ABOUT MAGES, THEN, CHAO-SAN...?
AS MUCH AS HAKASE, SURE.
SO WHO WAS IT THAT WAS AFTER YOU...?!
I CAN'T IMAGINE THERE'D BE EVIL MAGES ON CAMPUS...
A-HA, HA, HA! WELL-L-L...!
WAIT—I THINK THEY'VE CAUGHT OUR TRAIL. THEY'RE CLOSE.
THREE OF 'EM, I'D SAY...

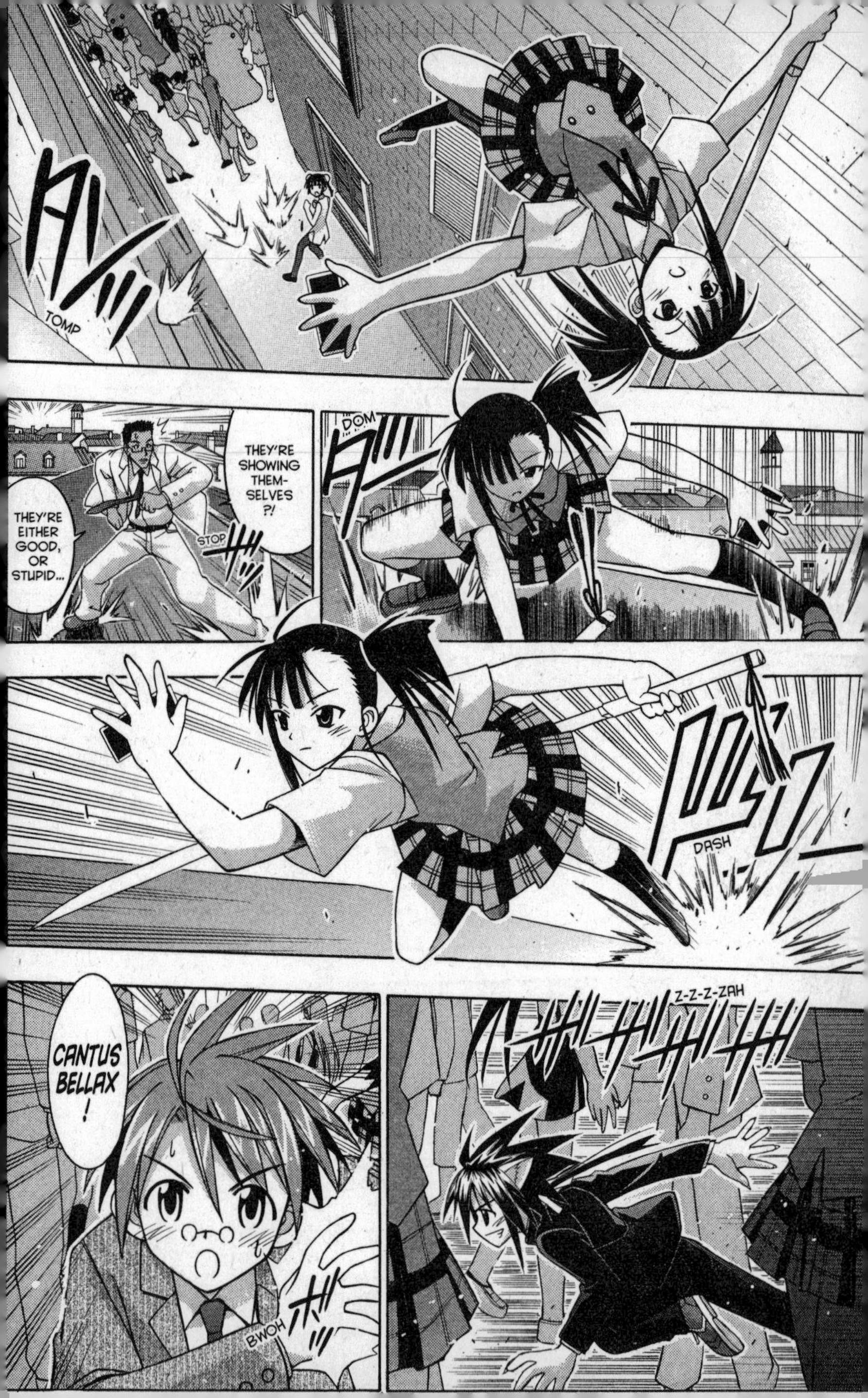
TOMP
DOM
THEY'RE SHOWING THEM-SELVES ?!
THEY'RE EITHER GOOD, OR STUPID...
STOP
DASH
Z-Z-Z-ZAH
CANTUS BELLAX !
BWOH

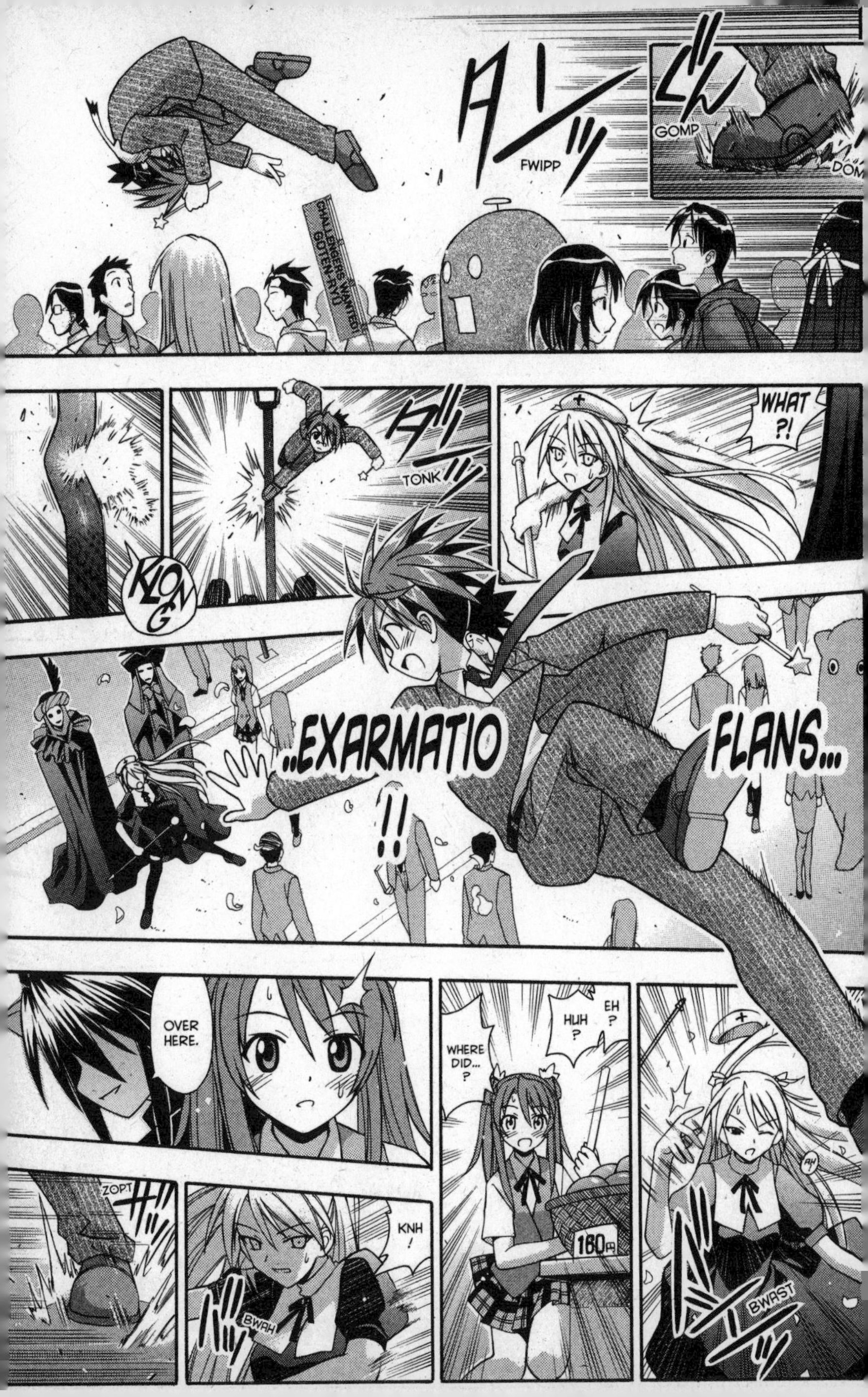
GOMP
DOM
FWIPP
CHALLENGERS WANTED! GOTEN-RYU
WHAT ?!
TONK
KLONG
FLANS...
..EXARMATIO
!!
EH ?
HUH ?
WHERE DID... ?
AH
OVER HERE.
BWAST
160円
KNH !
BWAH
ZOPT

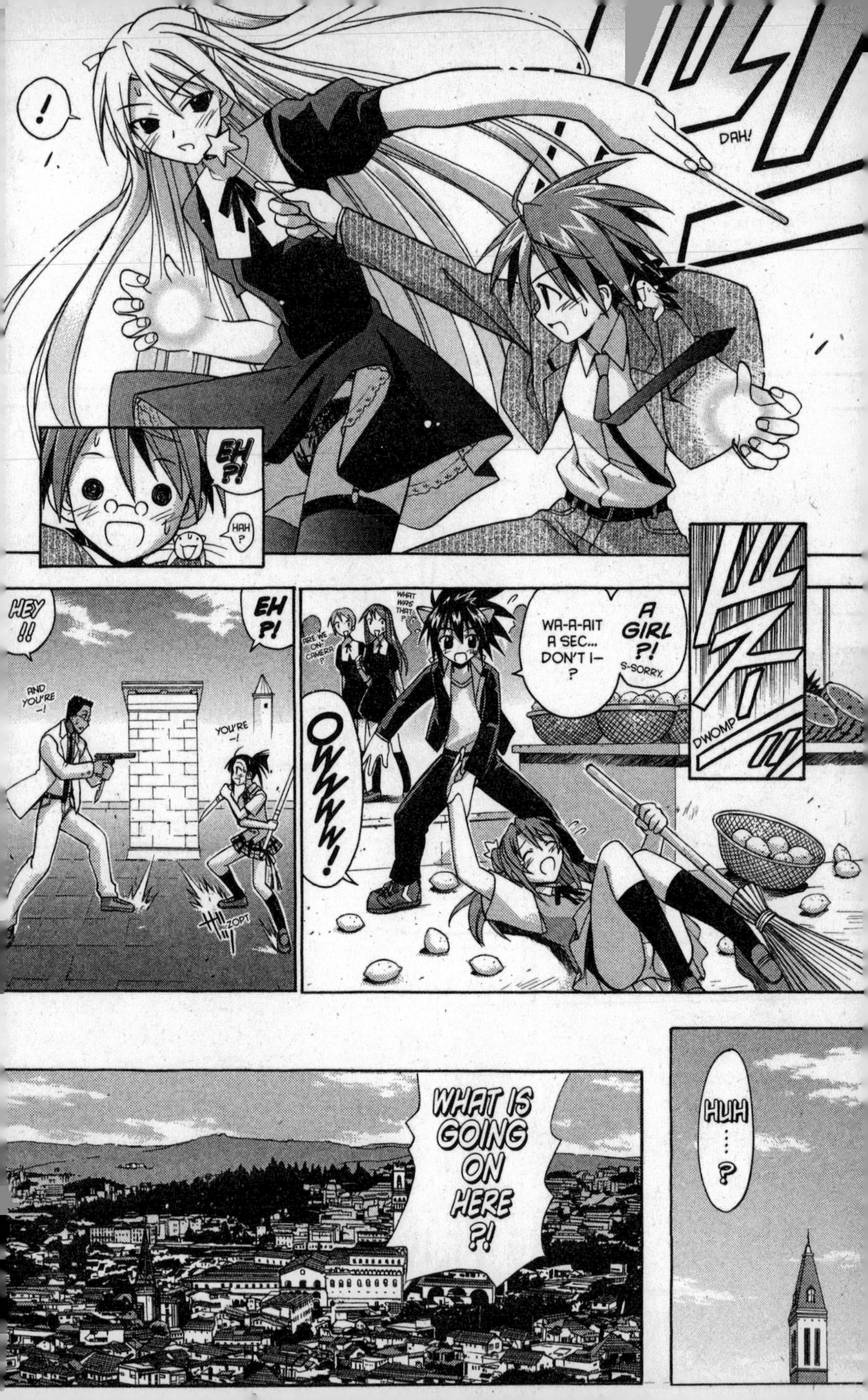
DAH!
!
EH ?!
HAH ?
DWOMP
A GIRL ?!
WA-A-AIT A SEC... DON'T I—?
S-SORRY.
WHAT WAS THAT?
ARE WE ON-CAMERA?
OWWWW!
EH ?!
YOU'RE —!
HEY !!
AND YOU'RE —!
ZOPT
HUH ....?
WHAT IS GOING ON HERE ?!

WH-WHAT DO YOU MEAN TO DO WITH CHAO-SAN?!

N-NEGI-BŌZU...

UGH.

OWW...

ZZZT

GRAB

ONE THING, THOUGH, IS CERTAIN—ALL MEMORY OF MAGES MUST BE WIPED FROM HER MIND.

NO ONE'S QUITE SURE, YET...

ACTUALLY, CHAO-KUN'S ALREADY ON HER THIRD WARNING, SO...

B-BUT IT'S SO SUDDEN!

AS IN, ERASE?!

"WIPE HER"...

I DID TRY TO ERASE ASUNA-SAN'S MEMORY WHEN WE FIRST MET, BUT...

THAT'S WHAT I WAS TAUGHT.

I-I KNOW THAT, BUT...

...YOU DO REALIZE THAT OUR EXISTENCE MUST BE KEPT SECRET?!

IT'S BEST THAT MUNDANES NEVER KNOW OF US.

NEGI-SENSEI, IN ORDER FOR US MAGES TO PEACEFULLY CO-EXIST IN THIS MODERN WORLD...

NOW, WE FIND SHE'S DEPLOYED A MECHANICAL DEVICE TO EAVESDROP ON AN AREA WHERE NORMAL PEOPLE WOULD NEVER BE ALLOWED.

IT'S NOT AS THOUGH WE CAN TELL HER ALL OF IT.

FOR OUR OWN REASONS, WE'VE ALLOWED CHAO-KUN SOMEWHAT IN ON THE SITUATION, BUT...

THEY *ARE* ONLY DOING THEIR JOB...

YOU SEE? WHEREVER I GO, THOSE TEACHERS ARE ALL THE SAME—ALWAYS THINKING THEY'RE BETTER THAN YOU.

KEH.

PHOO ....

....

HE SEEMS TO BE GROWING INTO A FINE YOUNG MAN.

HE'S HIS SON, ALL RIGHT...

THAT *COMBAT* WE JUST SAW, THOUGH... NOW THAT WAS *IMPRESSIVE*.

YES... I DUNNO.

YOU SURE ABOUT THIS?

HOO, HOO, HOO... THAT'S SECRET!

IF YOU DON'T SAY IT, IT'S ME THEY'LL HOLD RESPONSIBLE!

BUT, CHAO-SAN—FOR THEM TO CALL YOU A "PROBLEM-STUDENT"... WHAT IS IT THAT YOU'VE *DONE*?!

IT'S NOTHING I WOULDN'T HAVE DONE FOR...

NOW YOU'VE *REALLY* SAVED ME, NEGI-BŌZU! I OWE YOU MY LIFE! ♡

THE SCIENCE OF CHAO LINGSHEN IS AT YOUR COMMAND. ♡

LET ME SOLVE A PROBLEM FOR YOU, NEGI-BŌZU—YOU KNOW, TO PAY YOU BACK.

BY-THE-BY, NEGI-BŌZU, HAVEN'T YOU SOMETHING *ELSE* ON YOUR MIND...?

EH ?

NEGIMA! EIGHTIETH PERIOD: LEXICON NEGIMARIUM

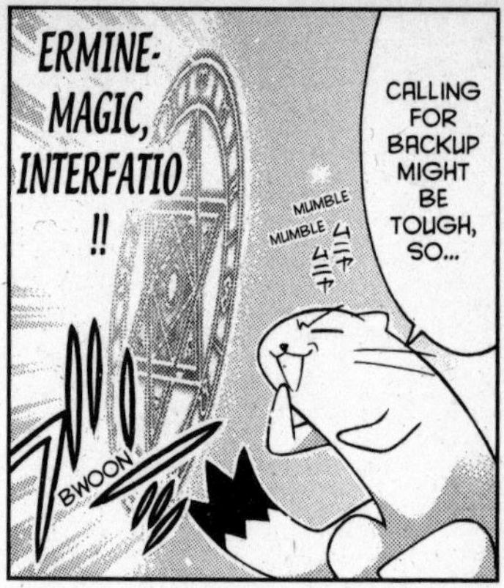
CALLING FOR BACKUP MIGHT BE TOUGH, SO...
MUMBLE MUMBLE
ムニャムニャ
ERMINE-MAGIC, INTERFATIO!!
BWOON

■「『念波妨害』」
インテルファーティオー

INTERFATIO

Many users of magic or Magi have ESP (*extrasensoria perceptio*) and are able to read the minds of others (1st Period, 16th Period), distinguish among particular magic powers (8th Period, 16th Period, 20th Period, 23rd Period, 42nd Period, 46–47th Periods, 49th Period, 68th Period, 79th Period), perceive future events (15th Period), detect infiltration into a specified area (18th Period, 67th Period), be aware when one's self is being observed (27th Period, 79th Period), sense the feelings of one to whom one is close (29th Period, 35th Period, 53rd Period, 55th Period), note the presence of a spiritual being (73–74th Periods, 78th Period), see through an illusion (78th Period), detect the presence and location of another Magi (80th Period), among other forms of truly extraordinary, extrasensory perception.

As phenomena without overt, outward manifestation which may be rationalized without empirical evidence even by those who are not of the magical world, those abilities which fall beneath the rubric "ESP" tend to be less popular than those of a more easily perceptible, external character (i.e., conflagration) insofar that, among the magically inclined, abilities of a perceptive or intuitive nature tend to be seen as rather more practical and, therefore, less exciting. Even in the quotidian world of corporate business, for example, it is not uncommon to retain (however discreetly) fortunetellers as company consultants. In this sense, the career path chosen by Negi's schoolmate, Anya, is not at all unusual.

ESP, as the acronym puts it quite plainly enough, refers to perception outside the realm of the "normal" senses (sight, hearing, touch, smell, taste). When the perception is sight, that which is sensed are electromagnetic waves—vibrations of electric and magnetic fields which form the visible spectrum; when auditory, vibrations in the air; when temperature (touch), vibrations on the molecular level. Each of the "ordinary" senses, then, is perceived across its various mediums, while ESP—being of an "extraordinary" nature—has as its home the spiritual plane, and therefore cannot be perceived by the common individual.

As regards the matter of telepathy between Magi, communication is effected across a similar medium—that of the spiritual plane. To explicate further, just as the commonborn communicate via voice (vibrations in the air), or through written words (characters relayed across the visible spectrum), so too do the magically gifted communicate, albeit in a manner wholly unlike "speech" or "words" appearing in the receiver's mind, but as something completely different.

In Latin, *interfatio* means "speaking between," or "interruption." The purpose of this spell, then, is to disrupt telepathic communication by filling the medium across which it travels with something like static, or "white noise." Another way to think of it would be to imagine a person right next to you, shouting in your ear, while you and someone else are trying to have a conversation.

- STAFF -

Ken Akamatsu
Takashi Takemoto
Kenichi Nakamura
Masaki Ohyama
Keiichi Yamashita
Chigusa Amagasaki
Takaaki Miyahara

Thanks To

Ran Ayanaga

NEGIMA! CHARACTER POPULARITY POLL

HERE ARE THE RESULTS OF THE FOURTH (ANNUAL?) *NEGIMA!* CHARACTER POPULARITY POLL, A.K.A. THE "NEGI-PRIX 4." BELIEVE IT OR NOT, SETSUNA'S TOPPED THE CHARTS TWO TIMES IN A ROW (!), ALTHOUGH THIS TIME, THE VOTES *ARE* MORE EVENLY DISTRIBUTED. THINK WE'LL SEE AN UPSET NEXT TIME 'ROUND...?

RESULTS OF THE THIRD *NEGIMA!* POPULARITY POLL

RANK	CHARACTER	TOTAL VOTES
1ST	SAKURAZAKI, SETSUNA	2,272
2ND	MIYAZAKI, NODOKA	2,051
3RD	KONOE, KONOKA	1,658
4TH	KAGURAZAKA, ASUNA	1,111
5TH	AYASE, YUE	807
6TH	NAGASE, KAEDE	803
7TH	SASAKI, MAKIE	750
8TH	MURAKAMI, NATSUMI	544
9TH	MCDOWELL, EVANGELINE A.K.	526
10TH	IZUMI, AKO	463
11TH	ASAKURA, KAZUMI	355
12TH	YUKIHIRO, AYAKA	283
13TH	KAKIZAKI, MISA	251
14TH	AKASHI, YŪNA	209
15TH	KUGIMIYA, MADOKA	198
16TH	SHI'INA, SAKURAKO	165
17TH	HASEGAWA, CHISAME	147
18TH	KARAKURI, CHACHAMARU	142
19TH	NABA, CHIZURU	122
20TH	KASUGA, MISORA	120
21ST	CHAO LINGSHEN	95
22ND	TATSUMIYA, MANA	87
23RD	RAINYDAY, ZAZIE	84
24TH	OKŌCHI, AKIRA	83
25TH	KŪ FEI	62
26TH	NARUTAKI, FUMIKA	56
27TH	AISAKA, SAYO	54
28TH	YOTSUBA, SATSUKI	51
29TH	SAOTOME, HARUNA	43
30TH	HAKASE, SATOMI	36
31ST	NARUTAKI, FŪKA	22

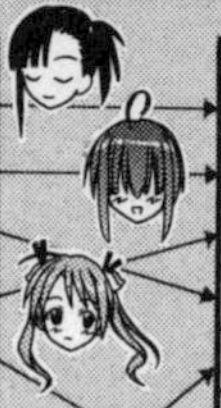

RESULTS OF THE FOURTH *NEGIMA!* POPULARITY POLL

RANK	CHARACTER	TOTAL VOTES
1ST	SAKURAZAKI, SETSUNA	1,633
2ND	MIYAZAKI, NODOKA	1,307
3RD	KAGURAZAKA, ASUNA	1,015
4TH	KONOE, KONOKA	966
5TH	MURAKAMI, NATSUMI	914
6TH	MCDOWELL, EVANGELINE A.K.	803
7TH	AYASE, YUE	628
8TH	SASAKI, MAKIE	604
9TH	NAGASE, KAEDE	593
10TH	KARAKURI, CHACHAMARU	583
11TH	IZUMI, AKO	567
12TH	YUKIHIRO, AYAKA	402
13TH	AKASHI, YŪNA	348
14TH	NABA, CHIZURU	321
15TH	CHAO LINGSHEN	320
16TH	AISAKA, SAYO	255
17TH	KAKIZAKI, MISA	226
18TH	OKŌCHI, AKIRA	223
19TH	SAOTOME, HARUNA	212
20TH	TATSUMIYA, MANA	198
21ST	KUGIMIYA, MADOKA	185
22ND	YOTSUBA, SATSUKI	176
23RD	ASAKURA, KAZUMI	124
24TH	HASEGAWA, CHISAME	113
25TH	KŪ FEI	105
26TH	RAINYDAY, ZAZIE	64
27TH	NARUTAKI, FŪKA	55
28TH	NARUTAKI, FUMIKA	53
29TH	HAKASE, SATOMI	42
30TH	SHI'INA, SAKURAKO	38
31ST	KASUGA, MISORA	27

NEGIMA! FAN ART CORNER

I'M GOING TO INTRODUCE THE FAN ART SENT IN BY YOU READERS THIS TIME, AS WELL. (^^)

TEXT: ASSISTANT Max

WELL WISHES MOST HUMBLY ACCEPTED (HEH).

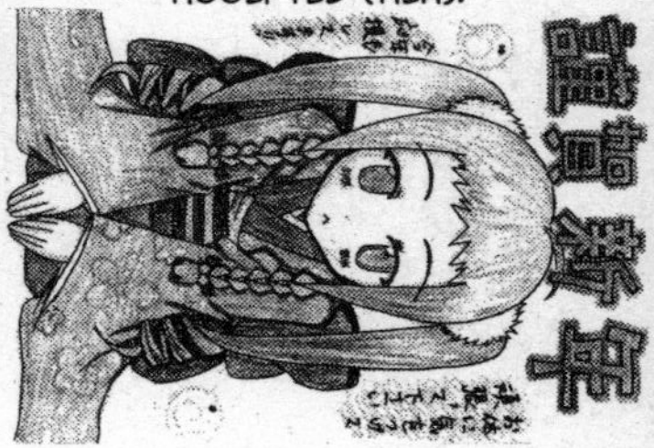
謹賀新年

YIKES! GUESS WE'D BEST NOT FORGET YOU NAGI FANS, HUH? (HEH.)

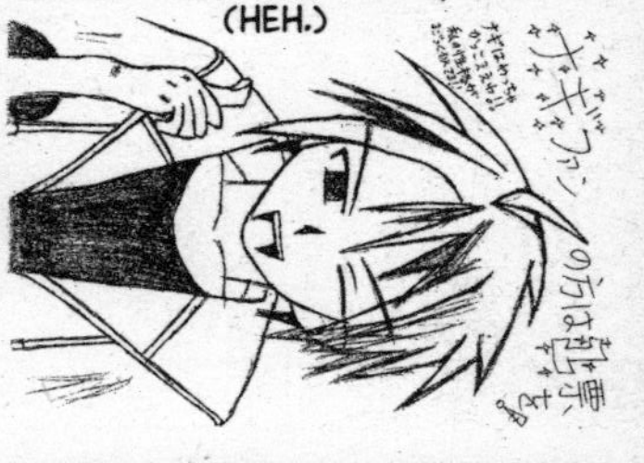

HOW CUTE IS THIS KOTARŌ, HUH?!

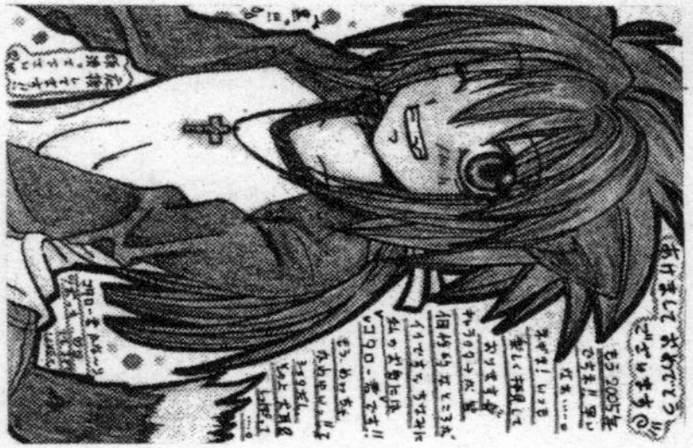
あけましておめでとうございます

LOVE THE WAY THE "BAKA BLACK" NICKNAME IS WORKED IN, HERE.

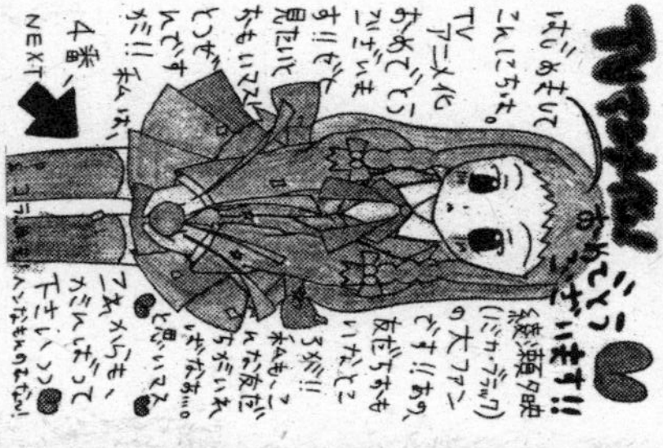
TVアニメ化!
おめでとうございます!!
はじめまして
こんにちは。
綾瀬夕映
(バカ・ブラック)
の大ファン
です!!
TV
アニメ化
おめでとう
ございます!!
4番
NEXT
これからも、
がんばって
下さいっっ

A PICTURE MADE FROM CUT-OUTS! VERY RARE, INDEED.

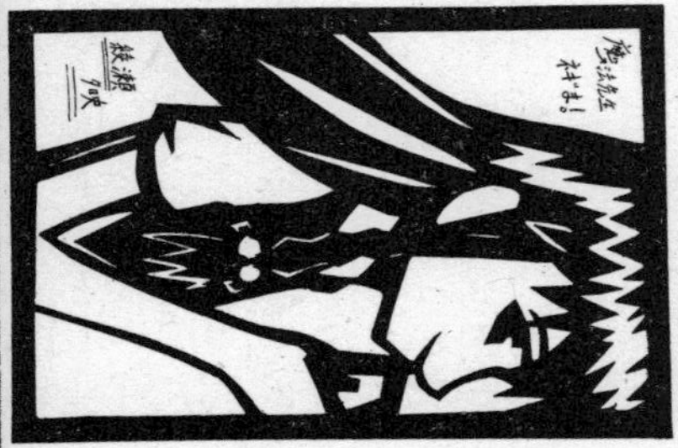
魔法先生
ネギま!
綾瀬
夕映

AYAKA LOOKS ESPECIALLY SPARKLY IN THIS ONE.

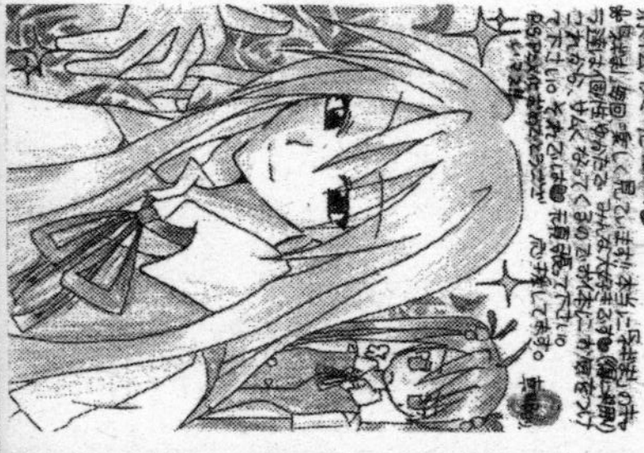
赤松健先生へ

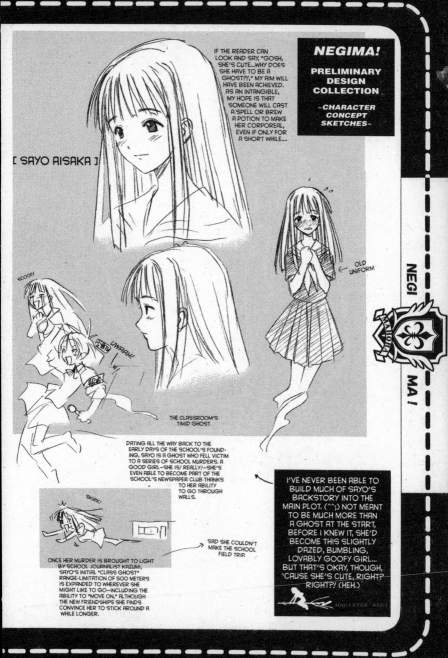

IF THE READER CAN LOOK AND SAY, "GOSH, SHE'S CUTE...WHY DOES SHE HAVE TO BE A GHOST?!," MY AIM WILL HAVE BEEN ACHIEVED. AS AN INTANGIBLE, MY HOPE IS THAT SOMEONE WILL CAST A SPELL OR BREW A POTION TO MAKE HER CORPOREAL, EVEN IF ONLY FOR A SHORT WHILE....

NEGIMA!

PRELIMINARY DESIGN COLLECTION

~CHARACTER CONCEPT SKETCHES~

[SAYO AISAKA]

OLD UNIFORM

SCOOP!

UWAAH!

THE CLASSROOM'S TIMID GHOST.

NEGI

MA!

DATING ALL THE WAY BACK TO THE EARLY DAYS OF THE SCHOOL'S FOUNDING, SAYO IS A GHOST WHO FELL VICTIM TO A SERIES OF SCHOOL MURDERS. A GOOD GIRL—SHE IS! REALLY!—SHE'S EVEN ABLE TO BECOME PART OF THE SCHOOL'S NEWSPAPER CLUB THANKS TO HER ABILITY TO GO THROUGH WALLS.

SKIRK!

SAD SHE COULDN'T MAKE THE SCHOOL FIELD TRIP

ONCE HER MURDER IS BROUGHT TO LIGHT BY SCHOOL JOURNALIST KAZUMI, SAYO'S INITIAL "CLASS GHOST" RANGE-LIMITATION OF 500 METERS IS EXPANDED TO WHEREVER SHE MIGHT LIKE TO GO—INCLUDING THE ABILITY TO "MOVE ON," ALTHOUGH THE NEW FRIENDSHIPS SHE FINDS CONVINCE HER TO STICK AROUND A WHILE LONGER.

I'VE NEVER BEEN ABLE TO BUILD MUCH OF SAYO'S BACKSTORY INTO THE MAIN PLOT. (^^;) NOT MEANT TO BE MUCH MORE THAN A GHOST AT THE START, BEFORE I KNEW IT, SHE'D BECOME THIS SLIGHTLY DAZED, BUMBLING, LOVABLY GOOFY GIRL... BUT THAT'S OKAY, THOUGH, 'CAUSE SHE'S CUTE, RIGHT? RIGHT?! (HEH.)

MAGISTER NEGI

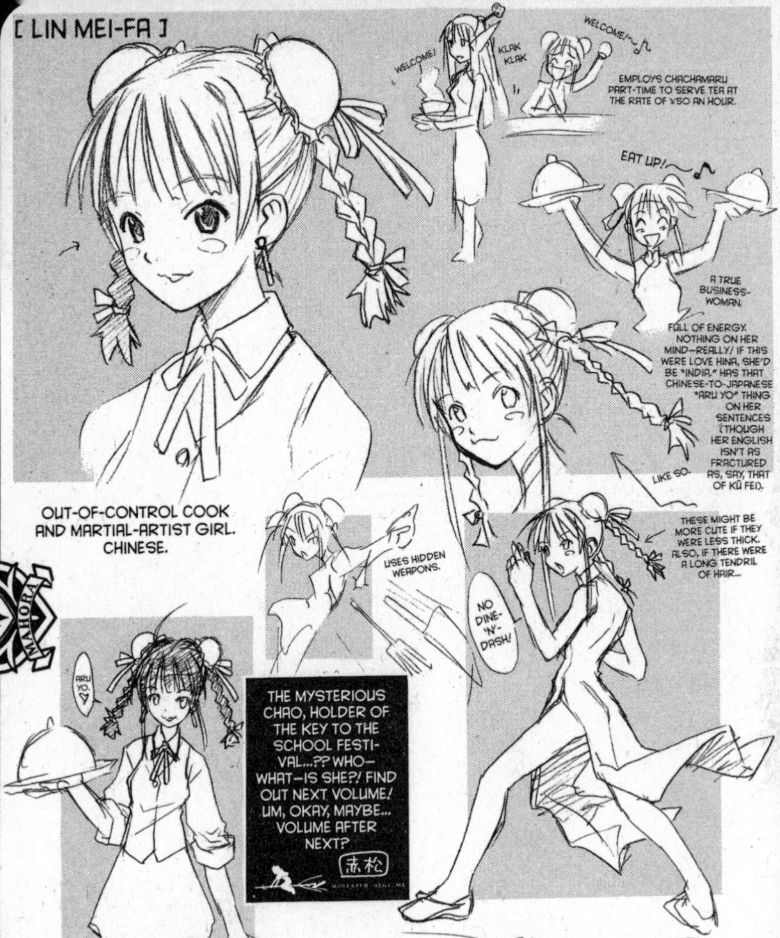

[LIN MEI-FA]
WELCOME!
KLAK KLAK
WELCOME!~♪
EMPLOYS CHACHAMARU PART-TIME TO SERVE TEA AT THE RATE OF ¥50 AN HOUR.
EAT UP!~♪
A TRUE BUSINESS-WOMAN.
FULL OF ENERGY. NOTHING ON HER MIND—REALLY! IF THIS WERE LOVE HINA, SHE'D BE "INDIA." HAS THAT CHINESE-TO-JAPANESE "ARU YO" THING ON HER SENTENCES (THOUGH HER ENGLISH ISN'T AS FRACTURED AS, SAY, THAT OF KŪ FEI).
LIKE SO.
OUT-OF-CONTROL COOK AND MARTIAL-ARTIST GIRL. CHINESE.
USES HIDDEN WEAPONS.
NO DINE-'N'-DASH!
THESE MIGHT BE MORE CUTE IF THEY WERE LESS THICK. ALSO, IF THERE WERE A LONG TENDRIL OF HAIR...
ARU YO. ♥
THE MYSTERIOUS CHAO, HOLDER OF THE KEY TO THE SCHOOL FESTIVAL...?? WHO—WHAT—IS SHE?! FIND OUT NEXT VOLUME! UM, OKAY, MAYBE... VOLUME AFTER NEXT?
赤松
VICE-CHAIRMAN, COOKING RESEARCH CLUB; FOUNDING CHAIRMAN, WATER-MELON-BREAKING CLUB
CHINESE NOODLES, ¥250!
ARMORED DINING-CAR RESTAURANT! (SHE LIVES INSIDE.)
OPEN FOR LUNCH, AND AFTER SCHOOL.

MAGISTER NEGI MAGI

● MAHORA ACADEMY JUNIOR-HIGH GIRLS' SCHOOL BUILDING
SCENE NAME: SCHOOL   POLYGON COUNT: 288,583

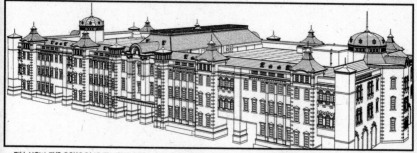

TILL NOW, THE SCHOOL'S ALWAYS BEEN A PHOTOCOPY OF THE INITIAL, HAND-DRAWN SKETCH, BUT WE FINALLY WENT AND MADE A PROPER 3-D VERSION OF THE MAHORA ACADEMY JUNIOR-HIGH GIRLS' SCHOOL BUILDING. IT'S REALLY BIG! AND COMPLICATED! IT TOOK MUCH LONGER TO RENDER THAN THAT OF THE WORLD-TREE SQUARE, WHICH WAS INTRODUCED IN THE PREVIOUS VOLUME (^_^;). MARVEL, IF YOU WILL, AT THE SHEER DETAIL OF THIS KEY LOCATION WITHIN THE SPRAWLING ACADEMY CITY.

HERE'S THE MOST RECOGNIZABLE DETAIL OF THE JUNIOR HIGH, THE CLOCK TOWER AT THE FRONT OF THE BUILDING. WE'VE EVEN DONE SOME FINE DETAIL-WORK IN THE MASONRY BUT, SINCE IT'S SO SMALL, MOST PEOPLE WON'T EVEN NOTICE. (^_^;)

SEE? SEE?! CHECK THE DETAILED STONE WORK!
(HEH.)

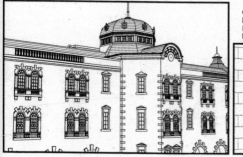

OUTSIDE OF CLASSROOM 3-A. THE PERSPECTIVE OF THE FACADE YOU SEE BELOW IS THE FIRST TIME 3-A'S EVER BEEN SHOWN FROM THE OUTSIDE.

• CHAO'S DINING-CAR RESTAURANT
SCENE NAME: CHAO'S_TRAM_   POLYGON COUNT: 34,885

TILL3-D COMPUTER GRAPHIC OF CHAO'S CONVERTED DINING-CAR RESTAURANT, CHAO BAO ZI. THE SCHOOL FESTIVAL REALLY SEEMS TO BE KEEPING THE PLACE HOPPING! I'D LIKE TO SEE IT SHOW UP IN THE MAIN STORYLINE, AS WELL.

ROUGH SKETCH OF THE TRAIN. SOME STRANGE DETAILS, HERE.... (^_^;)

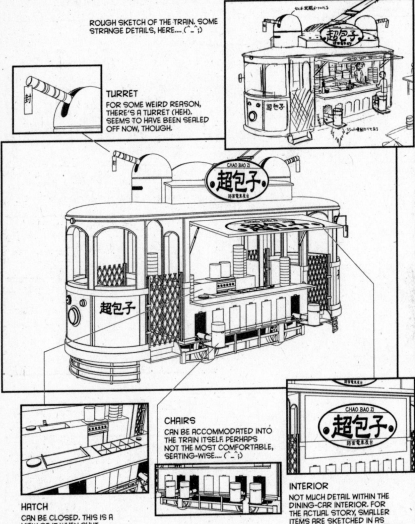

TURRET
FOR SOME WEIRD REASON, THERE'S A TURRET (HEH). SEEMS TO HAVE BEEN SEALED OFF NOW, THOUGH.

CHAIRS
CAN BE ACCOMMODATED INTO THE TRAIN ITSELF. PERHAPS NOT THE MOST COMFORTABLE, SEATING-WISE.... (^_^;)

INTERIOR
NOT MUCH DETAIL WITHIN THE DINING-CAR INTERIOR. FOR THE ACTUAL STORY, SMALLER ITEMS ARE SKETCHED IN AS NEEDED.

HATCH
CAN BE CLOSED. THIS IS A VIEW OF IT WHEN SHUT.

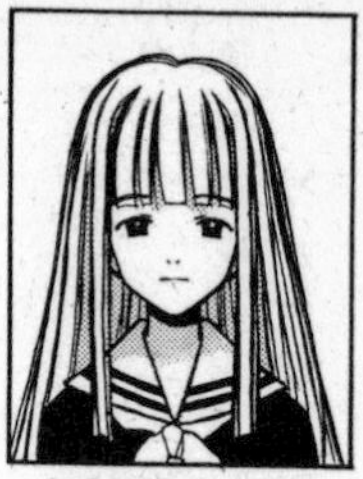

1. SAYO AISAKA

1940~
DON'T CHANGE HER SEATING

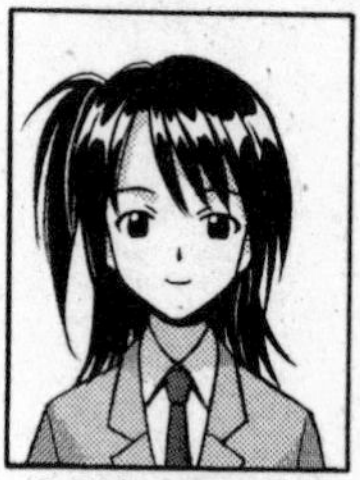

2. YUNA AKASHI
BASKETBALL TEAM

PROFESSOR AKASHI'S DAUGHTER

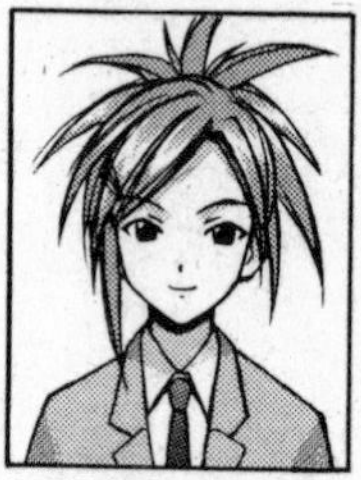

3. KAZUMI ASAKURA
SCHOOL NEWSPAPER

MAHORA NEWS (ext. B09-3780)

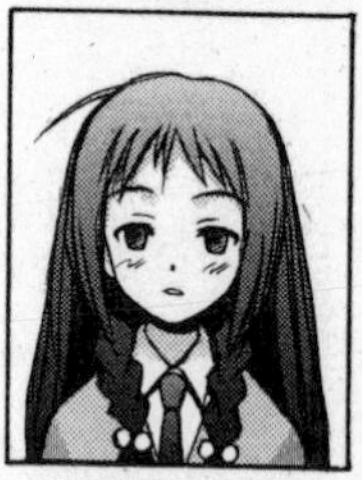

4. YUE AYASE
KID'S LIT CLUB
PHILOSOPHY CLUB
LIBRARY EXPLORATION CLUB

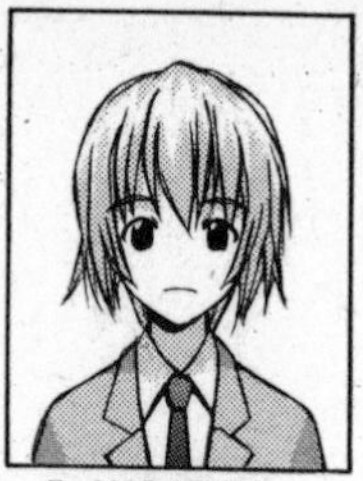

5. AKO IZUMI
NURSE'S OFFICE
SOCCER TEAM
(NON-SCHOOL ACTIVITY)

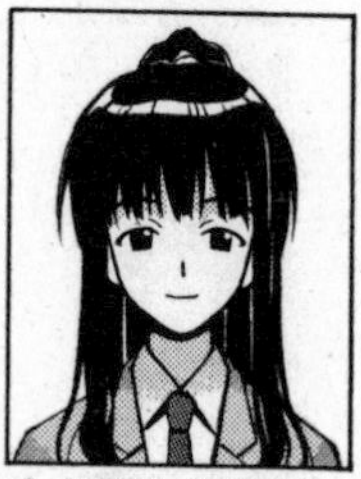

6. AKIRA OKOCHI
SWIM TEAM

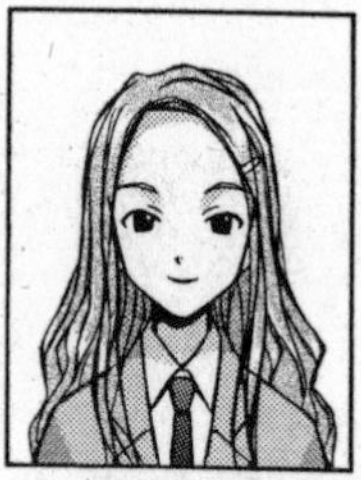

7. MISA KAKIZAKI
CHEERLEADER
CHORUS

A GOOD PERSON JUST
AS I THOUGHT.

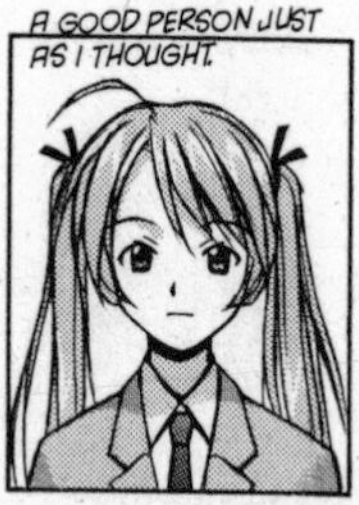

8. ASUNA KAGURAZAKA
ART CLUB

HAS A TERRIBLE KICK

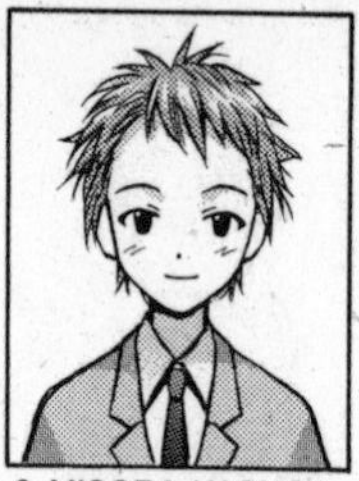

9. MISORA KASUGA
TRACK & FIELD

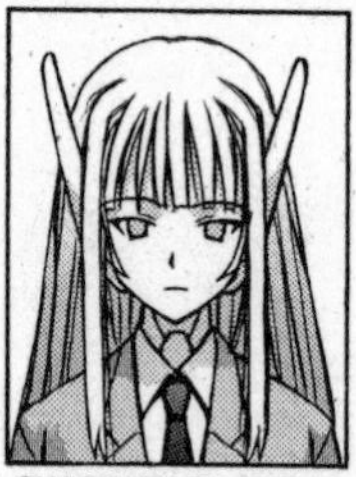

10. CHACHAMARU KARAKURI
TEA CEREMONY CLUB
GO CLUB

CALL ENGINEERING (ext. A08-7796)
IN CASE OF EMERGENCY

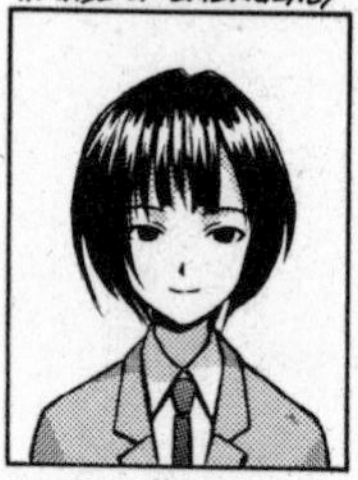

11. MADOKA KUGIMIYA
CHEERLEADER

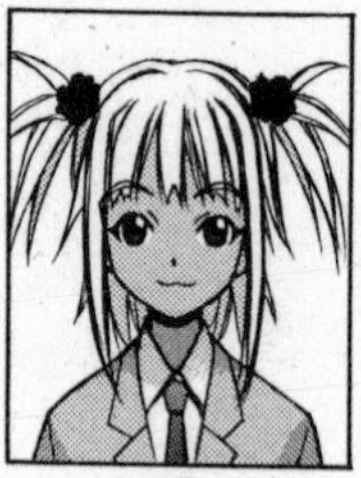

12. KŪ FEI
CHINESE MARTIAL ARTS
GROUP

GRANDDAUGHTER OF
SCHOOL DEAN

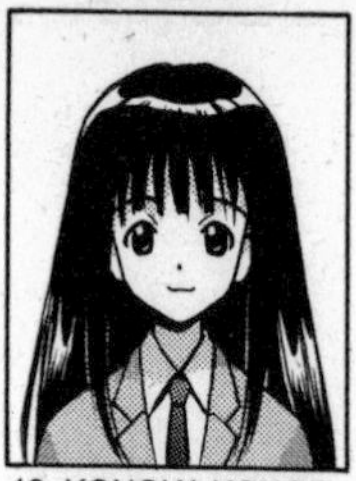

13. KONOKA KONOE
SECRETARY
FORTUNE-TELLING CLUB
LIBRARY EXPLORATION CLUB

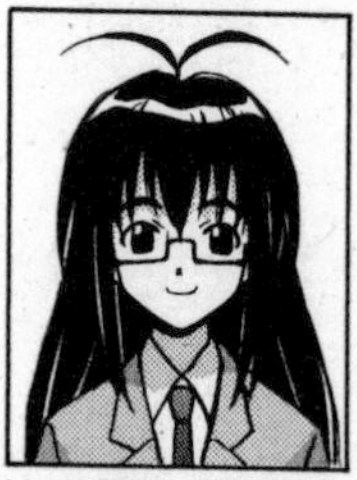

14. HARUNA SAOTOME
MANGA CLUB
LIBRARY EXPLORATION CLUB

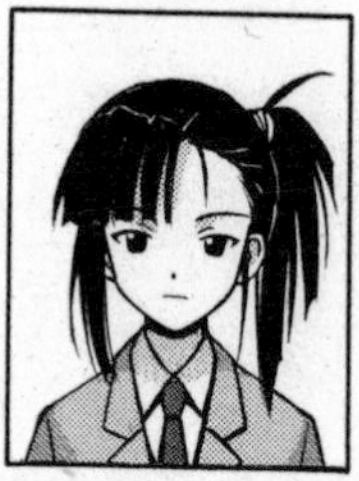

15 SETSUNA SAKURAZAKI
JAPANESE FENCING

KYOTO SHINMEI STYLE

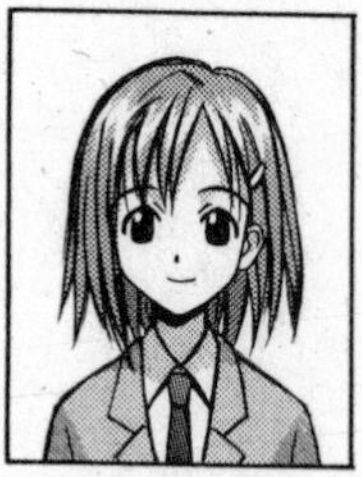

16. MAKIE SASAKI
GYMNASTICS

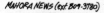

EMERGENCY CONTACT
(PRIMARY)

ASUNA'S
CLOSE
FRIEND.

29. AYAKA YUKIHIRO
CLASS REPRESENTATIVE
EQUESTRIAN CLUB
FLOWER ARRANGEMENT
CLUB

25. CHISAME HASEGAWA
NO CLUB ACTIVITIES
GOOD WITH COMPUTERS

21. CHIZURU NABA
ASTRONOMY CLUB
MORE OF A DANGO THAN A FLOWER

17. SAKURAKO SHIINA
LACROSS TEAM
CHEERLEADER

I WON!   LOST!

30. SATSUKI YOTSUBA
LUNCH REPRESENTATIVE

26. EVANGELINE
A.K. MCDOWELL
GO CLUB
TEA CEREMONY CLUB
ASK HER ADVICE IF YOU'RE IN TROUBLE

VERY
ADULT-LIKE
♥

22. FUKA NARUTAKI
WALKING CLUB
OLDER SISTER

18. MANA TATSUMIYA
BIATHLON
(NON-SCHOOL ACTIVITY)

31. ZAZIE RAINYDAY
MAGIC
SCHOOL ACTIVITY

VERY CUTE

27. NODOKA MIYAZAKI
GENERAL LIBRARY
COMMITTEE MEMBER
LIBRARIAN
LIBRARY EXPLORATION CLUB

SURPRISINGLY
SKILLED ♥

23. FUMIKA NARUTAKI
SCHOOL DECOR CLUB
WALKING CLUB
BOTH OF THEM ARE STILL CHILDREN

19. CHAO LINGSHEN
COOKING CLUB
CHINESE MARTIAL ARTS CLUB
ROBOTICS CLUB
CHINESE MEDICINE CLUB
BIO-ENGINEERING CLUB
QUANTUM PHYSICS CLUB (UNIVERSITY)

28. NATSUMI MURAKAMI
DRAMA CLUB

24. SATOMI HAKASE
ROBOTICS CLUB (UNIVERSITY
JET PROPULSION CLUB (UNIVERSITY))

20. KAEDE NAGASE
WALKING CLUB
NINJA

May the good speed
be with you, Negi.
Takahata.T.Takamichi.

キャラ解説

CHARACTER PROFILE

① 相坂さよ
SAYO AISAKA

大人気の ユーレイです。
THE EVER-POPULAR GHOST!

(しのむ + むつみ) ÷ 2 みたいな属性
IN LOVE HINA TERMS, I GUESS MAYBE SHE'D BE SHINOMU
でしょうか。 アワアワ ボケボケ ちゃう?
+ MUTSUMI ÷ 2 (IN OTHER WORDS, NERVOUS TENSION + AIRHEAD)...?

コノカ とかに 似た デザイン なので、
SINCE SHE'S SO POTENTIALLY SIMILAR TO KONOKA,

鼻 とか 瞳 のテカリ とかで 必死に
I WORKED REALLY HARD TO CHANGE THE "FEEL" OF HER NOSE,

違いを 出そうとしたのですが (笑)
AS WELL AS HOW THE LIGHT SHOWS IN HER EYES...DID IT WORK? (HEH.)

やっぱ 同じですよね。スミマセン ?
PROBABLY THEY STILL DO LOOK PRETTY SIMILAR...SORRY 'BOUT THAT.

声優は ベテランの 白鳥由里さん。
FOR THE ANIME, HER VOICE-ACTOR IS YURI SHIRATORI, A REAL VETERAN.

アニメでは 出番が 多いようで、
IT SEEMS SAYO WILL HAVE AN EVEN BIGGER PART IN THE ANIME THAN IN THE MANGA,

今から 楽しみです。
SO I'M LOOKING FORWARD TO THAT.
(主役の回も あるらしく…)
(SUPPOSEDLY SHE'LL EVEN HAVE HER OWN EPISODE.)

次の 10巻からは、いよいよ
AS OF VOLUME 10—NEXT VOLUME!—

学園祭の スタートです!
IT'S FINALLY THE START OF THE SCHOOL FESTIVAL.

ぜひ 見てね!
BE SURE NOT TO MISS IT!

赤松
(AKAMATSU)

About the Creator

Negima! is only Ken Akamatsu's third manga, although he started working in the field in 1994 with *AI Ga Tomaranai* (released in the United States with the title *A.I. Love You*). Like all of Akamatsu's work to date, it was published in Kodansha's *Shonen Magazine*. *AI Ga Tomaranai* ran for five years before concluding in 1999. In 1998, however, Akamatsu began the work that would make him one of the most popular manga artists in Japan, *Love Hina*. *Love Hina* ran for four years, and before its conclusion in 2002, it would cause Akamatsu to be granted the prestigious Manga of the Year award from Kodansha, as well as going on to become one of the best-selling manga in the United States.

Translation Notes

Japanese is a tricky language for most Westerners, and translation is often more art than science. For your edification and reading pleasure, here are notes on some of the places where we could have gone in a different direction in our translation of the work, or where a Japanese cultural reference is used.

P2 Robot, page 10

A prototype humanoid "walking robot" in development by auto manufacturer Honda since the mid '80s (starting with the E0 or "Experimental Model 0" in 1986 and continuing up to the E6 in 1991), the robot you see running alongside the students on this page is the P2. In 1993, Honda entered the prototype phase, and created the P1 (the frame of the P2 model seen in this panel was created in 1996). A year later (in the summer of '97), Honda created the first-to-look-mostly-humanoid P3; in 2000, the final evolution of the Honda robots culminated in the creation of the ASIMO (for more info, see asimo.honda.com).

Saratoga Cooler, page 15

The drink Madoka asks Negi if she may order during his "education" on the world of "Adult Cafés." A non-alcoholic beverage made with lime juice and grenadine, added to a glass of crushed ice, topped off with ginger ale and garnished with lime, a Saratoga Cooler is essentially the better-known Moscow Mule...except, of course, without the vodka.

"All-Girl Swimsuit Expo Café," page 27

Known perhaps more properly (and definitely more naughtily) in Japan by the proper title *DOKI! Onna-Darake no Idol Mizuki Taikai* ("BAH-BUMP! The Nothing-But-Idol-Girls Swimsuit Suit-Off"), the show itself is not only real but just one of a series of similarly titled programs featuring swimsuit-clad female idol-singers gamely attempting various pool-based obstacle courses while singing their latest hits in-between. (The Japanese sound-effect *porori*, incidentally, refers to a "wardrobe malfunction" of the type which, amazingly enough, happens only to "B"-list idols—never to those on the "A"-list.) Needless to say, ratings on this and other such late-nite TV "specials" in Japan are said to be very high with teenage and young adult male audiences.

"No-Panties Café," page 28

In the '80s, in the floating world known as Japan's colorful sex trade, there once was a place known as a "No-Panties Café (*No-Pan Kissa*)." Much like any other coffee shop but with two major differences, the point of a "no-panties café" was, of course, that the waitresses wore no undergarments...and that the floor was mirrored. With typical pricing for a cup of plain, house coffee—no refills!—said to have run around ¥2,000–3,000 (US$18.00–27.00 at today's exchange rates), one supposes the customer got what he paid for....

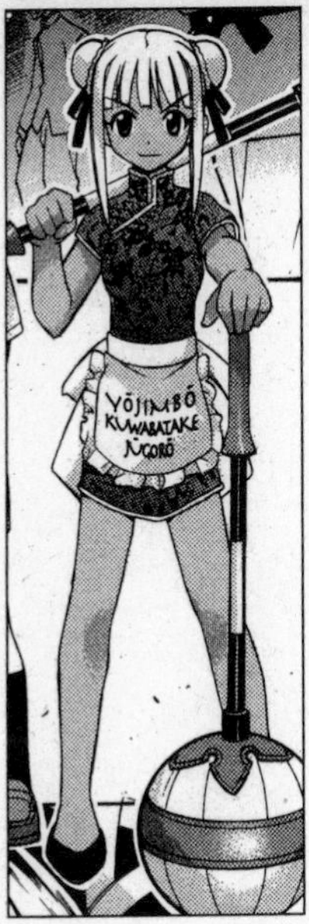
YŌJIMBŌ
KUWABATAKE
JŪGORŌ

Yōjimbō Kuwabatate Jūgorō, page 33

...is what's written on Kū Fei's apron. An obvious reference to the famed Kurosawa film of the same name, a *yōjimbō*, of course, is a bodyguard. In the film, when the Toshirō Mifune character is asked his name, he replies falsely, "Kuwabatake Sanjūrō...although I'm close to 'Shijūrō,' now"—the joke being, "Sanjūrō" refers both to a common Japanese first name as well as to an age, 30, while "Shijūrō" means 40. Kū Fei, whose apron reads "Jūgorō" (as in jūgo, 15), is Akamatsu's nod to Mifune's pun.

Satomi Hakase, page 62

In Japanese, *hakase* means "professor," so even though Satomi's last name is written with different *kanji*, interpreting her nickname as "Professor Professor" would not be, technically speaking, incorrect.

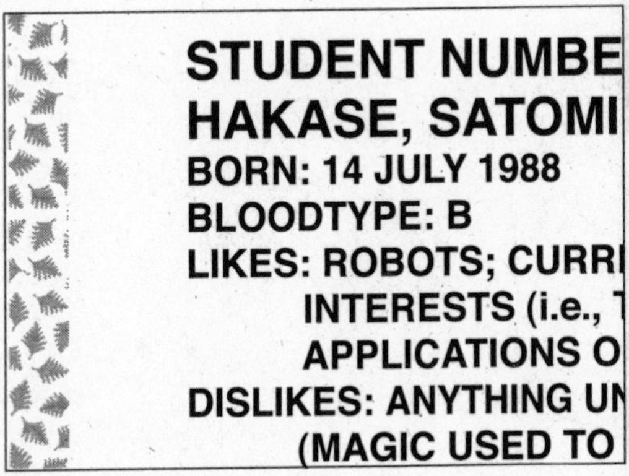
STUDENT NUMBE
HAKASE, SATOMI
BORN: 14 JULY 1988
BLOODTYPE: B
LIKES: ROBOTS; CURR
INTERESTS (i.e.,
APPLICATIONS O
DISLIKES: ANYTHING U
(MAGIC USED TO

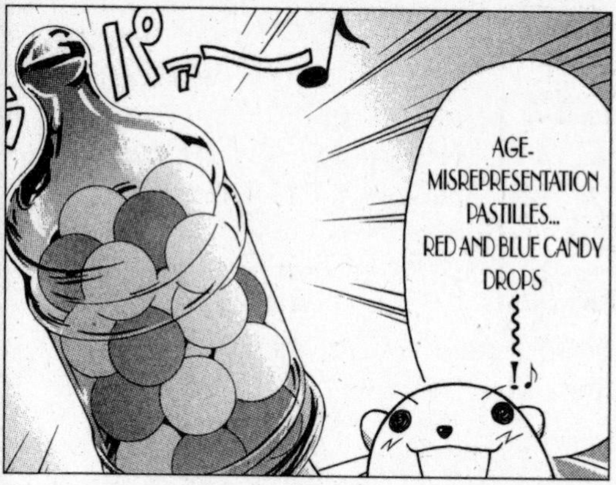
AGE-MISREPRESENTATION PASTILLES... RED AND BLUE CANDY DROPS

Red and Blue Candies, page 93

An homage to *Manga no Kami-sama* or "God of Comics" Osamu Tezuka's '70s manga *Fushigi na Merumo* ("Marvelous Melmo"), in which a girl is given a jar of red and blue candies by her mother (who is in Heaven), so that her daughter might overcome various obstacles. In Tezuka's original story, the red candies make Melmo ten years younger, while the blue make her ten years older. In *Negima!*, the effect of the colored candies is reversed, and there is no ten-year restriction.

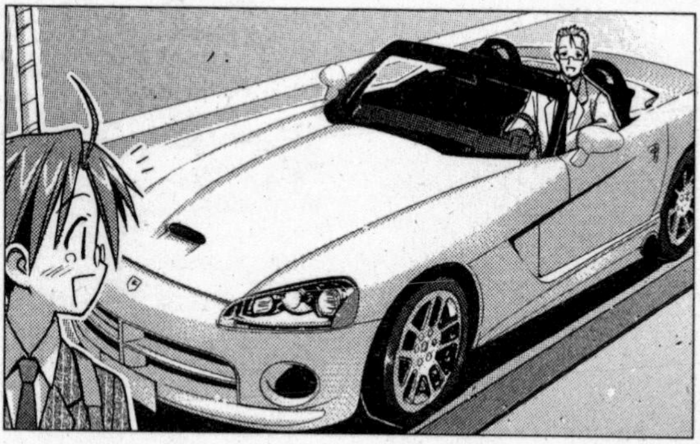

Takamichi's Tight Ride, page 119

A Dodge Viper SRT-10 Convertible, featuring a 500 HP 8.3 Liter V10 engine with a top speed of 306km/h... just in case you were wondering.

Seruhiko-sensei, page 144

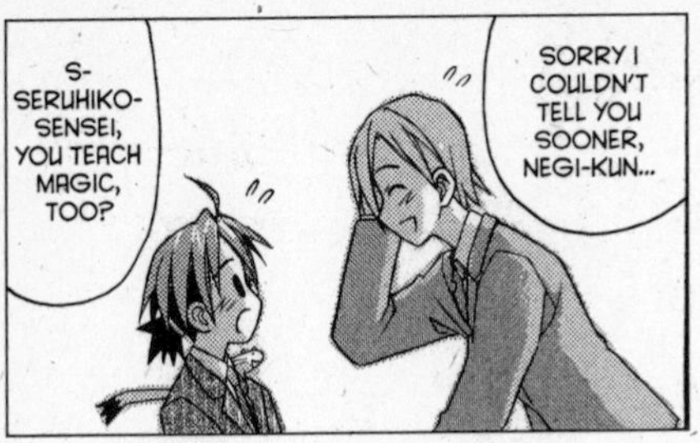
SORRY I COULDN'T TELL YOU SOONER, NEGI-KUN...
S-SERUHIKO-SENSEI, YOU TEACH MAGIC, TOO?

A character who's appeared (perhaps more mysteriously) several times in the past, now that it's been revealed that Seruhiko-sensei is a magic teacher like Negi, it can be noted that "Professor Seruhiko" is also Akamatsu's homage to the "Serpico" character in fellow author Kentarō Miura's manga, *Berserk* (note the resemblance?).

Sagitta Magica, page 160

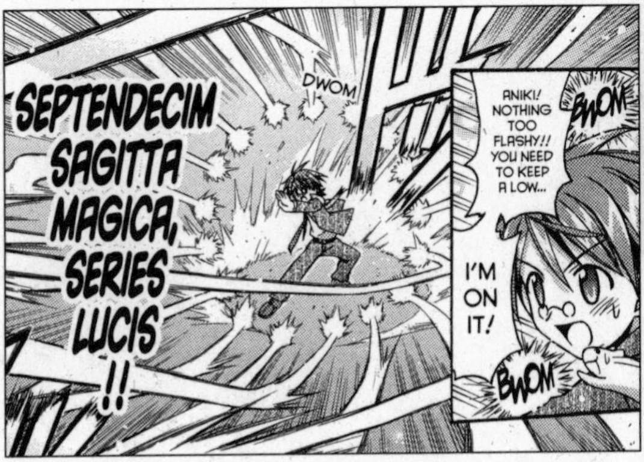
ANIKI! NOTHING TOO FLASHY!! YOU NEED TO KEEP A LOW...
BWOM
I'M ON IT!
BWOM
DWOM
SEPTENDECIM SAGITTA MAGICA, SERIES LUCIS!!

By now we know of course that "Sagitta Magica" means "magic arrow(s)," but here's something you may not have noticed—every time Negi casts the spell, *the number of arrows is always a prime number* (1, 17, 19, 199, et cetera). According to Akamatsu, although he'd decided to go with the prime-numbers concept for the manga, once the series came out for the PlayStation, for game reasons the idea had to be abandoned.

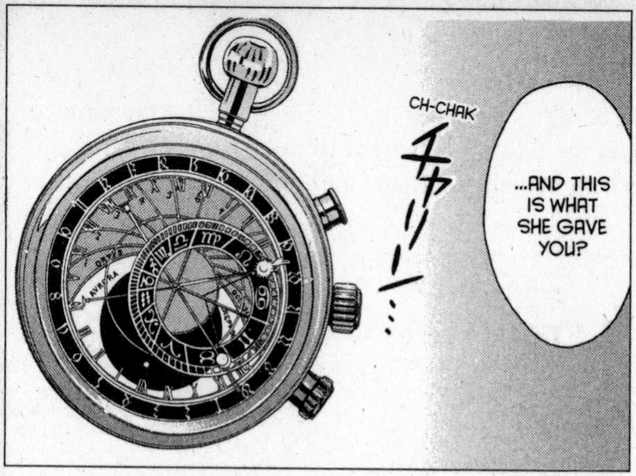
CH-CHAK
チャリ…
...AND THIS IS WHAT SHE GAVE YOU?

Chao's Watch, page 172

The timepiece given to Negi by Chao plays a major (more like *the* major) role in the next volume, but here's a bit of information ahead of time. Chao's watch is named "Cassiopeia," and though we won't give away what it does quite yet, we *will* tell you that the design for its face is taken from the Orloj, the world-famous Astronomical Clock located on the former City Hall of Prague (for more, Orloj.com).

Preview of Volume Ten

Because we're running about one year behind the release of the Japanese Negima! manga, we have the opportunity to present to you a preview from volume ten. This volume will be available in English on June 27, 2006.

BY CLAMP

Watanuki Kimihiro is haunted by visions. When he finds himself irresistibly drawn into a shop owned by Yūko, a mysterious witch, he is offered the chance to rid himself of the spirits that plague him. He accepts, but soon realizes that he's just been tricked into working for the shop to pay off the cost of Yūko's services! But this isn't any ordinary kind of shop . . . In this shop, Yūko grants wishes to those in need. But they must have the strength of will not only to truly understand their need, but to give up something incredibly precious in return.

Ages: 13+

Special extras in each volume! Read them all!

By HIROYUKI TAMAKOSHI

Kouhei is your typical Japanese high school student—he's usually late, he loves beef bowls, he pals around with his buddies, and he's got his first-ever crush on his childhood friend Kurara. Before he can express his feelings, however, Kurara heads off to Hawaii with her mother for summer vacation. When she returns, she seems like a totally different person . . . and that's because she is! While she was away, Kurara somehow developed an alternate personality: Arisa! And where Kurara has no time for boys, Arisa isn't interested in much else. Now Kouhei must help protect his friend's secret, and make sure that Arisa doesn't do anything Kurara would regret!

Ages: 16+

Special extras in each volume! Read them all!

Guru Guru Pon-Chan

BY SATOMI IKEZAWA

WINNER OF THE KODANSHA MANGA OF THE YEAR AWARD!

Ponta is a normal Labrador retriever puppy, the Koizumi family's pet. Full of energy, she is always up to some kind of trouble. However, when Grandpa Koizumi, a passionate amateur inventor, creates the "Guru Guru Bone," which empowers animals with human speech, Ponta turns into a human girl!

Ponta dashes out into the street and is saved by Mirai Iwaki, the most popular boy at school! Her heart pounds and her face flushes. Why does she feel this way? Can there be love between a human and a dog?

The effects of the "Guru Guru Bone" are not permanent, and Ponta turns back and forth between dog and girl.

Ages: 13 +

Special extras in each volume! Read them all!

VISIT WWW.DELREYMANGA.COM TO:
- View release date calendars for upcoming volumes
- Sign up for Del Rey's free manga e-newsletter
- Find out the latest about new Del Rey Manga series

TOMARE!

[STOP!]

You're going the wrong way!

Manga is a completely different type of reading experience.

To start at the *beginning*,
go to the *end*!

That's right! Authentic manga is read the traditional Japanese way—from right to left. Exactly the *opposite* of how American books are read. It's easy to follow: Just go to the other end of the book, and read each page—and each panel—from right side to left side, starting at the top right. Now you're experiencing manga as it was meant to be.